Political Forgiveness

Political Forgiveness

Lessons from South Africa

Russell Daye

ORBIS BOOKS

Maryknoll, New York 10545

Founded in 1970, Orbis Books endeavors to publish works that enlighten the mind, nourish the spirit, and challenge the conscience. The publishing arm of the Maryknoll Fathers and Brothers, Orbis seeks to explore the global dimensions of the Christian faith and mission, to invite dialogue with diverse cultures and religious traditions, and to serve the cause of reconciliation and peace. The books published reflect the views of their authors and do not represent the official position of the Maryknoll Society. To learn more about Maryknoll and Orbis Books, please visit our website at www.maryknoll.org.

Manufactured in the United States of America.
Manuscript editing and typesetting by Joan Weber Laflamme.

Queries regarding rights and permissions should be addressed to: Orbis Books, P.O. Box 308, Maryknoll, NY 10545-0308.

Library of Congress Cataloging-in-Publication Data

Daye, Russell.
  Political forgiveness : lessons from South Africa / Russell Daye.
    p. cm.
Includes bibliographical references and index.
  ISBN 1-57075-490-X (pbk.)
  1. South Africa. Truth and Reconciliation Commission. 2. Reconciliation—Political aspects—South Africa. 3. Amnesty—South Africa. I. Title.
  DT1974.2.D39 2004
  968.06—dc21
                          2003012105

*Dedicated to David and Val McAdam
and all the others
who carry the spirit of District Six*

Contents

Acknowledgments

There are a great number of people to whom I am indebted for help with this study and the research upon which it is based. Chief among them is Frederick Bird of Concordia University in Montreal, who supervised the doctoral research from which this book grew. His guidance and support were invaluable. I also want to thank Gregory Baum, Marguerite Mendell, and Walter Wink for their careful reading of my chapters, their suggestions, and their encouragement, and David McAdam and Tom Edmonds for their help with the text. Tina Montandon was a great source of aid. I am grateful to Sue Perry, Catherine Costello, and Robert Ellsberg at Orbis Books for their suggestions and for the care with which they have treated the book. Without the assistance of a number of South Africans, my research in their homeland would have been fruitless. They include Yazir, Ngululeko, and Thabo of The Direct Action Centre for Peace and Memory, Rev. Rob Robertson, Bishop Dwane, Rev. John Oliver, Stan Abrahams, and Ian and Lorraine Proedehl. Michael Forrester's friendship, hospitality, and lively debriefing sessions deserve special mention. Finally, I want to thank the person to whom I am most indebted, my research partner and life partner, Fiona McAdam. Her enthusiasm, her challenging opinions, and her commitment to this project have left their mark on every chapter.

Abbreviations

ANC	African National Congress
ANCC	All-Native Circle Conference
APLA	Azanian Peoples' Liberation Army
CCB	Civil Cooperation Bureau
G7	Guguletu Seven
HRV	Human Rights Violations
IFP	Inkatha Freedom Party
IJR	Institute for Justice and Reconciliation
MK	Umkhonto we Sizwe ("Spear of the Nation")
NGK	Nederduitse Gereformeede Kerk
NGO	Nongovernmental organization
PAC	Pan-Africanist Congress
PAGAD	People Against Gangsterism and Drugs
SACC	South African Council of Churches
SADF	South African Defense Forces
TRC	Truth and Reconciliation Commission
UCC	United Church of Canada
UDF	United Democratic Front
VOC	Dutch East India Company

Preface

Who would have thought at the turn of the millennium that in less than two years we would be looking back on the 1990s as a more peaceful time? I am writing in mid-2003. Tonight, from an aircraft carrier, George W. Bush will announce that the war in Iraq is all but over. I will not tune in. Instead, I will pray that fighting in the Middle East can come to an end, that the West does not fall into a broad and protracted conflict with the Islamic world, that the crimes and the curtailing of civil rights carried out in the name of the "war against terrorism" will not spread, and that my young children will not grow up in a century more violent than the one that encompassed my own childhood. Even the nineties, which saw so much blood spilled in the Balkans, Central Africa, and elsewhere, looks like a time of hope compared to our current moment in history. After all, it saw the end of the Cold War, the abandoning of apartheid, and the spread of democracy in parts of Europe, Asia, Africa, and Latin America.

The roots of this book go back to that time. It seemed that a significant number of nations were in transition, moving from oppression or civil war into an era of relative stability and democracy. We were beginning to ask how these societies could move beyond a peaceful stalemate to genuine reconciliation. The country that displayed the most ambition and daring on this front was South Africa. Its Truth and Reconciliation Commission was meant to break new ground in the exploration of national healing. Like many others from around the world, I decided to go and study this initiative. My observations, conversations, and experiences inspired me to try to build a model of political forgiveness. As you will see in the coming chapters, by political forgiveness I mean a form of deep reconciliation, a kind of social healing that is needed in so many places.

To build such a model it was necessary to work in an inter-disciplinary way. There are risks to such an approach, of course; it requires thinking "outside the box," and this kind of thinking can be messy or undisciplined. But it can also break new ground, which is certainly needed when we face the demanding task of repairing human relations. My choice was to take the risk, to draw upon exciting new work in such wide-ranging fields as political science, psychology, legal studies, and theology (to name a few), and to mix these insights with those arising from my own field research in South Africa. My hope is that the model born of this adventure will be useful to the practitioners of those disciplines and to the courageous people intervening in post-rending situations in contexts as small as a neighborhood or as large as the international community.

There is no shortage of such people. They labor in all corners of the globe, sometimes paying a heavy price. The world paid more attention to their efforts a few years ago, before the war-makers reclaimed center ground. But the new wars and the media obsession with them have not dissuaded the peacemakers. They work away. Let us hope that their pursuits, including political forgiveness, will once again capture the world's attention.

1

Introduction

Oliver is a Xhosa man with a strong high voice that reminds one of chai wallas at Indian train stations. His body and his emotions are marked by years of deep involvement in the anti-apartheid struggle; they show both a proud strength and a bitter weariness. Growing up in the Eastern Cape, Oliver was aware from an early age that whites lived in separate areas and that there was tension between them and his people. There was discussion of politics at home, and his mother, who supported the Pan-Africanist Congress (PAC, a liberation organization whose rhetoric was more explicitly anti-white than that of the African National Congress [ANC]), was especially critical of white authorities. One incident, which occurred when Oliver was seven or eight years old, made him understand that he was living in a deeply racist society. He and some friends were swimming in the local river. Police officers came along and made them leave the area. It was bluntly explained that blacks[1] were not allowed to swim upstream from the area reserved for whites.

After several harsh years of work in the mines, Oliver joined the ANC's military wing, Umkhonto we Sizwe (MK, "Spear of the Nation"). He was trained to operate within South Africa, recruiting members from the mixed-race community (he was assigned to this task because he spoke Afrikaans well) and hitting "soft targets"—mostly black police or municipal officials who cooperated with the regime. He also became a judge (and executioner) of the people's courts.[2] He was eventually captured by police, imprisoned for several years, and subjected to extreme mistreatment.

As apartheid came to an end (politically, at least), Oliver came to see himself as a person who had both received and done harm. He seeks forgiveness from the families of people he sentenced to death, and he struggles to forgive those who brutalized him. Suffering from a variety of physical ailments, he now works for a nongovernmental organization (NGO) that does educational and advocacy work in both African and mixed-race townships. He spends a lot of time with mothers

1

of those who never returned from the struggle. When he speaks of his former comrades who now inhabit "shiny government offices," he betrays a deep ambivalence. It is a joy that they have survived the struggle to make good, and they are helpful contacts for his work. But they have left him behind and no longer need the old network for friendship or to tell them who they are.[3]

When South Africa's Truth and Reconciliation Commission (TRC) was launched in 1995, there were heady hopes that it would serve as a secular equivalent to the ancient Christian Rite of Reconciliation—the ritual in which repentant sinners were returned to the embrace of Christian community and acknowledged as having received God's forgiveness. Instead, the commission functioned more like a national baptism. Repentance was given its place as were words and gestures of reconciliation, but the extended ritual also announced to the world that a birth had taken place, and that a new being would go forth to take its chances with success and failure, salvation and damnation. This new being was the Rainbow Nation, a dream as much as a real entity.

The TRC was a baptism in tears. Some of its critics called it the Kleenex Commission because of its many dramatic moments when mothers mourned publicly over disappeared sons and victims cried with rage at their tormentors, and because of Chairman Desmond Tutu's willingness to weep with those who wept. (Tutu was equally quick to laugh with the laughing, but these moments were more rare.) Tutu's leadership was extraordinary, and Western observers accustomed to the careful separation of church and state wondered at the freedom he was given to serve as a priest to the nation.

The pain of thirty-five years of bloodshed was poured out for all to see. It was hoped that this ablution would not only foster healing but would also unlock voices to claim responsibility. The optimism of early days has not been fulfilled, but rituals sometimes continue operating on the psyche for years or decades after. We are yet to know how many voices will be unlocked, or how many hands will reach across violence's chasms in search of those on the other side. What we do know is that the TRC was a bold experiment, a journey onto fresh political terrain. It was an attempt to advance the healing of one nation, but its successes and mistakes offer a growing body of wisdom as a gift to the world.

It is a gift of which we are in great need. By the end of the twentieth century it had become cliché to say that it was the most violent century in history. It is tempting to take comfort in the knowledge that we are in a new century, but this would be false assurance, given that we are a long way from breaking free of the factors that made the last one so bloody. While it has been more than fifty years since our last world war, and the Cold War has come to at least a temporary end, we are faced with an array of potentially explosive conflicts, many of which are taking new and confusing shapes. The types of discord that burden our world include religious, ethnic, and racial violence; civil wars in which opposing militias serve as fronts for competing multinational corporations; a daunting number of terrorist movements; and new "cold wars" between countries such as India and Pakistan. And this is just to begin the list. Upon close examination it becomes clear that many of these conflicts are not new, even if some of them are taking novel forms. The current strife in the Middle East, the land struggles in Central America, the communal violence in India, the massacres in Afghanistan, and the civil wars in Central Africa are examples of fresh twists and turns in old stories of opposing interests, unequal power relationships, and ghosts of violence past. Perhaps the most remarkable illustration of this point is the seemingly endless series of hostilities in the Balkans. To quote Donald Shriver: "The world cringes at a Serb's willingness to kill a Muslim in revenge for ancestors who fought the Battle of Kosovo in the year 1389."[4]

As technology provides larger numbers of people with the means to do great harm, and as tension-producing dynamics such as population growth, human mobility, and competition for resources become more and more a part of life, it is imperative that human beings, human communities, and human societies find effective methods for ending their stubborn conflicts and healing their wounds. In recent decades we have seen various attempts, in all corners of the globe, to develop these methods. Truth commissions have been employed in Latin America, Africa, Europe, and Asia, usually in the period of transition from a less to a more democratic government. Various amnesty processes have been tried. Apologies on behalf of governments, churches, and other institutions have become a common part of public discourse. Prime ministers and presidents have confessed the sins of the governments they lead, even sins committed long before they were elected.

When these healing processes and acts of contrition are examined closely, we find a theme that is common to most of them, but which usually lies under the surface. It informs the dialogue, but only occasionally in an explicit way. It comes to consciousness during testimony at an inquest but slips into the background again when jurists and officials produce final reports. This theme is the need for forgiveness. At least as early as 1958, with the publication of Hannah Arendt's *The Human Condition,* scholars have been pointing to the potential value of forgiveness for repairing past damage to the fabric of society so that it will not unravel into future chaos.[5] Why then has social and political forgiveness not been a larger part of public discourse?

There appears to be a cluster of reasons. The first is that there is no consensus on the meaning of the concept. What is forgiveness, exactly? A process? A transaction? A feeling? An internal state? A behavior such as a speech act or a performative utterance? Then there is the question of who has the power to forgive. Must it be the victims of the injustice, or can it be granted by a third party? Some would argue that it is granted not by any human being but by God. What are the necessary elements of forgiveness? Must there be confession? Repentance? Restitution? Must the "forgiver" truly *feel* that all is mended or are uttered words enough? Another reason is that forgiveness is often seen to be a theological concept, appropriate for communities of faith but not appropriate for the larger community whose politics are secular. In the church's treatment, forgiveness came to be associated with correcting one's actions in the private sphere but not the public sphere—an attitude institutionalized in the sacrament of penance.

There is no doubt that forgiveness holds a powerful place in the human psyche. It almost seems archetypal, coming to consciousness wherever people are hurt and relationships rent. I am not sure if this phenomenon is universal, but it is extremely far-reaching. It is true that theorists are still struggling to define forgiveness, but in everyday conflicts people seem to function with an inherent sense of its contours. We have an intuitive understanding of what makes for legitimate forgiving; dissonance arises when we stray from this understanding. This common wisdom has its limits, however. As we pass from the terrain of interpersonal relationships to the realm of political relations, the dynamics become more complex and institutional. On this ground our intuitive understanding of forgiveness is much weaker. Yet, forgiveness discourse is becoming increasingly common in politics.

Is there a legitimate place in politics for the pursuit of forgiveness? Can there be forgiveness between nations or other large groups of people? Should leaders try to foster large-scale forgiveness in contexts of transition from war and oppression to something better? Would they be wiser to keep their eyes on other prizes, such as peaceful coexistence, healing, and the reconstitution of society? These questions are being asked and debated in an expanding number of contexts. In the midst of these discussions there is a struggle to define *political* forgiveness, to clarify its parameters. The task of this book is to contribute to this work of defining and clarifying by articulating a working model of political forgiveness. The model has been given shape by my theoretical inquiries, by explorations of literature on early reconciliation initiatives, and especially by my field research in South Africa. My hope is that it will provide *an* answer to the following question: In light of what we have learned so far, how can we best portray political forgiveness? There is no pretension that this model will be conclusive. The terrain of political forgiveness is in the early days of exploration; its cartographers will be revising and refining their maps for a long time.

SOUTH AFRICA'S TRUTH AND RECONCILIATION COMMISSION

Later in this introductory chapter I will outline my model. At this point let me offer a few words about reconciliation in South Africa. After coming to power in 1994, the ANC government launched the largest and most intricately designed process of post-conflict healing that the world has yet seen. At the center of this process was the TRC, headed by Nobel Laureate Archbishop Desmond Tutu. In his first address to the TRC, Archbishop Tutu made the following remarks:

We are privileged to be on this Commission to assist our land, our people to come to terms with our dark past once and for all. They say that those who suffer from amnesia, those who forget the past, are doomed to repeat it. It is not dealing with the past to say facilely, let bygones be bygones, for then they won't be bygones. Our country, our society would be doomed to the instability of uncertainty—the uncertainty engendered by not knowing when yet another scandal of the past would hit the headlines, when another skeleton would be dragged out of the cupboard.

We will be engaging in what should be a corporate nationwide process of healing through contrition, confession and forgiveness. To be able to forgive one needs to know whom one is forgiving and why. That is why the truth is so central to this whole exercise.[6]

The hope for forgiveness is stated up front—not simply a transactional forgiveness between individual perpetrators and their individual victims, but a "nationwide process." Tutu is speaking of a directed, concerted attempt to come to terms with massive social disruption in the past so that there may be greater harmony in the future.

We are meant to be a part of the process of the healing of our nation, of our people, all of us, since every South African has to some extent or other been traumatized. We are a wounded people because of the conflict of the past, no matter on which side we stood. We all stand in need of healing.[7]

During a TRC amnesty hearing that I witnessed in 1997, the theme of forgiveness came up repeatedly. The following words are from a white woman whose daughter, then in her early twenties, was killed in what has come to be called the Heidelberg Tavern Massacre. She is speaking to three young black men who carried out the shooting under orders from their superiors in the Azanian Peoples' Liberation Army (APLA), a militant anti-apartheid organization.

And as I will say to the applicants, as I heard all the time, they acted under orders which I understand. I too act under orders as I sit here now, just speaking directly to you because I firmly would like to believe that we all do believe there is a God above our heads. If I can be allowed to say this, and because I believe that God is God and I act under His orders and for me, His orders are to say to you and to all here, yes, I have forgiven you. I will not oppose your amnesty because who am I, I am not your judge.[8]

During the course of the hearing another white woman, Mrs. Ginn Fourie, who also lost a daughter in the massacre, was given a chance to speak to the applicants and to hear from them. This was not the first such opportunity. She was given a similar opportunity at their criminal trial two or three years earlier. What is interesting is that the nature of their dialogue changed from the trial to the amnesty hearing. At the trial one of the three young men (Mr. Ggomfa) refused to speak to Mrs. Fourie. At the hearing he and the other applicants addressed her by saying "good morning, Mama"—*Mama* is a term of respect—and he apologized and showed concern for her suffering. Those of us present witnessed a rehumanization of Mrs. Fourie and white people in general in the eyes of Mr. Ggomfa, and an opening of dialogue not only between these individuals but between whole subsections of a society.

There were literally hundreds of these kinds of encounters during the life of the TRC. The commission was a bold new venture in political healing, one with forgiveness as one of its central goals. My observations of the TRC hearings in the fall of 1997 raised many issues relevant to the problematic of defining political forgiveness, outlining its parameters, and understanding the factors that foster and impede it. I found myself asking questions: When all these participants in the hearings—lawyers, clergy, Christians, Muslims, whites, blacks, poor people, rich people—speak of forgiveness, do they mean the same thing? What is the connection between amnesty and forgiveness? Can we expect that professions of forgiveness will be followed by changes in behavior or renewed dialogue? Which institutions within South African society are changing as a result of the TRC, and how? Now that formerly segregated groups have to deal with one another on a daily basis, is the national dialogue fostered by the TRC enabling more effective communication among them? Does this dialogue move only within societal subgroups or also between them? Are hostilities calming? Is vengeance being tamed? If so, can these developments be connected to the TRC in a convincing way?

During the first half of 2000 I was able to return to South Africa to seek answers to these questions. Interviews were conducted with a demographically wide range of South Africans. Most of the interviews were held in the Western Cape province (which includes Cape Town), but a number took place in other parts of the country. Most of the interviewees had not directly participated in the TRC (although a significant number had), but all were aware of it and were being forced to develop their own response to its revelations. As in 1997, I was able to witness amnesty hearings and to talk with a number of participants in those hearings. But it was not only at hearings or during interviews that I heard about the TRC and the larger process of coming to terms with South Africa's past. Discussion of these topics was ubiquitous. It was taking place every hour in restaurants and taverns, at dinner tables, at the office, on radio and television, in the newspapers. To be in South Africa was to be steeped in a national conversation about the conflict and violence of the past and what could be done to "put it behind us."[9] South Africa has "pushed the envelope" further than any other country in terms of political forgiveness. In the chapters that follow, we will be continually looking to see what can be learned from its endeavor.

Before moving on, a brief note about the time-line for the TRC. The commission was established with the passing of the Promotion of National Unity and Reconciliation Act of 1995. The list of commissioners was published in December of that year; their work began shortly thereafter. It was originally envisioned that the TRC would last only a couple of years, but due to an explosion of applications for amnesty and other factors, parts of the commission continued to function until 2002; its doors were finally closed in March of that year. After 1998, when the first five volumes of the TRC's *Final Report* were published, the work of the commission was dominated by the proceedings of the Committee on Amnesty, which had to process over seven thousand applications (even though only a few hundred were originally envisioned). The Committee on Reparations and Rehabilitation also continued its work beyond publication of the original volumes of the *Final Report*. As of mid-2002 the final two volumes of the report were still awaited, their release being delayed by court action taken by the Inkatha Freedom Party (ITP).

THE NATURE OF FORGIVENESS

In the next chapter we will explore the theoretical issues and challenges relevant to the articulation of a model of political forgiveness. For now, I would like to focus on one thesis, which is central to my model. It is my contention that forgiveness has a *core grammar*. Let me refer first to *interpersonal* forgiveness. By saying that forgiveness has a core grammar I mean that, even though the passage to forgiveness follows a wide variety of routes in real-life situations, there is a normative, underlying structure to processes of interpersonal forgiveness. Clusters of individuals who mutually seek the achievement of forgiveness are more likely to be successful if their actions adhere to this syntax.[10] A way to explicate this grammar is to describe a process of forgiveness as a *drama* that moves through a number of *acts*. I believe that there are three acts that must be played out, even while recognizing that these acts may be "scripted" in an almost infinite variety of ways.

The first act in a drama of forgiveness is *the naming and articulation of the harm done*. Somebody must point out that one party's unjust action (or inaction) has damaged another party or caused that second party to suffer. Usually it is the victimized party that makes this statement and begins the narrative of wrongs done. Sometimes an outside party names the unjust action—perhaps because the victimized party has been so oppressed that it has failed to see the injustice or because it has not been free to name it itself. On rare occasions the guilty party first names the offense, but its narrative usually begins in step two.

The second essential act is *an apology or confession* in which the guilty party admits to the wrong done and acknowledges its moral indebtedness to the party it has harmed. Very often at this stage the guilty party offers excuses or explanations along with the admission of guilt, but in the cleanest and best examples of a drama of forgiveness these qualifiers are abandoned and the party in the wrong stands "naked" before the narrative of its unjust action and asks for forgiveness.

The third act is *the offering of forgiveness* by the victimized party. Just as many offenders refuse to apologize, many victims refuse to forgive. They may offer a pardon that is qualified by calls for further repentance or some kind of restitution, but, in its ideal form, forgiveness is offered fully with no strings attached. Actually, it is surprising how often people are willing to forgive—even before apologies are offered. This may be because of a desire to break the bonds of suffering and start life anew. Many victims forgive not because their tormentors deserve it, but because they need to do it for the sake of their own inner freedom. Sometimes acts two and three are reversed, and it is an offer of forgiveness by a victim that sparks a heartfelt apology from a perpetrator.

It is important to point out that act three has both an *intra*-personal and an *inter*-personal dimension. The former involves the surrender of resentment and other antipathies by the wounded party. The latter involves a voicing of pardon. Of course, it is impossible for anyone other than the one offering forgiveness to know just how fully he or she has abandoned resentment. It is also possible, indeed likely in many instances, that resentment will return at a later time. Forgiveness is a process that often takes a long time. Sometimes it advances by two steps and then retreats by one.

This is one reason why I say that real-life processes of forgiveness usually do not adhere to the "normative" grammar as I outline it. My characterization of forgiveness as a drama in three acts is necessarily simplistic. It serves as an ideal in an almost Platonic way. Rarely do dramas of forgiveness fully conform, even in interpersonal relations. Sometimes the process begins in step three; it is after a gesture of forgiveness by the wounded party that the offender offers an apology and the harm is named. Other times the apology comes first. The sequence of acts is not the most important factor. What is more important is that all three be present and that their true natures be attended to.

When we move from the interpersonal to the sociopolitical realm, forgiveness becomes more complicated. In fact, there are some daunting theoretical challenges to such a shift. These will be discussed in the next chapter. In my opinion, the grammar of political forgiveness includes the same core elements as that of interpersonal forgiveness, but more elements need to be added as well. Staying with the metaphor of a drama of forgiveness, we can say that these additions constitute more "acts." Based on my investigations in South Africa, I have decided to add an act concerned with transitional justice and another concerned with healing.[11] We are left with a drama of political forgiveness in five acts. This drama is my model of political forgiveness. I have given the acts the following names:

- Act One: Truth-telling
- Act Two: Apology and the Claiming of Responsibility
- Act Three: Building a Transitional Justice Framework
- Act Four: Finding Ways to Heal
- Act Five: Embracing Forgiveness

To a limited extent the sequencing of the acts is flexible. This is not the case with the first and fifth acts. Truth-telling certainly belongs at the beginning of the drama; it is the foundation upon which the others are built. Similarly, the embracing of forgiveness in a comprehensive way can only come at the end of a drama of forgiveness. The middle acts, however, need not be seen as fixed in the sequence I give them. In a context like post-apartheid South Africa, the claiming of responsibility, the building of a justice framework, and the pursuit of healing will take place simultaneously and each will affect the others. Each of the five acts will be considered at some length in the chapters to come, but first let us make a quick passage through them with a view to the elements of interpersonal forgiveness that must be maintained as we shift our sights to the political realm, and to the new elements that must be added for such a shift to be feasible.

The first act in a drama of forgiveness is the articulation of the harm done. Any attempt to rush to the granting of forgiveness without a careful exposition of the unjust actions through documentation or through the generation of a broad narrative will bastardize the process. Truth-telling can be carried out in different ways, but *the victims must have voice.* An exposition of past actions and a public acknowledgment of its veracity by government leaders or other important persons can in itself be very healing for victims, especially if it rings true to their experiences.

An important issue is the selection of the community leaders or representatives who will guide any formal process of truth-telling. It is essential that they be people trusted by all segments of society, that they represent the experiences of diverse communities, and that their approach to truth-telling be balanced. After all, in a situation of mass conflict there will never be one fully innocent party or one fully guilty party. There are reprisals from the original victims. Collaborators blur the lines between oppressors and oppressed. Representatives are needed who can sort through ambiguities without being blinded by either a desire to expose one party as evil or an imperative to paint everyone as equally guilty so that an "easy" reconciliation can be achieved. The selection of Archbishop Tutu to head the TRC with Alex Boraine as his co-chairman is a prime example. The TRC's credibility among all sectors of South African society was given an immediate boost. Significantly, many whites who had supported apartheid began to believe that the formal truth-telling concerning South Africa's past would not be a one-sided witch hunt.

Gaining the trust of perpetrators is very important if they are going to assist in the documentation and narration of past wrongs, *apologize,* and *claim responsibility* for their actions. This is the second, and in many ways most precarious, of the acts in a drama of political forgiveness.

It is not realistic to hope that in a society which has suffered large-scale injustice all the perpetrators and their supporters and collaborators will step forward, confess their part in the damage done, and admit that they stand in need of forgiveness. This precludes the fulfillment of a nationwide process of forgiveness in a complete and clean way such as we sometimes witness at the interpersonal level. It may be hoped that some of the leaders who were most responsible for oppression would do this, but they are often the most reluctant. General Pinochet of Chile is a prime example. Even when leaders do offer apologies, they often qualify them with explanations or by referring to a prior injustice suffered by *their* constituency, which motivated them to act in extreme ways. F. W. de Klerk's apology to the TRC is a case in point. He apologized for apartheid and the pain it caused, but he refused to admit that it was a flawed and oppressive policy from the start, instead arguing that it was founded upon idealism. He also refused to admit that he authorized the violence of security forces during his time as prime minister.

Does this mean that political forgiveness can only take place and foster healing in exceptional situations and stalls at act two the rest of the time? I do not think so. In places like Chile and South Africa, confessions and apologies by *some* of the perpetrators, even if some of these are qualified, make a difference. They validate the perspectives and memories of victims. For those who have suffered torture, dislocation, appropriation of property, or loss of loved ones, this kind of validation is extremely important. It shows that the world is a place where truth is acknowledged, and it helps them move out of a state of perpetual fear and insecurity. It helps them break free of the ghosts and demons of the past and start building a new life. It also helps them move toward a time when they can stop hating and fearing their oppressors. They can begin to break the unholy bonds that have tied them to those who maltreated them.

One of the most frequently heard criticisms of political forgiveness is that it is incompatible with, and therefore impedes, justice. I disagree with this assertion. In fact, I have made the building of a *transitional justice framework*—a special, coordinated set of judicial measures for the period of movement from conflict to stability—the third act in my drama of political forgiveness. The pursuit of transitional justice involves the implementation of processes of both *retributive justice* and *restorative justice*. Retributive justice involves the punishment of those who have committed crimes. A good example is the Nuremberg tribunal, which tried and punished a number of Nazi leaders and German officers in the wake of the Second World War. Restorative justice involves attempts to compensate victims or repair communities and institutions that were damaged by unjust action or a time of strife. The Marshall Plan implemented a process of restoration. It was probably not seen as an instrument of restorative justice at the time, but more recent programs of restitution, like those for victims of Pinochet's terror in

Chile or for interred Japanese Americans, were understood to be such instruments.

It is a simple matter to see how ventures in restorative justice are compatible with political forgiveness—it is easier to forgive when our violation has been acknowledged and we have been compensated—but it is more difficult to see the connection between retributive justice and forgiveness. In Chapter 7 I will argue that there is a connection, one that relates to the emotion of resentment. The challenge for any society trying to recover from a period of civil war or acute oppression is to find the right balance between restorative and retributive measures, and to ensure that these measures are appropriate to the context. Meeting this challenge is very difficult in the best of situations. In most post-conflict contexts it is further complicated by a poverty of public resources.

When a nation has been rent by prolonged violence or tyranny, a number of kinds of healing are needed. Combined, they constitute act four of my drama. Where there have been gross human rights violations, individuals will suffer from traumatic stress disorders and will have particular therapeutic needs that center on issues of empowerment and security. It may be the case that whole communities, even societies, come to suffer from the dynamics of traumatic injury. Here, the issue of therapy comes to the fore. An important question is whether forgiveness interventions are more likely to advance or hinder the healing of individuals and communities.

Another kind of mending is also imperative. Here I refer to the repair of socioeconomic systems. Large-scale injustice usually arises from economic motivations, among others, and always has economic repercussions. In transitional societies there will be families who have lost their life savings, their livelihood, and even their breadwinners. What compensation do they merit? How can they be reintegrated into the economy? Also, many of the public and private institutions will need repair, as well as reformation where they contributed to the strife.

This brings us to the fifth act in my drama: the embracing of forgiveness. There is a reason why this is the final act: Nationwide forgiveness has a more distant horizon than truth-telling, responsibility-claiming, justice, or healing. It involves the reformation of whole communities at a level so deep that collective identities are transformed. This kind of communal "soul work" requires revision of the very myths and narratives that tell a people who they are and who their friends and enemies are. In a context of such deep reform all the symbol systems—cultural, theological, mythological, artistic, and so on—that influence identity construction come into play. For movement toward political forgiveness to occur, charismatic actors and creative thinkers will have to bend these symbol systems away from enmity and toward affinity.

I see forgiveness in two ways. First, as a social good, akin to justice or healing or the claiming of responsibility, that can be pursued with tangible policies—even if it will take longer to achieve than these other goods. Second, as something more mysterious materializing in crucibles that mix human pain, need, imagination, and good will. Throughout this book I will move back and forth between these two perspectives.

The remaining chapters of the book will be given structure by my drama, but with two preliminary chapters inserted at the beginning. After a review of theoretical considerations in Chapter 2, we will undertake a brief survey of South African history in Chapter 3. Chapter 4 will explore Act One: Truth-telling. Chapter 5 will be concerned with Act Two: Apology and the Claiming of Responsibility. Chapters 6 and 7 will be companion chapters, both relating to Act Three: Building a Transitional Justice Framework. Chapter 6 will focus on the controversial issue of amnesty, and Chapter 7 on the imperatives of retributive and restorative justice. Chapter 8 will examine issues related to Act Four: Finding Ways to Heal. Chapter 9 will be concerned with Act Five: Embracing Forgiveness. The final chapter will be a brief conclusion in which we take a final look at the TRC and review my model.

2

Theoretical Issues

Human beings seem to be programmed to raise the issue of forgiveness in situations where one person is harmed by another. People all around the world, people shaped and informed by radically different cultures, employ the concept of forgiveness in response to wrongdoing. Can we assume that all these actors are operating with a singular, universal definition of forgiveness? No, this does not seem to be the case. In recent years we have seen an increased interest in studying and defining forgiveness on the part of psychologists and philosophers. This growing body of work has made it clear that we are a long way from consensus.

Part of the problem is that different thinkers focus on different aspects of forgiveness. Some concentrate on its emotional aspect and understand forgiveness to be a feeling or an emotion. Others concentrate on the fact that forgiveness happens *between* people and describe it as a transaction. Still others employ a philosophy of action and define forgiveness as a speech act or a performative utterance. Some thinkers are very aware that forgiveness does not happen all at once and recognize that a series of actions is necessary before it can take place; they tend to understand it as a process. I will not side with any one of these camps to the exclusion of the others. Forgiveness is multidimensional. Losing sight of any of its dimensions would do disservice—especially to a study such as this one, which has society-wide forgiveness as its focus. At this level of analysis, ambiguity and complexity must be embraced.

That said, there is one thing about which we can be unambiguous: The human need for forgiveness can be very powerful indeed. Anyone who has had a highly valued relationship broken by hurtful action, and who has longed for the "good old days" before the rupture, understands the appeal of forgiveness. Anyone who has, in hindsight, been struck by the devastating realization that his or her actions were truly hurtful to innocent parties knows what a gift forgiveness can be. Anyone who has been able to cast off a long-carried burden of anger and antipathy and has felt the subsequent relief realizes how liberating forgiveness can be. When we are actors in a situation

13

in which the issue of forgiveness is raised, our most important beliefs are evoked. We have to find ways to give voice to our values and our morals because it has become necessary to define who stands in the right and who stands in the wrong. If we are the ones who need to forgive or be forgiven, then the very construction of our identities comes into play. The painful moment in which the need for forgiveness is articulated is an opportunity, certainly for healing, but also for the evaluation and even the reconstruction of relationships, beliefs, and identities. It is a moment full of risk. At such a time, clarity about the nature and dynamics of forgiveness will be of great value.

A number of philosophers and psychologists have understood this and have tried to provide clarity, each in his or her own way. In this chapter we will explore some of their work. First, we will try to come to terms with *interpersonal forgiveness*, its nature and definition. Then we will examine *political forgiveness* to see how it is similar to and different from interpersonal forgiveness.

INTERPERSONAL FORGIVENESS

One of the most important philosophical explorations of forgiveness in recent decades takes the form of a dialogue between Jeffrie G. Murphy and Jean Hampton in their book *Forgiveness and Mercy*.[1] Murphy makes the first attempt at defining forgiveness.[2] He follows the lead of eighteenth-century bishop Joseph Butler and asserts that forgiveness is the "forswearing" of resentment.[3] It is important to note that resentment is not surrendered because it is an inappropriate emotional response to being wronged. Both Butler and Murphy offer a defense of resentment. Butler, while pointing out the dangers of resentment, admits that it serves the function of reinforcing and defending the rules of morality. Murphy justifies resentment because it protects and bolsters self-respect. When a person willfully and wrongfully injures another, there is a double harm. The first harm is the injury itself. The second is the implicit statement by the wrongdoer that "I am essentially more important than you are. It is acceptable for me to trample your dignity or rights because I am a more important person than you." The generation of resentment within the injured person is a rejection of that claim. It is a counter-assertion of that person's worth.

If resentment serves this function, then, is there any value in its abandonment? Murphy believes that there is. Resentment has an unhealthy, even dangerous aspect. It stands as an obstacle to the restoration of relationship and may color the judgment of the one who resents. If forgiveness is the surrender of resentment, then it can perform the valuable functions of opening alienated parties to renewed relationship and averting the danger of skewed judgment. As such, forgiveness can be considered a virtue.

Murphy is quick to point out, however, that it is not always a virtue. We must remember the original purpose of the resentment: the protection of self-respect. Forgiveness is only a virtue when the abandonment of resentment does not compromise the wronged party's self-respect. This leads Murphy to consider the circumstances under which it is appropriate to forgive. These involve a decision to abandon resentment because a *moral factor* comes into play that serves to separate the harmful act from the one who committed it. Murphy acknowledges that he is describing situations akin to ones in which Christians decide to "hate the sin but love the sinner." He argues that there are five reasons why harmed parties may legitimately choose to separate the "sinner" from the "sin" and thereby abandon resentment toward those who injured them. Murphy writes:

I will choose to forgive the person who has willfully wronged me, because

1. he repented or had a change of heart *or*
2. he meant well (his motives were good) *or*
3. he has suffered enough *or*
4. he has undergone humiliation (perhaps some ritual humiliation, e.g., the apology ritual of "I beg forgiveness") *or*
5. of old times' sake (e.g., "He has been a good and loyal friend to me in the past").[4]

Murphy's list of reasons to forgive has great relevance to the dilemma of victims of tyranny in places like South Africa. It is certainly legitimate for these survivors of oppression to carry deep resentment toward their oppressors. But such resentment can corrode both their psyches and their relationships. Many truly desire to forgive, but most also disdain the notion of cheap forgiveness. They search for legitimate reasons to forgive. Based on my interviews, my impression is that heartfelt repentance on the part of the perpetrator is the most compelling and satisfying reason for a survivor to offer forgiveness. There seems to be a deep need within victims for their oppressors to know and to acknowledge the fact that they were wrong. Some South Africans understand their amnesty process to be a kind of political forgiveness in which applicants are forgiven after undergoing Murphy's item number four, humiliation. The idea is that the nation agrees to offer pardon those who are willing to lower themselves to the point of publicly begging for it. As we will see in Chapter 6, the situation is much more complicated than this. Among the people calling for forgiveness (or its refusal) in South Africa, recourse is being made to all of the reasons mentioned by Murphy.

Murphy's partner in dialogue, Jean Hampton, agrees that Murphy and Bishop Butler are onto something when they focus on resentment in their definition of forgiveness, but she thinks that Murphy's definition has a shortcoming. This lies in the fact that his definition deals exclusively with internal changes within the "forgiver."

Forgiveness must be defined so that it involves more than simply effecting certain psychological changes for moral reasons. Of course, it may presuppose such changes in order to be possible, but it is a response that is centrally concerned with the forgiver's *relationship to the wrongdoer*. Thus we speak of forgiveness as "bestowed upon" or "offered to" the wrongdoer.[5]

This is an important shift. Hampton is not taking issue with the assertion that forgiveness involves a surrender of resentment; rather, she is saying that the emotional transformation within the forgiver is only one dimension of the event or process that is forgiveness. Not only are the forgiver's feelings changed but also his relationship to the wrongdoer. My position, outlined in the previous chapter, that forgiveness is an interactive process with a standard "core grammar" causes me to agree with Hampton's criticism. I think Murphy's identification of the surrender of resentment as central to the *intra*-personal transformation that comes with forgiveness is correct. But, as he defines it, forgiveness can be unilateral. In other words, we can surrender resentment for moral reasons without being in dialogue with the one who harmed us. According to my model, a claiming of responsibility by the offender is necessary, as is a voicing of pardon by the one forgiving. Murphy's definition ignores this *inter*personal dimension.

Hampton criticizes Murphy for this omission and makes another good point as well. Her writings on forgiveness acknowledge that *preparation* is required before the forgiver can reach the point of forgiveness. She asserts that forgiveness should be analyzed as a process involving psychological homework.[6] Since the publication of *Forgiveness and Mercy*, and perhaps partly because of the book's influence, a small but dedicated cluster of psychologists has been analyzing forgiveness in just this way—as a process. This body of work is still young, and the range of data is far from comprehensive, but these studies may prove to be fruitful.

Everett L. Worthington Jr. and some colleagues have been developing a multi-step model, not of forgiveness in real-life situations, but rather of a process of forgiveness that can be stimulated and guided by a clinical intervention.[7] Unlike Murphy, who focuses on resentment, Worthington identifies *fear* as the greatest emotional obstacle to forgiveness. When people are hurt, says Worthington, they are fear-conditioned in a classical conditioning sense—like a rat in a cage. The rat hears a tone and is then given a painful shock. Later, when the rat hears the tone again, it becomes afraid. Likewise, a person who receives a hurt or an injustice from someone will experience fear when in the presence of that person at a later time. Following instinctual patterns, the wounded person is likely to flee from the offender, fight with the person, or make a gesture of submission. All of these responses are likely to impede forgiveness.

Worthington believes that the best way to reduce the fear response in a wounded person, as well as any desires for retaliation, is to engender empathy for the one who has caused the hurt. This is the central task of the five-step intervention Worthington recommends.

In step one the hurt is recalled within a supportive atmosphere. Clients are brought to the point where they can think of the person who injured them without feeling the full depth of the hurt. This serves to weaken the fear response so that wounded persons no longer employ the classical flight/ fight response. Step two is the key stage in the model. Here the goal is to generate other emotions in place of the fear response. In particular, a state of empathy for the offender is sought. Clients are helped to imagine what the offender might have been thinking and feeling during the hurtful event through such exercises as writing a letter of explanation that attributes reasonable motives to the offender. In step three clients are encouraged to go a step further and offer the "altruistic gift" of forgiveness. This is facilitated through the use of guided imagery and remembrance, which will bring clients to a state of humility. Steps three and four involve a number of procedures designed to reinforce the forgiveness and prevent clients from regressing to a state of fear and avoidance.

I have an ambivalent reaction to the model. On the one hand, the attention given to fear as a barrier to forgiveness strikes me as insightful and promising. Fear may not always be a part of one's response to an offense, but it very often is. This is especially the case for offenses like torture, rape, and murder, which are horribly common in places like apartheid South Africa. Also, what is a better antidote to fear than empathy? Worthington and his colleagues are on the right track here.

On the other hand, I wonder whether this tugging of wounded hearts toward forgiveness is not manipulative and sometimes inappropriate. Certainly one would expect that the volunteers for such a process would be persons who truly desire release from the negative emotions they feel toward the people who have harmed them. But, in a variety of circumstances, there may be other, more appropriate interventions to deal with these noxious emotions. Certainly, if I remember the victims of apartheid whom I met in South Africa, a number are so wounded that they might embrace any offered intervention that promised to harmonize their passions. I have serious doubts, however, that the pyramid model of forgiveness could foster a harmonization that would be true to the moral dynamics of their life situations. It lacks an important step: truth-telling, including acknowledgment by the offenders that they have done wrong. This highlights a danger with psychological models of forgiveness. They may be employed in clinical settings, but they are for people who were wounded in and who will return to real-life settings with their complex matrices of relations. Healing is moral and political, even if only at the level of family politics or office politics. To forget this would be to leave the moral consequences of intervention to chance.[8]

This does not mean that psychological models like those of Worthington and others have no place in the pursuit of political forgiveness; rather, it means that they must be held to standards of appropriateness that lie outside of the considerations that originally informed their creation. There are many victims of apartheid who carry strong, self-corroding emotions but do not suffer from extreme conditions like post-traumatic stress disorder. Perhaps they would be good candidates for an intervention like that outlined by Worthington, assuming that the model could be altered to include an element of moral and political analysis.[9]

In her article "Forgiveness in Context," Molly Andrews comments on the work of the psychologists of forgiveness in a manner that brings us back to an issue raised earlier: the importance of not losing sight of the forgiver's relationship to the wrongdoer. Andrews is critical of the psychological models because they construe forgiveness as a unilateral activity.[10] She contrasts them with a model of "negotiated" forgiveness and argues strongly for the superiority of the latter. Negotiated forgiveness transpires through dialogue between the offender and the victim. The wrongdoer admits an offense and seeks forgiveness for it. Andrews maintains that this entails (at least) the three steps of confession, ownership, and repentance. The wrongdoer must admit to committing the unjust and harmful action, take responsibility for it, and express remorse.

Why does Andrews prefer models of negotiated forgiveness? Like some of the other writers we have surveyed, she believes that a change of heart is central to the process of forgiveness, but she makes a shift: the change of heart must take place *in both the forgiver and the forgiven*. Andrews is unwilling to surrender forgiveness to the realm of intra-personal phenomena. She understands forgiveness to be a social phenomenon.

Andrews is correct in her shift of emphasis. Forgiveness is about the healing of the wounded party, certainly, but it is also about the transformation of the wrongdoer so that he or she will not repeat the offense (and, possibly, will also experience healing) and about the transformation of the relationship between them. This transformation may protect the forgiver in the future, and it may also protect other people. It is rare for two persons to act out a drama of rending and forgiveness in isolation from a larger matrix of relationships. Other parties have vested interests. While this is especially true for political forgiveness, it is very much true for interpersonal forgiveness as well.

We move now to a discussion of political forgiveness. All of the issues we have encountered in our survey of works on interpersonal forgiveness apply to political forgiveness as well, and are compounded by a number of others.

POLITICAL FORGIVENESS

Forgiveness is a difficult and dangerous concept to carry into the realm of politics. There are some obvious and formidable obstacles, perhaps the most important being that the core grammar of forgiveness belongs to the realm of interpersonal relations. Here forgiveness is usually thought of in one of two ways: (1) as a transaction between *two* parties, the offender and the victim; or (2) as a transaction among *three* parties—the offender, the victim, and a mediating third party (often God). When we try to carry the concept of forgiveness from such simple contexts into the multilayered world of politics, it is much more difficult to hold together.

Another obstacle is the long association between forgiveness and religion. In the West forgiveness has been so tied to Christian teachings and Christian institutions that some thinkers believe it is too colored by theology ever to be retrieved for application in such secular realms as national or international politics. This problem may not be as severe in some other parts of the world. The importance of Archbishop Tutu's rhetoric of forgiveness to South Africa's TRC serves to make the point. Even in South Africa, however, there was some resistance to Tutu's rhetoric just because he was a representative of the Christian community.

The problem of forgiveness' association with Christianity is compounded by the extent to which the Christian understanding of forgiveness was influenced by the sacrament of penance. This sacrament shifted the power to forgive from the victim to God (through the priest as mediator). In fact, the victim was often forgotten and removed from the equation. Emphasis was placed on the offender, who was required to bring the sinful act to confession and carry out the penance prescribed by the priest. The power to forgive was sometimes abused by the church—the extensive system of indulgences being the most prominent example. During the Protestant Reformation and the Counter-Reformation most of these abuses were curtailed, but many if not most Christians still understand forgiveness offered by God to be more important than that offered by the victim.

It is ironic that the very religious institutions that have valued and promoted forgiveness as a virtue are in danger of obscuring it because of their association with it. Exacerbating the problem is our memory that important Christian thinkers themselves, from Augustine to Luther to Niebuhr, have been complicit in the exclusion of forgiveness from politics by identifying separate sets of ethics for the "city of God" and the "earthly city." They thought it to be too much of a stretch to expect a place for the virtue of forgiveness in the rough world of earthly politics. There is room for forgiveness in our lives, but in the realm of private relations, not public ones.

As Hannah Arendt pointed out, Jesus "discovered" the indispensable role of forgiveness in the processes of social change.[11] The canonical gospels reveal that Jesus held forgiveness to be essential if fractured communities were to survive, or, even better, to heal. Despite this, in Christian treatment, starting with the New Testament itself, there is a steady drift away from this perspective to one in which forgiveness is a private matter between transgressor and victim or between parishioner and priest. Fortunately, in recent years there have been a number of excellent works by Christian theologians and ethicists that have gone a long way toward correcting these problems.

The writings of Miroslav Volf, Robert Schreiter, L. Gregory Jones, and Donald W. Shriver Jr. serve as prominent examples.[12]

Another obstacle to the importation of forgiveness into the realm of politics is its association with forgetting. Forgive and forget is a cliché that we have all heard. But in contexts of mass injustice or great rending, forgetfulness is very dangerous. When the wounds and the rage left by violent oppression are ignored or pasted over, they resurface and cause new unrest. Thinkers like Donald Shriver have tried to sever the mental link between forgiving and forgetting, but others, even some as adroit as Miroslav Volf, have reinforced the connection. Legal and political philosopher Martha Minow has argued that, while there are particular and limited situations in which a political process of forgiveness is appropriate, large-scale reconciliation processes need to situate themselves somewhere between vengeance and forgiveness, which, because of its association with forgetfulness, can push toward facile amnesties and can interfere with justice.[13]

The work of Shriver is very helpful in terms of responding to the difficulties outlined above. In *An Ethic for Enemies: Forgiveness in Politics* he champions political forgiveness as a rebuttal of what he considers to be a lamentable and pervasive frame of mind in humanity today:

> I have written this book chiefly to address the frame of mind which resists dealing with the leftover debris of national pasts that continue to clog the relationships of diverse groups of humans around the world. The debris will never get cleaned up and animosity will never drain away until forgiveness enters these relationships in some political form. To dismiss this concern as a preoccupation with ancient history is to miss all the evidence for the truth that William Faulkner put on the lips of one of his characters: "The past is not dead and gone; it isn't even past."[14]

In the introduction to *An Ethic for Enemies* Shriver offers a definition of political forgiveness by outlining its four constituent elements. In opposition to the popular wisdom that associates forgiving with forgetting, he asserts that forgiveness begins with memory, in particular memory that contains a moral judgment of wrong, injustice, and injury. Here we confront the first challenge of political forgiveness. Without an agreement between two or more parties that serious wrongdoing has taken place, forgiveness "stalls at the starting gate." This consensus can take a long time, which is not surprising given general antagonism that usually marks a post-conflict situation. The eventual agreement may well describe a culpability—and associated need for forgiveness—that is bilateral or even multilateral. Even in contexts where one social group has clearly been oppressed by another, there will probably be memory of human rights violations by both sides.

The second element of Shriver's definition of forgiveness is the abandonment of vengeance. This is where the cycle of violence is broken. Without a commitment to the forbearance of revenge, moral judgment (element one) may actually heat up a situation of conflict by arming one or more parties with the knowledge of having been wronged. It is important to note that a forbearance of vengeance does not necessarily include an abandonment of punishment for evildoers, but this punishment would be decided upon and administered by formal institutions that adhere to due process.

Shriver's third element of forgiveness is no less difficult than the first two: empathy for the humanity of the enemy. He is careful to distinguish empathy from sympathy, especially sympathy for the enemy's cause or actions. The combination of moral judgment of wrong and empathy for the wrongdoer's humanity may be rare, but it is this combination that can lay the groundwork for the reconstruction of human community.

Empathy can open former enemies to the final element of forgiveness: the renewal of human relationship. True forgivers will be prepared to begin living with the enemy again on some level of mutual affirmation. In politics this would be coexistence. At the least it would entail a civil relationship between strangers in community. According to Shriver this relationship may or may not embody reconciliation. He places reconciliation at the end of a process that forgiveness begins.[15] Coexistence may be little different from passive tolerance, but even this would be a move away from a violent or destructive past toward a more hopeful future.

Shriver could have added other elements to his list of four. Restitution is one. He makes reference to restitution as a desirable end that becomes possible when memory suffused with judgment has been established, but he does not include it as an essential or definitive part of the process. There is some historical precedent for the exclusion. There have been a number of reconciliation-oriented political processes that have not included restitution or reparations. Some of the Latin American truth commissions serve as examples. I would argue, however, that the absence of restitution was to the detriment of these commissions and the nations they served. As time passed, some of those nations were forced to revisit the issue of reparations and to implement compensation programs. When there has been wrongdoing and rending at a communal or societal level, the issue of reparations cannot be avoided, at least not in the consciousness of the victims.

Two general comments need to be made about the movement of forgiveness from the domain of interpersonal relations to a much larger one. First, the time-line becomes different. While interpersonal forgiveness can take a lifetime, it usually happens more quickly. Political forgiveness can take *generations*. We see this in the United States with the reemergence of calls for apologies and restitution related to the legacy of slavery. This phenomenon not only demonstrates that the ghosts of oppression past do not go away but also shows that statements of repentance and forgiveness can be decades, even centuries in coming. While this fact may be daunting, it is also a source of hope. If the agents of apartheid are slow to confess, they may be moved to do so later, benefiting from the emotional distance provided by time elapsed, or their children may do it for them. A traditional Mi'Kmaq chief on Canada's east coast once explained to me that the wisdom of his people teaches him to take fifteen generations into consideration whenever he speaks to an important decision: the current generation, the seven that preceded it, and the seven that will follow. Not bad advice for students or promoters of political forgiveness.

Second, the language appropriate to the drama of forgiveness is not the same at the interpersonal and societal levels.[16] At the interpersonal level emotive language that gives voice to remorse and reveals the angst of the perpetrator is essential. This can also be true in a large context of reconciliation when a specific perpetrator meets his or her own victims, such as in the amnesty hearings of the TRC. But when a leader of a people, a community, or a constituency offers an apology or forgiveness, it is less important that the language be emotive. Instead, *symbolic* language that acknowledges the breadth of past wrongs or the depth of contrition is more important. Not that emotion is irrelevant, but it must have a different horizon. Perhaps the best example of such language is the *body* language of Willy Brandt when he laid a wreath upon the monument at the Warsaw Ghetto. Instead of bowing to lay the wreath, he knelt. All across Europe this was seen as a sign of repentance on behalf of the German people.[17]

This is not a bad image with which to close our chapter. In the wake of war or oppression the debate and rhetoric about forgiveness can grow well beyond the point of confusion. Sometimes an adroit gesture can cut through the clamor and give a gift of clarity. South Africa had at least two public figures who were masters of such gestures: Nelson Mandela and Desmond Tutu. In the next chapter we will survey the history that not only brought that country to the precipice of disaster but also produced such extraordinary rescuers as Mandela and Tutu.

3

Historical Overview

This chapter will concentrate on South African history during the second half of the twentieth century. In 1948 the first National Party government was formed and embarked upon its policy of apartheid. Its reign lasted until 1994, when the country held its first free and fair election and the Government of National Unity was formed, being led by the ANC and Nelson Mandela. Historical developments in the latter half of the 1990s will not be considered except to provide a description of the socioeconomic conditions with which the post-apartheid regime was forced to wrestle and which provided a backdrop to the TRC. Most of the themes and dynamics of the historical period we will consider were firmly rooted in earlier developments—going back at least as far as the first European settlement in 1652. I will offer only the very briefest sketch of these earlier developments; there are a number of good books available to those who would explore them more fully.[1]

Human beings have been living in the territory now called South Africa for many thousands of years, perhaps as many as 125,000. Middle Stone Age toolmakers may have existed there forty thousand years ago. Six hundred or so sites belonging to Late Stone Age peoples (twenty thousand years ago) have been uncovered. The San hunter-gatherers, who came to be called Bushmen by Europeans, were likely their descendants. The San, whose population probably never exceeded twenty thousand, lived in highly mobile bands of twenty to two hundred people. It was their absolute dependence on game that caused them to organize this way and to be widely dispersed in southernmost Africa.[2]

The Khoikhoi, called Hottentots by Europeans, whose numbers may have reached 100,000, are thought to have been hunter-gatherers related to the San. They obtained cattle from an outside source about two thousand years ago and by 1652 were firmly established in a cattle-herding way of life. They lived mainly along the Atlantic and Indian coasts of what are now Namibia and South Africa, and along the Orange River.[3]

The majority of South Africans, called Africans, belong to the Bantu-speaking peoples—the Zulu-Xhosa-Swazi, the Sotho-Tswana, the Venda, the Shona, and others. A myth has long been propagated that these peoples

23

arrived on the plains of Southern Africa at the same time that the Dutch became implanted on the Cape of Good Hope. Archeological research has shown this to be false; Bantu-speaking chiefdoms were present much earlier. They appear to have sustained themselves as mixed farmers. In the Late Iron Age their population increased, more livestock was kept, sociopolitical organization became more complex, and communities grew up around deposits of gold, copper, and iron.[4]

At the end of the fifteenth century the Portuguese circumnavigated the Cape of Good Hope and began the European association with southern Africa. Although the Portuguese rarely landed on the Cape, English, French, and Dutch companies trading with the Far East all considered building a settlement there. It was the Dutch who decided to follow through. Jan van Riebeeck established a base for the Dutch East India Company (VOC) at what is now Cape Town in 1652. It was to be a modest settlement that would provide fresh food and a hospital for sailors on their way to Asia. In 1657 plans changed, and the granting of permission for nine company servants to establish private farms amounted to the planting of a full-fledged colony. Over the following years more and more free burghers established their homesteads.

From the beginning, relations among the three groupings of people—Khoikhoi, Bantu-speaking peoples, and Europeans—were marked by great conflict. Added to this mix were slaves brought from further north on the African continent and from parts of Asia where the VOC was active. The Khoikhoi, squeezed between the Bantu-speaking kingdoms and the advance of white settlement, were the first victims of that conflict; forced into service to Europeans or into flight to the frontier, they eventually disappeared as a distinct people.

Dutch settlers were joined by other northern Europeans, notably Huguenots. Their numbers, and the territory they put under cultivation, grew rapidly. Tensions developed between the so-called Boers and their VOC governors, whose first concern was the company's interests, not the welfare of the settlement. Over the course of the eighteenth century Cape Town grew to become a pluralistic city more open to Enlightenment values. The farmers, who were conservative people guided by Dutch Reform religion, did not look kindly upon this change. Then, in 1806, the entire colony was taken over by the British, who interfered in the ways the burghers settled disputes with the Khoikhoi and treated their slaves. As a result of these strains and the desire for more and better land, "trekboers"[5] began venturing further and further afield, surveying vast areas of land to the north, and encountering the Bantu-speaking peoples there.

The nineteenth century was marked by several periods of intense conflict, between Europeans and Africans and among African groups themselves. During the early decades a major period of upheaval took place among the Bantu-speaking chiefdoms. It is not clear to what extent this crisis emerged from developments within African society and to what extent it was precipitated by contact with whites. In any case, there appears to have been what T. R. H. Davenport calls "massive human tragedy." The Xhosa word for this time is *mfecane*—"to be weak, emaciated from hunger."[6]

The entire century was marked by wars between Africans and European groups. Early on, there were skirmishes on the eastern frontier of the Cape Colony with the Xhosa. As trekboers moved north in greater numbers, there were battles with various Bantu-speaking groups. Guided by their Calvinistic religion, the trekkers felt that their fate was in the hands of God. They suffered massacres but ultimately won more fights than they lost, sometimes against numbers much greater than their own. Their defeats and victories were woven into a mythology of divine selection as the "white tribe of Africa." Later, British armies entered the fray, trying both to moderate the conflicts between Boers and Africans and to advance colonial interests. Eventually, the British presence became entrenched in areas such as Natal, where the British imported large numbers of workers from the Indian subcontinent, further diversifying the racial mix of what is now South Africa.

Over the course of that violent century, the collection of whites who ventured north forged a cohesive identity and a distinct language; they became Afrikaners and their tongue Afrikaans. The Dutch Reformed Church became the central institution in their communities. They formed a number of independent republics, the most notable being the South African Republic, led by Paul Kruger. As the nineteenth century gave way to the twentieth, their interactions with others did not become less violent; the opposite happened.

The British seemed willing to tolerate Afrikaner self-rule but were keen to ensure access to the rich diamond and mineral (especially gold) deposits on the large swath of land upon which the trekboers had settled. Economic disputes intensified, and war broke out on October 11, 1899. It was a horrible war. Heavy casualties were suffered on both sides. Its most appalling character was the number of civilians who became the victims of violence and starvation. Of the at least twenty-five thousand Boers who died, most were women and children who had been forcibly removed from their homesteads and placed in British concentration camps. Twelve thousand Africans lost their lives as well, and the British colonial forces lost more than twenty-two thousand.[7]

The war was a crisis of epic proportions for the newly formed Afrikaner people. The horrible loss of life was devastating, as was the military defeat for people who had believed themselves to be on a divinely ordained mission. Much farmland was no longer suitable for cultivation, and many Boers fell from their position as landowners to join the burgeoning proletariat—an economic status no higher than that of the Africans to whom they felt innately superior. Afrikaner society was struck such a powerful blow that it was in danger of disintegration, but, digging deep into its Calvinist religion for fortitude and themes with which to rebuild its national myth, it rebounded with considerable vigor. The result was a reintegration that was striking in its swiftness, its comprehensiveness, and its brutality toward nonwhites. There are many signs that the myth of apartheid, which guided the Afrikaner people for most of the twentieth century, and which would become a cohesive national policy in mid century, was born during this postwar reintegration.

Only eight years after the war, the Afrikaner-led Union of South Africa was formed with the blessing of the British. It included the former Afrikaner stronghold of the Transvaal and stretched as far as Natal in the east and all the way to the Cape in the South. All of the previous political unions in this territory had enforced policies of racial segregation, but the forms and extent of such policies were greatly exaggerated in the new state. The breadth and depth of the economic exploitation of blacks grew in proportion. For blacks, and especially Africans, the first half of the twentieth century was a time of loss: loss of political power, loss of land, loss of freedom of movement, loss of personal autonomy, and loss of dignity.

There was a concerted and progressively thorough attempt to restrict African contact with whites to situations in which the Africans were providing service or labor. To a lesser but still significant extent the same goals were pursued in relation to people of mixed race and to Indians. Pass laws, which excluded blacks from urban areas designated for whites, had existed since the time of the original Cape colony, but now they became national policy.

Even more striking was the separation of races in agricultural areas. White farmers were competing with African peasants for land to cultivate, and mining interests in pursuit of cheap labor were pressuring the government to loosen the Africans' ties to the land. These combined interests were successful in their lobbying, and the government passed the Native Land Act of 1913. Even though Africans represented the majority of the population, they were given only 7 percent of the land. In 1936 the amount of designated land would increase, but only to 14 percent. Typically, this land was neither highly fertile nor close to urban markets. Many thousands of African men were forced to leave their families and become part of the migrant labor pool that serviced the mines and, to a lesser extent, manufacturing. Like their white co-workers, they unionized, but unions were race specific, and the higher-paying skilled jobs were largely reserved for whites.

During the last years of the 1800s and the first decades of the twentieth century, some important loci of black solidarity began to form. One was the unions. Their struggles were very difficult and few short-term gains were achieved, but a foundation was being laid for a labor movement that would play a key anti-apartheid role decades later. Similarly, among the churches, which were also segregated by race, black leadership began to grow. African Independent Churches began to establish themselves as early as the 1890s.[8] Some of their leaders began to push for political gains for their constituency, becoming harbingers of later anti-apartheid crusaders like Alan Boesak and Desmond Tutu. Finally, I will mention the formation of black organizations of political activism. Most notable was the ANC, which was created in response to the segregationist policies of Louis Botha, the first president of the Union of South Africa. None of these instruments of black aspiration were able to make substantive gains for their people, and what they did achieve was largely torn down by the National Party governments after 1948, but the modest achievements of the early century planted seeds that would germinate into powerful liberation initiatives a few generations later.

1948–1994: THE APARTHEID ERA

Racial segregation reached a new level after the election of the National Party in 1948. This party, which held uninterrupted power until 1994 and which was led by men who sympathized with Hitler's National Socialism, embarked on a program of social engineering that was remarkable in its boldness, its scope, and the violence with which it was implemented. The ideology that fueled this program certainly included a potent element of white supremacy, but it was also marked by an oft-voiced belief that all races would best flourish if they were left to evolve unfettered by each other. The ideology, and the program, were given the name *apartheid.* When that label became infamous, it was replaced by the more banal *separate development.* But the entire economy that made white South Africans the richest people on the continent was based on integrated development, albeit a form of integration that was exploitative in the extreme. This left the architects of apartheid with the confounding task of designing a society, or cluster of societies, in which whites and blacks followed distinct paths of social-cultural-political development, but which kept blacks from full independence and self-reliance. A measure of dependence was needed to maintain the great pool of cheap labor. Despite Herculean efforts, they were ultimately unsuccessful.

Before the 1948 election South African society had actually been showing a trend toward racial integration. The new government moved swiftly to reverse this. Legislation was drawn up to establish distinct biological categories of human beings—African, coloured (mixed race), Asian, white—and to make it illegal for members of different categories to live in the same neighborhoods, to marry each other, or to have sex. The bureaucracy put in place to provide a racial designation for people whose "identity" was in dispute performed such absurd practices as measuring their hips and lips and sticking a pencil in their hair to see if it would be held. These labeling procedures had dire consequences for mixed-race families, which often saw their members earmarked to different groupings. A kind of racial Berlin Wall was being erected.

Other walls were torn down. Certain urban and suburban neighborhoods, long populated by blacks, were now designated for whites. The forced removals from Sophiatown (Johannesburg) and District Six (Cape Town) are legendary. In the latter case an ethnically diverse body of people, which had developed a very strong sense of community and a cultural vibrancy, disproving many of apartheid's assumptions, was broken up and dispersed into new townships far from the city. Save for a few places of worship, the entire borough was leveled.

Blacks suffered further political disenfranchisement. Africans had already been limited to electing a small number of white representatives to speak for them in Parliament. This "privilege" was stripped away. Mixed-race persons in the Cape had previously maintained the right to vote. This was lost.

The professional and entrepreneurial activities of nonwhites were also closely regulated. Blacks were subjected to limitations in terms of the kinds and sizes of businesses they could own and the areas where those enterprises could be located. Restrictions were also put in place regarding the numbers of blacks who could enter certain professions and the population to which they could offer their services.

Perhaps the most dramatic apartheid policy was the development of semi-autonomous homelands. The pieces of South African territory set aside for various African groups in the 1913 Native Land Act—7 percent of the national land mass, later expanded to 14 percent—were granted a measure of independence. The idea was for Africans, a clear majority of the population, to pursue their separate future on this fraction of the land, while whites forged theirs on the rest. African independence did not come without the South African government maintaining a measure of control, or without Pretoria reworking the structures of governance in the homelands. A system of patronage was put in place that kept the leaders of the homelands in the pockets of the National Party government, guaranteeing for Pretoria enduring influence.

Despite commissions and studies appointed to prove the contrary, the homelands were not economically viable. Natural resources were too scarce. They were located too far from commercial centers. It was inevitable that large numbers of African men would depart to work in the mines or other industries that thrived on cheap migrant labor and that an equally significant number of women would leave to perform domestic service for whites. These migrants became totally dependent on and vulnerable to their employers, who signed the passes that gave Africans permission to reside and travel outside of the group areas. Persons caught without a pass were routinely deported to one of the homelands. This kind of leverage enabled many whites to exploit and abuse with impunity Africans in their employ.

Africans, Asians, and people of mixed race responded to the National Party initiatives with protest and civil disobedience. By December 1949 the ANC had approved a program of resistance that urged the use of boycotts, strikes, and noncooperation and demanded African self-determination and freedom from white domination. Other organizations, including the South African Indian Congress, joined the resistance program. Protest intensified in 1952, the three-hundred-year anniversary of Jan van Riebeeck's arrival at the Cape. There was an attempt to throw the "administration of the law into confusion by Gandhian methods."[9] Protests focused on the removal of legislation related to pass laws, livestock limitation, Bantu authorities, group areas, the separate representation of voters, and the suppression of communism. This last issue was becoming increasingly important. The Communist Party was gaining support and becoming particularly influential among black leaders and their organizations. In response the government passed the Suppression of Communism Act (1950), which gave it broad powers to ban organizations and to prohibit specific individuals from taking part in other organizations. These powers were used to curb black political organizations and to break multiracial trade unions, a few of which had survived earlier bans.[10]

During the ensuing decades black political resistance moved through a series of cycles in which it heated up and then cooled off. As time passed the "hot times" became more intense and lasted longer, and the cooler periods started to disappear.

In the 1960s a campaign of passive resistance was launched, this time with a particular focus on the hated pass laws. The most tragic episode of that time was the massacre of sixty-nine nonviolent protesters in the township of Sharpeville near Johannesburg. After the massacre, positions on both sides hardened. The government banned the ANC (and the PAC), which then turned to guerrilla tactics.

Actually, the ANC waited until 1961 to launch its military wing, the MK. This decision was taken after Nelson Mandela wrote to Prime Minister Hendrik Verwoerd, probably the most important designer of apartheid policy, requesting a meeting. When Verwoerd failed to reply to the letter, the ANC leadership decided that it was time to try new tactics. Three years later Mandela and several other senior ANC officials would be given life sentences for their roles in sabotage operations.[11] These figures, especially Mandela, became the focal point of anti-apartheid sentiment in South Africa and abroad.

For more than a decade after the Sharpeville-era protests the government was successful in imposing a measure of "law and order" in South Africa. This stability was an important factor in the attraction of foreign investment to the country, and the economy grew steadily. In 1976 things changed. Student demonstrations broke out in Soweto against the imposition of Afrikaans as the language of instruction. A number of schoolchildren, some of them quite young, were killed when the police opened fire. Protests erupted around the country and lasted for more than a year. More than six hundred people died. Spasms of protest continued to break out until 1980.

There were three or four years of relative quiet in the early 1980s, but in September of 1984 youth again sparked a wave of defiance. Through the second half of the 1980s President P. W. Botha's government was forced to deal with a constant state of emergency as youth-led protests erupted around the country and organizations such as the United Democratic Front (UDF, a close affiliate of the ANC) and the PAC expanded their networks and their operations.[12]

During the 1980s clear divisions within the collection of liberation organizations began to appear. These were marked by philosophical differences and by conflicts between groups such as the UDF-ANC and the IFP (Inkatha Freedom Party).[13]

One of the philosophical fault lines drove a wedge between the ANC and the PAC. The PAC had been formed in 1959 when, upset with the influence of communists and frustrated that more radical action was not being taken, a group of "Africanists" left the ANC to form their own organization. Leaders among the Africanists were oriented toward an African cultural renaissance and held that "Africa is for the Africans"—a perspective pointedly different from the communist one, which attributed South Africa's racial injustice to class conflict. During the 1960s and 1970s the ANC and the PAC each established military wings, in-country cell groups, and international headquarters. At times they tried to cooperate, but their differences always prevailed.[14]

By the late 1980s and early 1990s these differences were plainly manifest in the actions of their military wings. ANC and MK operatives certainly committed human rights violations against South African citizens, black and white, but the philosophy that guided their actions identified racism, not whites, as the enemy. ANC policy was to attack military and infrastructure targets and to minimize civilian casualties.[15] By the final years of National Party reign, the PAC had progressed to a "one settler, one bullet" policy, and its guerrilla organizations were committing commando attacks against civilian targets like churches and taverns.

The Black Consciousness movement, of which Steve Biko was the most important figure, contributed to the philosophical debate by challenging blacks of all constituencies (Indians and mixed-race people included) to free their minds from the brainwashing of their white oppressors. The movement was launched in the early 1970s in an effort to "rebuild and recondition the mind of the oppressed in such a way that they would be ready forcefully to demand what was rightfully theirs."[16] This movement had far-reaching influence among blacks and also impressed some whites who were disillusioned with their country's politics of race. Biko was beaten to death in prison and became one of the internationally known martyrs of the anti-apartheid movement.

The rift between the PAC and the ANC was of small consequence compared to the conflict between the ANC and the IFP. The IFP was led by a Zulu prince named Mangosuthu Buthelezi. Buthelezi had formed ties to Nelson Mandela and other ANC figures during his student days; he had been expelled from Fort Hare University because of his involvement in an ANC Youth League demonstration. Later, through clever political moves, he had become chief minister of the Zulu homeland called KwaZulu. ANC leaders supported his acceptance of this position and hoped that he would aid their movement. Relations between Buthelezi and the ANC deteriorated, however, and he turned the IFP into a Zulu ethno-nationalist party opposed to the

ANC. Buthelezi became an important national figure in the mid-1970s, bringing the heads of the various homelands together, along with Indian and mixed race leaders, to resist the territorial disintegration of South Africa planned by the National Party.[17]

Through the 1970s and 1980s, Buthelezi tried to play the dual cards of Zulu nationalism and political realism. Despite continued opposition to apartheid, the IFP began to collaborate with the security apparatus of the South African government. Confrontations between IFP supporters and those of the UDF escalated in townships near Durban and Pietermaritzburg, the two large urban centers in what is now KwaZulu-Natal. By the late 1980s the conflict had intensified almost to the level of a civil war. Massacres became common. Years later the TRC was able to reveal the extent to which apartheid security forces provided resources and tactical support to IFP operatives during this strife.[18]

By the 1980s a couple of other factors were coming to shape the anti-apartheid movement. One was the growing strength of this movement in other parts of the world. While I give very little attention to developments outside South Africa in this chapter, it must be noted that international pressures were crucial to the ending of white rule. The expulsion of South Africa from the British Commonwealth and the exclusion of its teams from athletic competitions like the Olympics had strong symbolic value, but the implementation of economic sanctions by many countries and bodies like the Commonwealth were probably of greatest importance.

Another significant development was the increased activism of Christian organizations and leaders. The South African Council of Churches took a place of leadership in the resistance, causing the security forces to bomb its offices. Black clergy became important figures within the struggle. Desmond Tutu and Alan Boesak were popular speakers at rallies in South Africa and widely known personalities abroad. Tutu's receipt of the Nobel Peace Prize and Boesak's election to the presidency of the World Alliance of Reform Churches in 1982 gave increased international attention to apartheid and signaled to South African whites and blacks alike that the world was becoming intolerant of their political system. Organizations like the World Council of Churches and the World Alliance of Reform Churches added their weight and resources to the pressure being piled on the National Party government.

P. W. Botha had become prime minister of South Africa in 1978, and then president after the constitutional reforms of the mid-1980s. During his tenure anti-apartheid resistance grew stronger on all fronts. He responded by becoming progressively more stubborn in his defense of apartheid. This growing stubbornness was matched by willingness to employ violence to maintain law and order. By 1989 the country was in a continual state of emergency, the economy was in trouble as a result of international sanctions and other pressures, and members of the National Party caucus and cabinet were advocating negotiations with Nelson Mandela and other black leaders. Botha held a perfunctory meeting with Mandela but backed off from sincere negotiations. After Botha suffered a stroke, he was maneuvered out of office and replaced by F. W. de Klerk, a long-time member of the cabinet who had proved himself to be a conservative.

On February 2, 1990, de Klerk opened Parliament with a speech that had been rumored to be reformist. The rumors fell far short of the mark. Allister Sparks explains the importance of the address:

> He didn't just change the country, he transmuted it. In those thirty-five minutes de Klerk unleashed forces that within four years would sweep away the old South Africa and establish an altogether new and different country in its place. Another country with another constitution and another flag and another national anthem. And above all, another ethos.
>
> He demolished the old Afrikaner vision of a white South Africa, of a *volkstaat* that was theirs by divine right and without which they could not survive as a national entity, and ensured that in its stead a new black-led South Africa would arise, as alien to traditional Afrikaner thinking as Palestinian majority rule to Israelis.[19]

De Klerk did not intend to open the country to black majority rule. He made this clear in speeches after his dramatic remarks of February 1990. He envisioned a system of power sharing embodied in a House of Representatives elected by universal franchise, a Senate in which all racial groups would have equal representation (African tribal groups being counted as separate entities), and an all-party "collegiate" cabinet with a presidency that rotated annually among the parties with the most support. By freeing antiapartheid leaders and unbanning liberation organizations, however, he had unleashed forces that swept away his plans. Black leaders balked at the power-sharing plan and its format of group representation based on racial categorization. Negotiations between the National Party, the ANC, the PAC, the IFP, and other groups dragged out until November 1993. Piece by piece de Klerk gave up his plan for a government that would have kept Afrikaners from being subjected to majority rule. In the end the parties agreed that the first democratic elections would be followed by the formation of a Government of National Unity that would include all parties receiving more than 5 percent of the vote.[20]

The ANC won an overwhelming majority in the 1994 elections. Mandela became president and de Klerk one of his two vice-presidents. Part way through the term, the National Party withdrew from the government. The ANC won another large majority in 1999 and was no longer required to keep other parties in the cabinet, but some representatives of other parties, including Buthelezi of the IFP, were invited to stay.

The period of transition between de Klerk's famous speech and the elections of 1994 was not a peaceful one. The National Party tried to garner support for its power-sharing plan among black organizations that stood to lose ground to the ANC under majority rule. Chief among these was the IFP, which was already in continual violent conflict with ANC supporters. Security police provided extensive support to Inkatha groups and in return asked them to carry out specific missions against ANC or UDF targets. The PAC was getting muscled to the edges of the negotiations. Its guerrilla organizations stepped up attacks against civilian targets, perhaps in an effort to seize political ground. Afrikaner nationalist groups were formed and turned to terrorist tactics. With peace and democracy within reach, and apartheid in the throes of death, many of the country's worst episodes of bloodshed took place.

It was a surprise, then, when the 1994 elections were relatively peaceful and political violence almost disappeared in their wake. As Sparks said, a new country was being born; its transition to relative political peace and stability was swift. But this new country was, of course, unable to make a clean break with the past. Economic apartheid had not been overthrown. Political violence was replaced by criminal violence, much of which arose from the same socioeconomic dynamics that had fostered the political strife. South Africa was still a place of dramatic poverty, both relative and absolute. At the same time, there was great confidence to be gleaned from the defeat of oppression. Huge challenges lay ahead but also behind. The new country, the Rainbow Nation, was to be a place of hope as well as struggle.

THE NEW DISPENSATION

The new country born in April of 1994 is marked by stunning diversity and miserable inequality. Strong regional differences are compounded by racial, ethnic, and class differences within each region. The life of some African farmers living in Venda can be characterized as pre-industrial and tribal.[21] This way of life can be contrasted with the cosmopolitan, post-industrial lifestyle of people (mostly white, but increasingly black) in Cape Town, Johannesburg, Durban, or Pretoria. But residents of Cape Town need not travel to Venda, or any of the other former homelands, to find communities and cultures radically different from their own. A trip of only a few miles to the Cape Flats (a sprawling area of black townships) or to Afrikaner farms in the Stellenbosh area would do the trick. A strong case could be made for the position that these are not subgroups of one society but are instead distinct societies themselves. South Africa has eleven official languages. Until the new dispensation, it had ten semi-autonomous homelands.

As recently as a dozen years ago an equally strong case could be made for the position that there were *two* societies in South Africa. One was composed of people who had basic human rights, such as the franchise and freedom of movement. The other was composed of a much greater number of people who had no such rights. With the new constitution and the democratic elections of 1994, these two societies have not simply melted into each other in a seamless union.

According to a 1989 survey, apartheid produced the world's most unequal society.[22] In 1995, a Danish government document offered the following statistics:

The richest ten percent of South Africans account for 51 percent of the national income, whereas less than four percent goes to the poorest 40 percent. The distribution of wealth is even more distorted; five percent of the population lay claim to almost 90 percent of total assets. In the rural areas of the former homelands, two thirds of the blacks live below the official poverty line. Whites earn ten times as much as blacks on average, and they live an average of ten years longer. The infant mortality rate among whites is ten (in 1000) as compared to 100 for blacks.[23]

The dramatic political transformation of the 1990s has not been matched by similar socioeconomic change. Since the election in 1994 nonwhites have come to dominate the legislative and administrative branches of government at all levels, and progress is being made at making the bureaucracy representative of the population at all levels of seniority, but the ascension of mixed-race persons, Indians, and especially Africans to senior positions in the private sector is happening much more slowly. Similarly, wage levels for whites are still much higher than for others. Blacks (especially Africans) are much more restricted in their access to quality education and training programs, and many or most work places are still characterized by vertical and adversarial relations between members of different races.

This imbalance in income is both a cause and an effect of the remarkably large amount of internal migration, especially among Africans who are forced to leave the former homelands where there has been economic collapse. Thousands of rural poor are pouring into urban areas each week, staking out tracts of unused land in the hope of making a better life. Every urban center in the country and many smaller towns have adjacent townships where many residents live in shacks under very difficult conditions.

Perhaps the most dramatic effect of inequality in South Africa is the country's levels of crime. The violent crime rates in Johannesburg and Cape Town are among the highest in the world, and the rest of the country does not lag far behind. Much of the media attention and research on crime victims in South Africa focuses on suburban residents and businesses, and their risks are indeed high by any international standard, but those living in poor areas are even harder hit.[24] In some parts of South Africa a form of warlordism has become endemic, and it appears that this situation will remain for the foreseeable future. Police acknowledge a countrywide increase in vigilantism, including the stoning of family members of those accused of crimes. The international visibility of South Africa's crime rates discourages investment, clearly having a negative economic impact. The most important cause of this crime is unemployment among young males, especially Africans (and those from the mixed-race community in the Cape). In many areas unemployment among these demographic groups runs greater than 50 percent. Their proximity to large numbers of wealthy South Africans and easy access to guns (a legacy of the anti-apartheid struggle) exacerbate the situation.

Another consequence of the great amount of social dislocation in South Africa is a soaring HIV infection rate, among the highest in the world. Migrant labor, poor health education, and the world's highest incidence of rape are contributing factors, as are a number of social ills that usually accompany widespread poverty: alcohol and drug abuse, family breakup, and promiscuity.

In 1994 the new African-led government was handed the challenge of alleviating these problems and transforming the socioeconomic structure that produces them. It is nothing less than a heroic task. Despite the close association between the ANC, socialist trade unions, and the South African Communist Party before the political transition of the early 1990s, the government of Nelson Mandela rejected the option of a shift to a socialist state and the redistribution of wealth through such measures as the nationalization of industry or the collectivization of land. Indeed, while the social safety net has been extended to a modest degree, the new government has surprised observers with its broad embrace of market capitalism. Likely because of a concern to avoid "white flight" and the accompanying loss of expertise and capital, ANC policies designed to redress inequality have rarely been radical or dramatic, and it could be argued that the government is doing more to confront absolute poverty than relative poverty. Broad initiatives in housing, education, health, water services, and other social-service areas have been launched, but these suffer from a lack of capital, and the government has been reluctant to increase corporate income taxes or private taxes for the wealthy to fund them.

Perhaps the most impressive legislative initiatives have been the ones that confront the dynamic of inequality in the work place. The passing of the new Labour Relations Act of 1995 was a watershed. It is true that the ANC surprised many observers with its broad embrace of market capitalism and its cooperation with the structural adjustment programs of the International Monetary Fund (IMF), but the Labour Relations Act bucks some of the major trends of economic globalization. In this legislation the right to strike is greatly expanded. Workers, other than those in essential services, can strike on most collective bargaining issues without fear of losing their jobs as long as they follow some relatively simple procedures.[25] The rules of collective bargaining are much more thoroughly spelled out—with a shift toward the interests of labor.

At the beginning of this decade the most visible and controversial piece of labor legislation was the Employment Equity Act. This is an affirmative action initiative designed to counter the forces that have relegated "designated groups" to unemployment or the least remunerative echelons of the work force and have denied them equal pay for equal work. The act identifies the following "designated groups": blacks (this category includes Africans, Indians, and people of mixed race), women, and disabled people. All employers with fifty or more employees (legislation for smaller firms is pending) must abandon any policies or practices that exclude members of designated groups and implement practices that foster the hiring, advancement, and provision of equal pay to members of those groups.[26]

The new labor legislation has been fairly high profile in South Africa, but its visibility has come nowhere near that of the TRC. This venture dominated news coverage and public attention in South Africa for much of the late 1990s and garnered considerable notice around the world. It has been a source of intense controversy as well as profound hope. In the chapters to come we will view this bold initiative from the perspectives provided by each of the acts in our drama of political forgiveness.

4

Act One: Truth-telling

The first act in our drama of forgiveness is about opening a good conversation. Truth-telling about harm done in the past needs to happen such that the appropriate people are talking (in the appropriate way) and the appropriate people are listening (in the appropriate way). This is as true for forgiveness among tens of millions of people as it is for forgiveness between two people. Every context has its own contingencies that determine what it means to have a good conversation. Those who design processes of truth-telling would do well to discover these contingencies, but this is no mean task.

THE NEED FOR TRUTH

Reflecting on the process of coming to terms with the politics and history of their country, South Africans of all races often recount a singular moment when they became aware of apartheid as something radically anomalous—when they realized that their lives, their communities, and all their relationships were embedded in and distorted by a bizarre and dark social system. For many, this moment came when they were children; for others, it was later. From that time on, the ground under their feet never seemed quite solid. Those who chose to give a lot of attention to this realization inevitably experienced more such moments as they discovered the grotesque contours of race relations in their country. Many others had further revelations imposed on them as the politics of apartheid invaded their lives.

For most South Africans it was extremely difficult to know what was really happening in their country. Yes, it was clear to those who cared to look (and to the many blacks who had no choice but to look) that there was official, systematic, and violent repression of nonwhites. Beyond acknowledging that reality, however, it was difficult to fill in details other than the ones stumbled upon in daily life. The government-sponsored media, such as the South African Broadcasting Company, was essentially an extension of the National Party's propaganda machine, and the rest of the formal media was under censorship. Those involved with liberation organizations were privy to other sources of information, but there were also rumors about atrocities in the ANC camps, and some of the other liberation organizations used these to their own advantage. By the 1980s anti-ANC rhetoric from organizations such as the IFP was almost as strong as that from the government. In the midst of this ambiguity, all parties fought public relations battles along with the physical battles. One's perceptions of "the truth" was largely influenced by such factors as the part of the country where one lived, one's exposure to international media or publications (which was tightly restricted), one's type and level of education, and to whom one chose to listen.

Thus it comes as no surprise that many millions of South Africans were totally captivated by the TRC hearings and by the general work of uncovering past events conducted by the commission. This fascination was undoubtedly related to the many experiences of having one's world turned upside down by a political fact.

A great discourse about truth-telling—its urgency, its primacy, and its proper nature—was launched in South Africa in the early 1990s. As apartheid was coming to an end, millions of South Africans found themselves in a strange relationship with truth; they were on existentially unstable ground, unsure of the "facts" that had served as foundations for their lives. "Truths" in almost all areas of their lives came into question. Assumptions, dogmas, and myths that shaped their nation, their churches, their system of commerce, and most other institutions were being pounded into dust.

It would be natural to assume that this was the case more for whites than blacks, which is true to a certain extent, but the beliefs that undergirded many black institutions also came into question. The many black churches that told their members to stay apolitical and portrayed liberation activists as troublemakers serve as examples. Of course, great numbers of blacks, especially those that were active in liberation organizations, saw the opposite process occur as well; their beliefs, long challenged, were now moving into the mainstream.

"District Six" was the location of South Africa's most famous (and infamous) forced resettlement. When it was first occupied, District Six was actually on the outskirts of Cape Town, but as the city grew, it became enfolded in the urban center. Most of the people who lived there were neither white nor African. In apartheid terminology, they were called coloured, but this labeling did injustice to the cultural and ethnic diversity that thrived there. When listening to accounts of life in that borough, it is difficult to sift history from legend; a powerful and beautiful mythology has grown up about the community, aided by the work of such figures as Richard Reeve—a District Six boy who was educated at Oxford and became an internationally celebrated playwright before his murder in the late 1980s.

One thing is clear: a very diverse collection of peoples, including Christians, Jews, and Muslims, lived together with a harmony and a vitality that disproved the fundamental tenets of apartheid. Even the quasi-criminal youth gangs like the Seven Steps Gang are remembered with more fondness than fear. Religious celebrations and cultural festivals from many traditions were performed in the streets, often with neighbors from different backgrounds joining in.

As Cape Town grew, the land in District Six became more valuable, and white developers and officials began to covet it. The National Party government was already offended by the extent to which District Six demonstrated the power of cross-cultural engagement and the possibility of interracial friendship. Besides, it was becoming a center of anti-apartheid activity. In the late sixties bulldozers were sent in and the entire borough, save for a few houses of worship, was razed. Residents were dispersed throughout new townships that were being constructed at greater distances from the city. In fact, some people were sent so far away that their daily train or bus commute to work in Cape Town took hours. The new settlements were more race and class specific. Today they are awash in poverty and report some of the highest violent crime rates in the world. Many of the people who were resettled describe the experience as heartbreaking or even soul shattering. Younger generations speak of the old folks who never recovered.

The sparing of churches and mosques by the government was a tactical mistake. Former residents continued to travel there to worship, and they became key to the resistance against new development. Even today much of the land has not been redeveloped. The movement to revitalize District Six as a cultural ideal and as a community is very much alive. Congregations like St. Mark's Anglican Church and the local Moravian fellowship, along with a number of community groups, are involved in efforts to reclaim the land and have it used for purposes true to the spirit of the community. The District Six Museum is known around the world for its commemoration of what was and for the resources it provides to artists and cultural rebuilders. It is housed in an old Methodist church—a building that was no longer needed by its mixed-race congregation when it amalgamated with a white congregation in Cape Town. The new congregation, Central Methodist Mission, is carrying former residents of District Six and their children into new adventures of interracial camaraderie.

FINDING A WAY TO NAME THE HARM DONE

South Africa initiated the most ambitious process of historical remembering that the world had ever seen. The South Africans who designed this process realized that truth-telling about the past involved a lot more than the sharing of memories. The how and why of such a sharing would have to be thought through with great care. Who would have power to speak? Who would design the forums in which the speaking would take place? Who would preside over them? Who would be given the task of shaping the documents that would record the process? Given that there is an imaginative element to reconstructions of the past, what kinds of media, academics, and artists should be involved in the process?

The designers of the truth-telling process had to come to terms with the fact that the question What is truth? has no simple answer. Truth looks different from different perspectives. The TRC would have to be a forum that allowed for multiple perspectives but also demanded a certain level of rigor in terms of the verification of historical facts. When dealing with the attack that killed eleven worshipers at St. James Church in a white Cape Town suburb, for example, the TRC would have to establish such facts as who did (and ordered) what during the attack and its preparations, but it would also have to make space for the anti-apartheid commandos to explain why they felt the killing of worshipers advanced their struggle, for victims to relate their experience of the attack as well as the impact it has had on their lives, and so on. Out of these discussions would arise plural, even competing truths.

One relevant issue was the extent to which the truth-telling process would be oriented toward the discovery and disclosure of "hard facts," and alternatively, the amount of space that would be given to imagination in interpretation of those facts. I juxtapose here a kind of truth that gives primary attention to forensic, detailed evidence with another kind that seeks to interpret evidence so as to paint an evaluative history in broader strokes. The latter, by nature, must make room for a certain fictive element. Writing (with his co-authors) during the early days of the TRC, Kader Asmal, later the ANC minister of education, made it clear that he was aware of this tension. Asmal acknowledged that "history is fiction, subject to a fitful muse, memory."[1] He also acknowledged the important role of imagination but was eager to put strong boundaries around it:

> This is a workaday exercise, involving academic controversy, political debate, media revelations, processes of proof and of disproof. . . . Thus the process of forging collective memory is a flaring up of debate; it is the creation of a public atmosphere in which the seemingly unimportant memories and annals of the past achieve a new public importance. New incentives are unleashed so that forgotten or neglected private thoughts and evidence enter the domain of public acknowledgment. For the first time, seemingly worthless private reminiscence achieves public currency and manifest worth. This is a precise, not a sentimental process.[2]

Commissioners wrestled with the enigma of the nature of truth throughout the life of the TRC. In its *Final Report*, four different kinds of truth are acknowledged. The first kind is *forensic* or *objective* truth. This understanding is closely related to the commission's mandate to make public findings on specific events and the individuals involved in them. The investigative unit was deeply involved in this work. The second kind of truth acknowledged is *personal, narrative* truth. Hearings included a strong element of storytelling, as did the *Final Report*, and both victims and perpetrators were given leeway to interpret the events they described and to articulate their motivations and emotions. The third kind of truth is *social* or *dialogical* truth, the kind generated through extensive debate. Finally, the report also highlights the importance of *restorative* truth. This is truth that heals the ruptures of the past and repairs the nation for a better future. It acknowledges the pain people have suffered and includes an acceptance of responsibility.[3]

A painful challenge for the designers of the truth-telling process was the setting of parameters to the discussions. Many important stories would have to go untold in public forums, and many important perspectives would not be shared. Even if the TRC went on for ten years, the whole truth of the apartheid era would not be told. The architects and administrators of the TRC had the unenviable job of deciding who would receive attention and who would not, knowing that the exclusion of some would mean that parts of the past would go unexamined.

One thing was certain: Many of the people who had been enemies of apartheid were eager to begin the process. Kader Asmal offered (along with his co-authors) the following perspective:

> This country must hold up a mirror to the old protagonists, passive and active, of apartheid to show them their actions in the light in which these were seen by the majority of the people of South Africa, and indeed by most people of the world.
>
> The majority of people in South Africa lived and breathed the truths of apartheid. They suffered the indignities and humiliation of statutory inferiority. They suffered the pain of being forced out of their homes and off their land, away from their loved ones. They were imprisoned and detained in thousands. They require not revelations, but acknowledgment from the perpetrators and beneficiaries. They require a collective renunciation, by society as a whole, of apartheid's acts, systems, and beliefs.[4]

It is fascinating to witness the spirit of hope with which Asmal, one of the intellectual heavyweights of the ANC, embraced the idea of a truth commission. He asserted that South Africa's process of forging collective memory would, at least to some degree:

- enable the country to achieve a measure of justice for victims of the past by acknowledging the atrocities that they had suffered;
- provide a basis for a collective acknowledgment of apartheid's illegitimacy;

- facilitate the building of a culture of public ethics, and make room for genuine reconciliation;
- provide a basis for the decriminalization of the anti-apartheid resistance;
- ensure a sound basis for corrective action in dismantling the apartheid legacy;
- lay bare the roots of the violence that was still plaguing parts of the country;
- illuminate the long-standing humane values of the anti-apartheid resistance;
- demonstrate the morality of the armed struggle against apartheid;
- establish a new equality of all citizens;
- place property rights on a secure and legitimate footing;
- enable privileged South Africans to face up to their responsibility for the past;
- offer an acknowledgment of the wrongs done to the other countries of southern Africa;
- and clarify the important international implications of apartheid.[5]

Now that the TRC has completed its work, this list seems a bit heady and optimistic (it also shows the extent to which Asmal was invested in the legitimation of the ANC). On the other hand, very substantial strides have been made toward a number of these goals. Indeed, given the movement of the old liberation organizations—especially the ANC—into the center of political life, it is now surprising to remember that objectives such as "provide a basis for the decriminalization of the anti-apartheid resistance" or " demonstrate the morality of the armed struggle against apartheid" needed to be stated.

Mama Mxinwa is a gentle woman with big strong hands from decades of domestic service. She grew up in the Eastern Cape aware that her family was not very wealthy and that white people generally were better off. She was fairly apolitical in her disposition, however, and remained that way until middle age. At this time she was living in one of the African townships near Cape Town, the mother of eight children. There was a lot of talk about ANC organizing in her township, but, out of fear, she stayed away and advised her family to do the same.

One day one of her sons did not come home from school. It was a week before she learned of his fate. A man posing as an ANC recruiter had enlisted several young men, gathered them together, and led them to a pre-arranged confrontation with police. The boys were massacred and, after the shooting, had weapons planted on their bodies. This event became widely known as the Guguletu Seven, and then simply the G7.

THE PROMISE, LIMITS, AND STRUCTURE OF TRUTH-TELLING

Praise for the value of the TRC and similar projects of truth-telling has not been restricted to South Africa. Commentators and scholars from around the world have welcomed the new emphasis on truth-telling as a sign that we are moving into a new era of accountability. Echoing the voices of many others, Walter Wink has this to say:

In sum, a society recovering from the trauma of state violence needs as much truth as possible. Truth is medicine. Without it, a society remains infected with past evils that will inevitably break out in the future. Domination cannot exist without the Big Lie that persuades the many to offer their lives for the protection of the privileges of the few. Truthtelling not only exposes that lie, but establishes a sacred space where others may gather who will no longer tolerate the lie, as in the churches of East Germany.[6]

Priscilla B. Hayner is a prominent chronicler of truth commissions and similar processes. In *Unspeakable Truths* she carefully documents the value of truth-telling, but she also laments that "many comfortable assumptions have been restated over and over again in untested assertions by otherwise astute and careful writers, thinkers, and political leaders."[7] The first assumptions she refutes are that truth always leads to reconciliation and that it is always necessary to know the truth to advance reconciliation. There is plenty of evidence to support the link between truth-telling and reconciliation, but there is also evidence that a clear end to the threat of further violence, a restitution program for victims, efforts to remove structural inequalities, the existence of civic capacity, and simply the passage of time are also important. She also challenges the assumption that giving victims a public forum in which to tell their stories always fosters healing.

Hayner's larger point on making assumptions is well taken, but it is important to state that, while truth-telling may not always advance reconciliation, it is almost always of enormous import to those who have been oppressed by an unjust government or system. Nonwhite interviewees in South Africa repeatedly told me that the revelations of the TRC's human rights violations hearings gave them a feeling of a great burden lifted. After decades of having their everyday reality denied by a vast blanket of state propaganda, it was liberating to have this blanket torn away. Hayner would not deny this, but she asserts that there are contexts of reconciliation where a truth-telling process could do more harm than good. She points to Mozambique as a prime example.[8] When that country's war ended, the various parties quickly came to a state of peaceful coexistence. After years of brutal fighting in which the civilian population suffered horribly, this state of affairs is cherished with a sense of wonder. It is feared that a process of historical inquiry would jeopardize this. Given the number of atrocities that occurred and the number of people with blood on their hands, the danger of endless cycles of vengeance is all too real.

Despite her call to be careful about truth-telling, Hayner is convinced of its benefits. Echoing Asmal, she states the value of having such a reality check as the prime purpose of a truth commission:

> The most straightforward objective of a truth commission is sanctioned fact-finding: to establish an accurate record of a country's past, clarify uncertain events, and lift the lid of silence and denial from a contentious and painful period of history. The great number of interviews with victims, typical of these commissions, allows a detailed accounting of the patterns of violence over time and across regions, literally recording a hidden history. The detail and breadth of information in a truth commission report is usually of a kind and quality far better than any previous historical account, leaving the country with a written and well-documented record of otherwise oft-disputed events. . . . The official and public recognition of past abuses serve to effectively unsilence a topic that might otherwise be spoken of only in hushed tones, long considered too dangerous for general conversation, rarely reported honestly in the press, and certainly out of bounds of the official history taught in schools. In effect the report of a truth commission reclaims a country's history and opens it for public review.[9]

There are a number of options available to a nation in a state of transition and seeking to set the historical record straight. Often the goal of truth-telling is modified by or joined with other goals, such as preventing further violence or finding international credibility. And the search for truth can be conducted in a number of different ways. In 1992 the newly unified Germany decided to create a *research-based* commission to document the practices of the German Democratic Republic between 1949 and 1989. Most of the commissioners appointed were politicians and historians. They commissioned over one hundred papers from academics who were given access to the files of the former East German government. Unlike most other formal truth inquiries, the focus was not exclusively on human rights violations; instead, there was a broad range of political-historical analysis and ethical assessment of government policy and practice.[10]

In 1994 Sri Lankan president Chandrika Bandaranaike Kumaratunga appointed three separate commissions of inquiry. Each was to restrict its investigation to a distinct geographical region. All three focused on "the involuntary removal or disappearance of persons." Although the impact of the final reports was hampered by renewed warfare, their contents were eventually used in prosecutions of alleged perpetrators, and some of the victims received modest financial compensation.[11]

The Commission on the Truth for El Salvador was a product of the UN-brokered peace accord of 1991 and was administered by the United Nations using contributions from member states. It took testimony from two thousand victims and witnesses on cases of assassination, disappearance, torture, rape, and massacre. It also received information from human rights groups and other secondary sources. When the commission's report, *From Madness to Hope*, was published, it was a major political event in El Salvador. But only five days later a sweeping amnesty law was passed protecting those it named from prosecution. This considerably dampened the enthusiastic spirit in which Salvadorians had received it.[12]

These examples show just some of the choices that must be made regarding a commission of inquiry: Will commissioners be selected from the home country or the international community or both? Who will administer the commission (this depends on the perceived credibility and stability of the government as well as its available resources)? What range of transgressions will be considered? What primary and secondary sources of information will be used, and who will have access to this information? Will victims, perpetrators, and witnesses be questioned in open hearings? Will perpetrators be named in final reports? Will the information gathered be used in criminal prosecutions or will there be an amnesty process? Will some kind of reparation be offered to victims?

In the mid-1990s the new South African government worked its way through these choices. It designed and launched a truth *and reconciliation* commission amid much controversy over the relative importance of the two objectives. In the next section of this chapter we will survey the historical developments that led to the formation of the commission and examine the work of one committee of the TRC, the Human Rights Violations Committee, which was charged with launching South Africa's truth-telling process.

Yazir, a man currently about thirty years of age, grew up in one of the boroughs near Cape Town that had been designated for coloureds. He is thin, with penetrating eyes. His intensity of purpose and intellect are quickly apparent, as is his deep woundedness. During his preschool and elementary school years, he became increasingly aware that race was a dangerous issue because his questions about it were almost always met with silence.

Near the beginning of his secondary schooling, when he was about twelve years of age, Yazir was taken on a bus trip that passed through African and white areas. He was struck by the fact that people of different races lived under such different conditions. The range of wealth exhibited by the houses and neighborhoods amazed him. The reality that access to these things was determined by color deeply disturbed him.

By the time Yazir was fifteen years old, he had become involved with the ANC, and within a couple more years he was an MK soldier being trained in the Soviet Union. After a period of service outside South Africa, he returned for a mission in the country. One day, when he was nineteen years old, he was captured by security police and subjected to a period of harsh imprisonment. The police offered him an obscene choice: Give up the location of one of his MK comrades, or they would kill his mother and four-year-old nephew. When he revealed the location of the MK operative, Yazir was taken to the house in a car and forced to witness what he assumed would be an arrest. Instead, the police stormed the house with guns, grenades, and heavy weapons. The operation was not an arrest but an execution.

TRUTH-TELLING AT THE TRC

In December 1993, after years of negotiations, South Africa's Interim Constitution was agreed upon. This document formalized the negotiated peace between the apartheid government and the liberation organizations, particularly the ANC. The final part of the constitution to be agreed upon was the epilogue entitled "National Unity and Reconciliation." Representatives of the apartheid government were unwilling to come to a settlement that did not include amnesty and were pushing for a blanket pardon. The ANC was under pressure from many of its allies in the resistance movement to refuse. Finally, on December 5 a compromise was struck and the amnesty provision was inserted in the midst of paragraphs that dealt with the need to heal the nation and build a new and just foundation beneath it. The epilogue:

This Constitution provides a historic bridge between the past of a deeply divided society characterized by strife, conflict, untold suffering and injustice, and a future founded on the recognition of human rights, democracy and peaceful co-existence and development opportunities for all South Africans, irrespective of colour, race, class, belief or sex.

The pursuit of national unity, the well-being of all South African citizens and peace require reconciliation between the people of South Africa and the reconstruction of society. The adoption of this Constitution lays the secure foundation for the people of South Africa to transcend the divisions and strife of the past, which generated gross violations of human rights, the transgression of humanitarian principles in violent conflicts and a legacy of hatred, fear, guilt and revenge.

These can now be addressed on the basis that there is a need for understanding but not for vengeance, a need for reparation but not retaliation, a need for *ubuntu* but not for victimisation.

In order to advance such reconciliation and reconstruction, amnesty shall be granted in respect of acts, omissions and offences associated with political objectives and committed in the course of the conflicts of the past. To this end, Parliament under this Constitution shall adopt a law determining a firm cut-off date which shall be a date after 8 October 1990 and before 6 December 1993, and providing for the mechanisms, criteria and procedures, including tribunals, if any, through which such amnesty shall be dealt with at any time after the law has been passed.

With this Constitution and these commitments we, the people of South Africa, open a new chapter in the history of our country.[13]

We can see from the epilogue why South Africa did not settle for a commission of inquiry that focused only on the construction of a historical record. First, amnesty was part of the negotiated agreement. The National Party was unwilling to surrender power peacefully without it. It did not get its blanket pardon, however. In a bold move, the amnesty process was inserted into the larger truth and reconciliation process in a manner that forced applicants to contribute to the search for historical truth. Second, the epilogue forcefully articulates the goals of national reconciliation and healing. Building a historical record would be a key goal of the truth-telling exercises of the commission, but it would not be the only one. The repair of hearts, relationships, and communities would also be pursued.

As agreed, free elections were held in April 1994. The ANC won an overwhelming majority. Both the National Party and the IFP, which had only decided at the last moment to participate in the elections, agreed to join the ANC in a government of national unity. Among the many great challenges that faced the new government was the design of the formal reconciliation process.

The ANC already had some familiarity with commissions of inquiry. During the 1980s and early 1990s there had been reports of torture and other abuses in ANC camps. In 1991 a group of thirty-two former detainees in ANC camps set up a committee to confront the ANC about these abuses. In March 1992 ANC president Nelson Mandela appointed the Commission of Enquiry into Complaints by Former African National Congress Prisoners and Detainees. After seven months the three appointed commissioners produced a report documenting "staggering brutality" in the camps. Shortly afterward Mandela appointed a second commission of inquiry. Public hearings were held during the summer of 1993, and the final report reached conclusions similar to the earlier one.[14] In September 1993 the National Executive Council of the ANC took a policy decision to advocate a much more comprehensive commission of inquiry. It called for a truth commission to investigate human rights abuses throughout South Africa during the decades of apartheid.[15]

When Mandela became the new president of South Africa, he decided not to follow the examples of Raul Alfonsin of Argentina and Patricio Aylwin of Chile, who had established commissions by presidential decree. Instead, the new government spent about a year holding consultations and drafting the terms of the coming commission. Two international conferences were held to look at the transitional justice policies developed by other countries that had moved from authoritarian and abusive regimes to fragile democracies. Hundreds of hours of public hearings were held in Parliament.[16] NGOs were invited to make submissions, and many of their recommendations were heeded.

Finally, the Promotion of National Unity and Reconciliation Act was passed in mid-1995, and the seventeen commissioners to the TRC were named in the *Government Gazette* the following December. The men and women selected represented a broad cross-section of South African society. Archbishop and Nobel Laureate Desmond Tutu was named the chairperson of the commission, and Dr. Alex Boraine, a white former Methodist minister and politician who had played an important role in the consultation process leading to the formation of the TRC, was named vice-chairperson. The work of the TRC was to be directed by three committees: the Committee on Human Rights Violations (eight commissioners), the Committee on Amnesty (three commissioners), and the Committee on Reparation and Rehabilitation (five commissioners). An investigative unit with broad powers was also established and was headed by prominent African lawyer Dumisa Ntsebeza. The TRC was granted a budget of approximately US$18 million a year for two and one-half years. It employed a staff of about three hundred persons and set up four large regional offices.

At this point we will take a look at the mandate and work of the Committee on Human Rights Violations. In later chapters we will examine the Committee on Amnesty and the Committee on Reparations and Rehabilitation.

The Committee on Human Rights Violations was charged with providing a comprehensive accounting of gross human rights violations committed by the apartheid state and its supporters as well its opponents between 1960 and 1993. Its purview included violations committed in South Africa and in other countries. The committee was to name individual victims and expose the violations they had suffered, such as murder, kidnapping, and torture. This would not only provide psychological validation for the victims or their surviving relatives and comrades, but it would also clarify who was entitled to receive benefits under the program that was being designed by the Committee on Reparations and Rehabilitation.

This individual accounting became an important part of the task of establishing a historical record that painted a picture of South Africa's conflict and oppression in broad strokes. Many of the individuals and groups who had contributed to the consultations on the formation of the TRC emphasized the need to describe and judge the comprehensively unjust system of apartheid and the web of lies that concealed its true nature. They argued that there was such a legacy of legitimization of criminal activity and criminalization of legitimate protest that the new South Africa would have to construct intentionally a foundation for public morality and a culture of respect for human rights, and that the coming commission would be a good place to start.

When I attended some of the TRC hearings, I began to understand this imperative. South Africans in attendance showed no surprise at revelations that made my head spin. Among them was the existence of a government department called the Civil Cooperation Bureau (CCB), which masked itself as a government-business liaison office but really employed the most devious of security agents. These agents have admitted responsibility for such acts as the bombing of a day-care center and the murder of an African lawyer; they are suspected in letter bombings and poisonings. One amnesty hearing I attended was derailed when a witness claimed to have seen Dumisa Ntsebeza, the head of the TRC's investigative unit, participate in the massacre for which the applicants were seeking amnesty. It was eventually revealed that the witness was lying, having been prompted by an apartheid-era police official who was still on the job. I began to see how deeply deception and violence were embedded in the country's institutional life, and how these things would have to be exposed and challenged if communities and institutions were to have greater measures of sanity in the future.

Individuals who felt that they had been victims of gross human rights violations were invited to make submissions to the Committee on Human Rights Violations. Family members made submissions on behalf of people who had been killed. Statements from twenty-one thousand people were received and tested to determine whether the applicant would receive "victim status." The process of taking statements, frequently from people who could not write, and seeking verification was laborious. Dumisa Ntsebeza offers the following description:

> For example, if a person alleged that in May 1987 he was one of a group of protesters that marched to Pollsmoor to demand the release of Nelson Mandela, that during this march they were tear-gassed and assaulted and fired at by police, that his brother died in the incident and so on, the verification process would involve what came to be known as low-level corroboration. This would be done by the Investigative Unit. It would involve enquiries made at police stations, libraries, hospitals and mortuaries around the dates in question to establish if, in fact, there had been such an incident, if there were death certificates and/ or post-mortem results relevant to the death mentioned. Details would be checked and double-checked to establish if they are verifiable.[17]

Special investigations were launched into violations that showed a high level of authorization or that demonstrated a pattern of institutional complicity. Public HRV hearings were called for some of these investigations. Many of the hearings focused on particular incidents, such as the one in which Mrs. Mxinwa's son was murdered (this was called the Guguletu Seven hearing). Other hearings, such as the hearings on chemical and biological warfare and those on secret state funding, were topical. It is important to underscore that the investigations and hearings dealt with human rights violations by all parties to South Africa's prolonged conflict, not just the state security forces or other organizations that had been instruments of apartheid. This went a long way to legitimize the commission in the eyes of white South Africans, many of whom had feared that it would serve solely as a witch hunt or a prolonged public humiliation of whites.

The topical hearings conducted by the Committee on Human Rights Violations helped to identify the broad contours of the history of apartheid and also provided a forum in which judgments of that history could be debated. There was a set of hearings that invited submissions from political parties. The political party hearings gave the National Party, the ANC, and other organizations opportunities to offer their own interpretations of the events and legacies that were being uncovered by the TRC. They also gave apartheid-era leaders an opportunity to offer apologies. As we will see in the next chapter, an apology by F. W. de Klerk generated a fair bit of controversy. A set of hearings on the state security apparatus allowed a comprehensive examination of the broad, well-funded, and often hidden system of police, soldiers, and sanctioned terrorists. Institutional hearings were held on business and labor, the faith community, the legal community, the health sector, the media, and prisons. These paralleled the political party hearings in that representatives from these sectors could offer their interpretations, accusations, or apologies. There were also special hearings on compulsory military service, children and youth, and women.

In its *Final Report* the TRC offered thematic interpretations of all these hearings. The report has been criticized for being too spotty and lacking sufficient documentation, but, given the scope of its investigation and the easy availability of transcripts from all the hearings, this criticism seems unwarranted. In general, the report offered a broad and balanced interpretation. The opening paragraphs of the chapter that deals with the faith community hearings serve as an example:

1. Some of the major Christian churches gave their blessing to the system of apartheid, and many of its early proponents prided themselves in being Christians. Indeed, the system of apartheid was regarded as stemming from the mission of the church. Other churches gave the apartheid state tacit support, regarding it as a guarantor of Christian civilisation. They were the beneficiaries of apartheid, enjoying special privileges denied to other faith communities.

2. Religious communities also suffered under apartheid, their activities were disrupted, their leaders persecuted, their land taken away. Churches, mosques, synagogues and temples—often divided amongst themselves—spawned many of apartheid's strongest foes, motivated by values and norms coming from their particular faith traditions. They were driven by what has been called the 'dangerous memory' of resistance and

the quest for freedom, often suppressed but never obliterated from their respective faiths.[18]

Perhaps the most regrettable feature of these paragraphs is that the language is tepid, but in the report as a whole it is not consistently so, and the writing sometimes becomes more pointed as the report moves into the thick of things. In a way, the report represents a microcosm of the larger process of unveiling and debating South Africa's history that Asmal was calling for. Those responsible for the report, the commissioners, represented all sectors of society. They spent many months having evidence placed before them, and then they discussed and debated, cooperated and quarreled until they had a document that they could live with. One of its most valuable assets, and the same can be said of the hearings that it documents, is that it represents an extended dialogue between whites and blacks, former supporters and opponents of apartheid, Muslims and Dutch Reformed Christians, and so forth. For the first time all sectors of South African society are included as equals in the debate about where they have been and where they should go.

Lynn, an English-speaking white person, is now in her late twenties. At first her friendly manner and quick smile mask her intense attachment to social justice, but her words become fierce as she speaks of political machinations in either the new or the old South Africa. In the mid-eighties she was given sharp insight into the violent racial politics of Kwazulu-Natal. Her mother was a social worker who had earlier been active in support of the ANC but had discontinued that activism when her children were born. When Lynn was about nine years old, her mother decided that she could no longer stay politically disengaged. Lynn often accompanied her on trips to Umlazi and other African townships. This was a time of violent conflict between the ANC and the IFP, which was receiving arms and tactical support from state security forces. Lynn frequently visited encampments for refugees of the fighting and was given a firsthand education about apartheid in its most bloody manifestation. She was also marked by the distance other whites, especially members of her church, placed between themselves and her family when her mother became known as an agitator.

Her psychic distance from (and resentment toward) her fellow church members dramatically increased when she was fifteen. Some refugees of the IFP-ANC violence had sought shelter in Lynn's church, which was located in a privileged, white suburb. The congregation refused to sponsor them, and they were forced to leave the safety of the white enclave and seek a hiding place in Umlazi. They left on a Saturday morning, with a promise to send word of their new location. The following evening, at the church's Sunday night service, a young black man came to Lynn and her mother and informed them that the refugees had been discovered and massacred, probably by security policemen.

Lynn became deeply troubled and angry. She suffered a crisis of identity, which was compounded by the fact that her father, long since divorced from her mother, was a member of the defense forces involved in operations against the ANC and other liberation groups. Lynn and her mother were self-declared Communists. Her father was so strong in his conviction that Communists were enemies of the state that he reported Lynn's mother to the security police. For a time Lynn distanced herself from her roots to such an extent that she came to understand herself as a black South African.

Looking back, she now characterizes that identity construction as having an unhealthy element of denial. Listening to her and learning about the work she does, one is impressed by the amount of strength and wisdom she has gathered during her years of struggle and doubt. She is one of those rare people who can dynamically empathize with people of all stripes. Her commitment to social justice is informed by concern for those who dwell in all niches of South Africa's social geography.

LESSONS FROM THE HRV INVESTIGATIONS

It would be difficult to overstate the impact of the HRV hearings, which were widely broadcast and reported on the radio, on television, and in the papers. Many, many South Africans, especially whites and to a lesser extent Indians and mixed-race people, have indicated that they were shocked by the magnitude and character of the violence that had taken place in their country. Commentators have frequently argued that, despite government censorship and propaganda, information concerning the human rights violations against blacks was widely available during the apartheid era; South Africans who were "unaware" of the violent oppression were in denial. If these commentators are correct, then millions opted for ignorance, because there was widespread and painful surprise over what came out of the HRV hearings. Before 1995 these people may have been complicit in their own deception. Once the hearings began, such complicity was no longer an option.

What about the people who had had direct experience of state oppression or had suffered violence at the hands of liberation organizations? How did they experience the HRV hearings, either as participants, spectators, or from among the millions following through the media? How do they now feel about this aspect of the TRC's work? It is, of course, impossible to know the feelings of the millions of victims around South Africa. My investigations were of a limited scope and were largely conducted in one part of the country, the Western Cape (which includes Cape Town), but I am left with the impression that most value the extent to which the hearings fostered truth-telling. While there is a lot of resentment toward both the amnesty and reparations processes, there seems to be a general view that the HRV hearings uncovered a wealth of historical facts that would have otherwise remained hidden or at least disputed.

Mama Mxinwa and some of the other mothers of the Guguletu Seven certainly hold this opinion regarding the investigation of that massacre and its associated hearing. They say that, despite the intense pain of opening those old wounds, they are happy and relieved that the real nature of the event has finally been uncovered and that "we know where we are now." A reporter who was one of the first on the scene of the Guguletu Seven shooting expressed to me an opinion that was guarded but positive. At the time of the shooting he talked to several (African) witnesses of the event and reported a version very different from that put forward by the police. He subsequently took a lot of heat from the government as it tried to force him to reveal his sources (who would have been put in great danger) and attempted to prosecute him when he refused. Speaking of the G7 episode and others like it, he said "we can see a bigger tip of the iceberg than before."

The part that remains uncovered includes information about which senior officer(s) ordered, planned, and approved of the shooting. In many ways this example is representative of the HRV investigations in general. Those who suffered under apartheid could take comfort in the fact that their experiences were being acknowledged and that their beliefs and actions were being vindicated. They could also rest assured that many of the former regime's servants had been exposed and forced to admit to their actions. But even today they rest uneasy with the knowledge that most of apartheid's elite agents and architects remain in the shadows.

Others have different sources of ambivalence about the hearings. Yazir, the young man forced to choose between revealing the location of an MK comrade or the deaths of family members, spoke to a hearing at the urging of his therapist. Half a dozen years after he led his captors to the home of his former partner, he was on the precipice of physical and psychological collapse. It was hoped that the TRC would create a space in which he could find a measure of freedom from this story by telling it publicly. The telling was excruciating; at numerous points he broke down and had to pause to collect himself. At the end he was helped to a debriefing room. For some time afterward he could interact only with members of his immediate family. The experience had consumed all his courage and strength.

Looking back, he sees that the TRC created a space for him to confront his story. During his time of retreat after giving testimony he realized that he had survived this confrontation and that he would be able to get on with his life. The pain was far from gone, but there was a new sense of hope. The experience "convinced me that it is possible to create a space where we are able to face each other as human beings." But Yazir is also deeply disturbed by the ways his testimony has been appropriated, edited, and used by media outlets and writers. He found himself portrayed in a number of media stories and one best-selling book as "the agonized confessor" and the "informer who should be pitied." The lack of background and lack of subtlety in these pieces have left him bitter about the distortion of his testimony and the characterizations that were imposed on him.

Yazir feels the same frustration with the *Final Report* of the TRC. He feels that the document redacts his story and many others to fit the contours of a political agenda. There are victims in this process: those whose histories are distorted, and those whose histories are buried.

This frustration is not shared by all of the other victims who participated in the hearings. Mama Ngewu, like Mama Mxinwa, lost a son at the G7 massacre. She recounts her experience of speaking to the HRV hearing as very difficult. When asked if she felt relief after her testimony, she said simply, "It was bad at that time." But she feels that the pain was worth it because the participation of the mothers was part of the process of finding the truth. In their case there was an added element: The ANC *askari* (traitor) who had led the young men to the police ambush asked for an opportunity to apologize to the mothers privately. Under Archbishop Tutu's leadership, these kinds of encounters were encouraged and facilitated.

Father Michael Lapsley was the victim of a letter bomb almost certainly sent by someone within the apartheid government's security apparatus. He lost both hands and an eye and suffered much damage to his face. He voices yet another kind of ambivalence about the TRC's truth-telling process. He is not sure that he wants to know the identity of the bomber (and his accomplices), saying that the truth makes new victims and creates new burdens. On the other hand, he was happy to tell his story to a hearing; he felt that it was becoming a part of "the South African mosaic."

The impressions and opinions of the G7 mothers, Yazir, and Father Lapsley represent the qualified but generally positive evaluation of the HRV hearings that apartheid's old enemies seemed to be voicing. In terms of the overall work of the TRC, the Committee on Human Rights Violations did the most for these people. Other aspects of the committee's work have not been mentioned. Locating burial sites and recovering remains for a proper burial are an important example.

The limitations of the HRV process need stating as well, the most important being that the largest group of victims did not have its stories told. Its members were the millions of black South Africans who suffered systemic oppression every day of their lives but were not direct victims of "gross human rights violations." They included the millions who worked for appalling wages, the residents of District Six in Cape Town, Sophiatown near Johannesburg, and so many other communities that were forcibly relocated, the bright young people who were excluded from their preferred vocations, and those prevented from marrying someone they loved who happened to be of a "different race." This comment is offered not as a criticism so much as an acknowledgment of the limitations of truth commissions. The TRC had a much broader scope and many more resources than most, but it still had to set parameters to its explorations. The choice to restrict investigations to the realm of gross human rights violations precluded other important kinds of inquiry, while making the work of the commission manageable. The negative consequences of this choice were moderated by the fact that the committee, in institutional hearings and elsewhere, did examine the apartheid system as a whole as a human rights violation.

Those who were not victims or enemies of the apartheid regime also paid close attention to the HRV hearings. Many whites expressed shock at the actions of their former government. It is not uncommon to hear Afrikaners voice anger over a sense of betrayed trust. They lived in, and most of them accepted, a paternalistic society in which there was a kind of unspoken contract. Essentially, the authorities said "give us your support and leave us to the difficult task of running this conflicted country, and we will protect you and advance the destiny of the Afrikaner people." Most Afrikaners accepted these terms, even if unconsciously. Now many feel that the destiny of their people has run into a wall and its honor has been tainted. There is a crisis of conscience within Afrikanerdom. Their special mission as a people apart has turned to dust, and many are acutely aware of the extent to which they became anathema to the international community.

There are a number of responses to the crisis. Some hold to the old vision and advocate a withdrawal into an Afrikaner homeland where it can be lived out, even if in modest form. Others call for the abandonment of the Afrikaner language and culture. Most fall between these two extremes. Of course, this crisis was present before the TRC was launched. But the hearings seem to have served the purpose of tearing off some of the veils of self-deception. Many are glad for this. They sound a bit like Yazir as they assert that the TRC has created a space in which the Afrikaner people are forced to face their past. Others gave up on the TRC because they felt that it had become "too politicized." Some believe that the TRC became an ANC-led witch hunt, but they are the uninformed minority.

Before the commission began its work, many whites had this exact fear, but they have mostly changed their minds as they have witnessed investigations into human rights violations committed by the liberation organizations alongside the investigations into state-sponsored atrocities. The leadership of Archbishop Tutu has also helped. His rhetoric of forgiveness and his willingness to stand up to the ANC government left many whites with an impression of fairness.

As mentioned at the beginning of this chapter, a basic challenge of a truth-telling process is to ensure that the appropriate people are talking (in the appropriate way) and the appropriate people are listening (in the appropriate way). Tutu's leadership was strong in this regard. He was an engaged and empathetic listener who was willing to show his own emotional vulnerability. Because of his stature, those who testified before him had the sense that the nation was listening. His speeches expressed a powerful desire for reconciliation, but he did not shy away from the horrific nature of the incidents being discussed. He offered respect to all participants, but did not flinch from prodding perpetrators toward contrition or victims toward forgiveness.[19] Leadership from other commissioners was also helpful in most cases.

With the HRV hearings the TRC got off to a strong start. Representatives of the majority population of South Africa, which had been made largely powerless and voiceless for so long, were telling their stories, and the whole nation was listening—the privileged and the marginalized alike. As the work of the commission progressed into the later HRV hearings and the seemingly endless amnesty hearings, however, many South Africans reached a point of information (and emotion) overload. This weariness, combined with a progressive politicization of the process (not in the hearings themselves, so much, but in the public and media response), has left many citizens less than enthusiastic about the TRC. It may be that this fatigue was inevitable, given the scope of the history to be uncovered, but one wonders if a better time-line could have been found. Perhaps the annoyance felt toward the TRC will fade as time passes and be replaced in significant measure by a gratitude for the truth that has been uncovered. It is hard to imagine a country going through an inquiry of this magnitude without some short-term burn out.

Willie is an earnest young man working on an undergraduate degree at an Afrikaner university. His father was an important official in the apartheid government. He went to school and socialized almost exclusively with other Afrikaner children. Like many white children, he was isolated by his parents, teachers, and the media from the explosive reality of life in South Africa during the 1980s. When he was a young teen, he was climbing Table Mountain (the mountain that rises behind and towers over Cape Town) with some friends. The father of one of his friends pointed to a small island in the waters off the Cape and said: "There is Nelson Mandela." He was pointing to the infamous Robben Island, which served as a prison for Mandela and many of South Africa's other important political prisoners. The physical reality of Mandela's exile struck a nerve.

In the 1990s, after Mandela was released, Willie attended a school where many of the other students were sympathetic to the ANC. Because of his father's prominence in the National Party, his relations with his fellow students were sometimes awkward. During discussions with his father he has raised the issues of how much officials like his father knew about the activities of the security apparatus and why actions were not taken to curb them. Today he shows both pride for his father's accomplishments and a concern to find a history of his people that is truthful. He seems dedicated to the task of finding a world view that embraces both the new South Africa and the legacy of his forbears. He says that the HRV investigations have been helpful in this regard.

THE HRV INVESTIGATIONS AND FORGIVENESS

Did the truth-telling facilitated by the Committee on Human Rights Violations advance the cause of political forgiveness in South Africa? Did it help make the people and peoples of South Africa more forgiving? These are extremely complex questions, and it may be too early to attempt to answer them, but a few comments can be made.

In Chapter 1 I asserted that forgiveness has a core grammar and that forgiveness processes that adhere closely to this grammar are more likely to be fruitful. Naming the harm done, apology or confession, and the offering of forgiveness are important parts of any drama of forgiveness. All three of these were acted out many times during the course of the HRV hearings. Witnesses named the harm done and powerfully communicated its effects on their lives. Perpetrators frequently admitted to and apologized for their acts. A surprising number of statements of forgiveness were made by victims or their surviving relatives. Does this mean that the HRV investigations and hearings constituted a process that embodied the full grammar of political forgiveness? No, they did not. Many dramas of *personal* forgiveness with significant political implications did reach fruition during the hearings, but there has been no comprehensive consummation of forgiveness on a national scale. It would, of course, be folly to think that this could be accomplished in such a short time. Instead, what the Committee on Human Rights Violations achieved was to help begin and to give no small amount of momentum to the process of truth-telling that constitutes act one in the drama of political forgiveness. The curtain has also been partially raised for act two, but as we shall see in the next chapter, more apologies and admissions of culpability are needed.

Has the work of forgiveness been advanced in any other ways? Philosophical definitions and psychological models of forgiveness have highlighted resentment and fear (especially the former) as emotions that need to be overcome in a drama of forgiveness. What can be said of the HRV hearings in this regard?

Unfortunately, it is clear that the deliberations of the Committee on Human Rights Violations have fostered resentment. Surprisingly, a significant source of this resentment has been the ANC government, which gave birth to the TRC, and the segment of the citizenry that identifies with the ANC. Consternation with the TRC (this includes all committees, not just the Committee on Human Rights Violations) on the part of the ANC leadership was so strong that the party made an unsuccessful bid to block the release of the *Final Report* in 1998. To understand the bad feelings of the ANC leadership, it is helpful to recall Kader Asmal's hopes for the TRC. He predicted that it would generate a discourse that legitimized the ANC's actions during the years of struggle, including violent missions, and that it would place those actions on a different moral plane than the actions of the apartheid regime.

Many observers, myself included, feel that the TRC and its *Final Report* have fulfilled this hope. Some others, including many party faithful, feel that the TRC gave something akin to equal attention to all gross human rights violations, no matter who committed them. They argue that the holding of special hearings into ANC abuses alongside abuses by the security apparatus gave the impression that the two were of the same ilk. While this development is unfortunate and has had lamentable consequences in terms of the ANC's abandonment of the TRC reparations work, it is not the whole story. It can equally be said that the HRV inquiries have helped South Africans to surrender a measure of resentment.

The South African whites who had supported or accepted apartheid were already tired of being portrayed at home and around the world as anathema. Many did not feel optimistic about their future as a minority in a country run by people who saw them as such. But those who had assumed that the commission would simply serve as a large-scale indictment of the white minority were surprised to see that the investigations were more nuanced, and that the commission might actually serve as a watershed. Resentment is often an emotional cover for feelings of guilt. The hearings offered a forum to acknowledge and deal with that guilt. Perhaps they have helped white South Africa to move on toward a newly important place in the country's future. The tone of the TRC leadership and the emphasis on reconciliation also caused many former supporters of apartheid to let go of some of their rancor, but the most important factor was probably the revelations of the HRV hearings themselves. There was a realization that, even if only half of the reported atrocities were true, the majority population of the country had been wronged in a profound way. With this in mind, it was more difficult for members of the privileged minority to nurture resentment about their own difficulties.

Many blacks were able to surrender long-held frustration and bitterness when agents of apartheid were exposed for all the nation and the world to see, and when the privileged were forced to acknowledge the evils of the system from which they had benefited. Few things cause as much resentment as forces of oppression that hide behind a facade of legitimate national service. Even those who were not given the public exposure of the G7 mothers, for example, seemed to feel vindication by proxy. We were right! they are now free to cry. The receipt of vindication can lead to the surrender of resentment. Even more important than vindication, perhaps, is the length that the HRV inquiry went to reestablish the dignity of the majority population. Those who had portrayed nonwhites (especially Africans) as less than fully human were now being forced to acknowledge that they were the ones who had committed inhuman acts or supported a blasphemous system. The victims of this system were now being heard, empathized with, honored, and memorialized daily. Not all black South Africans have experienced the truth-telling as balm for their bitterness, but no small number have.

Although fear has not received as much attention as resentment in the forgiveness literature, it may well be of equal importance, especially for political forgiveness. It is difficult to forgive those you suspect may inflict harm again. We are only a decade from the transition to democracy in South Africa, but the reestablishment of the apartheid regime seems impossible. Black South Africans did not have the comfort of this perspective during the early days of the TRC. They had been living for decades with the knowledge that the government, the bureaucracy, the security forces, the judicial system, and other institutions were filled with their enemies—most of their faces unseen. These agents of apartheid were not only men and women; in the psyches of millions of blacks, they were also ghosts and monsters, hidden beings with unknowable power over their lives. After the transition to the new government, most of these people (except for the politicians) kept their jobs. It was quite reasonable for black citizens to wonder what they were up to. Would they continue to serve their old masters, only now in a more covert manner? When the security agents were exposed and interrogated at HRV hearings, their stature diminished. They no longer had the power of the unseen. When the institutional hearings put a spotlight on the judiciary, the police, the military, and the media, the shadows began to disappear, and South Africans were comforted with the realization that there would be no return to the old way. It was at this point that black South Africans could at least begin to see their former enemies as *former* enemies. Before this had been achieved, there was not much point in contemplating political forgiveness.

As whites witnessed the HRV hearings they began to realize that there would be no witch hunt. The new government had chosen vindication through truth-telling rather than vengeance. This said a lot about the intentions of the new regime. Combined with the rhetoric of reconciliation coming from President Mandela and the absence of drastic moves by the new government—such as purging public institutions, nationalizing industry, or imposing massive land reform—the tone and format of the TRC helped to reassure whites that their citizenship would be fully acknowledged in the new South Africa. They would not be treated as they had once treated their black neighbors. Many felt not only relief but also gratitude for the grace they were receiving. As their fear lessened, their capacity to empathize with those crushed by the old regime grew. It is important not to overstate this shift in attitude. Many observers, myself included, feel frustration that whites are not more aware of the gift they have received or of their responsibility to atone. It is disconcerting that more whites are not willing to acknowledge their support for the apartheid regime. There has been a shift, however, and significant steps are being made by some Afrikaners and English South Africans, including some important leaders, to enter into the dialogue of forgiveness as those making confessions.

5

Act Two:
Apology and the Claiming
of Responsibility

AN ALMOST-APOLOGY BACKFIRES

President F. W. de Klerk's decisions to decriminalize anti-apartheid organizations and to accept free and fair elections hastened the end of apartheid
and probably prevented a bloody civil war. These actions earned him a Nobel
Prize (shared with Nelson Mandela) and much international acclamation. To
a large extent, however, he shares the fate of Mikhail Gorbachev: He is respected internationally as a courageous and wise statesman but is the object
of much contempt at home. It may not come as a surprise that hard-line
Afrikaner nationalists feel contemptuous of de Klerk, but many human rights
advocates and former foes of apartheid are equally derisive. Why is this? Part
of the reason lies with the support state security forces under his authority
gave to the IFP during its prolonged and bloody clash with the ANC. But
there is an equal amount of scorn for de Klerk's actions (or lack thereof) since
leaving the presidency. There is a broad perception that he has not accepted
responsibility for his contributions to the apartheid state and its violence while
serving as a minister and later as president. When de Klerk made a statement
during a TRC political party hearing in May 1997, he spoke to an issue at
the heart of this perception; that is, whether or not he had apologized for
apartheid.

Firstly, a number of commentators as well as my political opponents
continue to claim that I have not apologised for apartheid. This is simply not true. . . . They equate the efforts that I made, and may I say at
the Commission's request, to try to explain in context the circumstances
which gave rise to apartheid with some or other attempt to defend or
justify the policies of the past. The latter has never been my intention.

60

Let me place once and for all a renewed apology on record. Apartheid was wrong. I apologise in my capacity as leader of the National Party to the millions of South Africans who suffered the wrenching disruption of forced removals in respect of their homes, businesses and land. Who over the years suffered the shame of being arrested for pass law offences. Who over the decades and indeed centuries suffered the indignities and humiliation of racial discrimination. Who for a long [sic] were prevented from exercising their full democratic rights in the land of their birth. Who were unable to achieve their full potential because of job reservation. And who in any other way suffered as a result of discriminatory legislation and policies. This renewed apology is offered in a spirit of true repentance, in full knowledge of the tremendous harm that apartheid has done to millions of South Africans.[1]

This is a powerful statement, which appears to represent an unqualified apology. One would think that words such as these, from a source such as this, could serve as an example for the kind of statements needed from South Africa's former leaders. In an earlier essay I made just this point and praised the statement as a model apology.[2] It seems that Mr. de Klerk's many critics saw things differently. Many South Africans who had lived through decades of bloody episodes for which the former president was admitting no foreknowledge or personal responsibility felt that he had not gone far enough. He failed to mention the many murders committed by the security forces during his presidency and the time he was a senior minister. Later in his statement he distances himself from these crimes. His detractors convincingly argue that a president who does not know the actions of his government forces is making a choice to be ignorant. By looking the other way, he gave them free reign. Many felt that it would be more honorable to own up to this fact and to apply for amnesty than to hide behind ineffectual denials.

Was de Klerk's apology a failed act, indeed a failed sequence of acts? Did he put an obstacle in the way of the goodwill he was trying to advance? Perhaps so. In any case, this is a fascinating example of a speech act that is increasingly common in political and institutional discourse: the official apology. Recently there have been many other cases. Cardinal Sin has apologized to the poor of the Philippines, saying the church has neglected them, leaving them as easy prey for selfish, powerful people. Pope John Paul II has apologized for the sacking of Constantinople and Christian culpability in the Holocaust. American presidents have apologized for the internment of Japanese Americans and predatory medical testing programs.

NICOLAS TAVUCHIS'S SOCIOLOGY OF APOLOGY

Apologies by powerful figures like presidents and popes can be of great importance in contexts where political forgiveness is sought, but they can backfire if done unskillfully. What makes a good apology? Sociologist Nicholas Tavuchis explores this question in his book *Mea Culpa: A Sociology of Apology and Reconciliation*.[3] Tavuchis's analysis of apology begins at the level of interpersonal dynamics and works from there. Even at this level apology is not a private matter between offender and injured; it "speaks to something larger than any particular offense and works its magic by a kind of speech that cannot be contained or understood merely in terms of expediency or the desire to achieve reconciliation."[4] The "something larger" is the grounds for membership in a moral community. Any person's relationships and group affiliations are dependent upon conformity to the specific and general norms of the moral community that encompasses those relations. Apology becomes relevant when those norms are violated and one's membership in the moral community becomes less secure or stable. When an apology is offered and accepted, there is an often painful re-membering of the moral community and a reinforcing of its norms. The offender recalls, and is recalled to, the moral fabric of the community by personally acknowledging responsibility for the breach, expressing genuine sorrow and regret, and promising to keep the rules in the future. This secular ritual serves not only to reconcile alienated parties, but also to reinforce moral standards and make them more visible.[5]

Tavuchis's grounding of apology in moral community speaks to the power of apology in the context of the TRC's HRV hearings, especially apologies from former supporters of apartheid to members of the majority population. An apology offered by a white offender to a black victim contains a subtext that says, "I was wrong to believe that we were not members of the same (moral) community," or, in other words, "I was wrong to believe that my humanity and your humanity were not of the same order."

In *Mea Culpa* Tavuchis examines a number of acts of public repentance, but one serves as an especially helpful example for those seeking to clarify the dynamics of formal apologies. This is an apology from the United Church of Canada (UCC) to that country's First Nations. It arose out of a long and ambiguous history of interaction between the two parties. A dozen years later it was followed by a second apology, and in between there was a "statement of repentance." At times the words and actions of the UCC and its leaders were gracious and well-chosen; at times they were quite the opposite. An examination of this behavior and the concerns and contingencies that stood behind it promises to teach us much about the politics of apology. To begin, let us take a brief look at the history of relations between the UCC and Canada's Native Peoples.[6]

The UCC was founded in 1925, but its history of exchange with Native Canadians extends back even further, into the 1800s. The UCC was formed by the amalgamation of Methodist, Presbyterian, and Congregational denominations. Methodist contact with aboriginal peoples in Upper and Lower Canada led to the formation of Native congregations around Montreal and some parts of Ontario. By 1840 British Methodists were working in northwest

Canada as chaplains to the Hudson Bay Company and missionaries to the Indians. According to the UCC's brief to the Royal Commission on Aboriginal Peoples (1993), most missionaries in this period adapted to the Native way of life rather than expecting the reverse, and Native ministers and teachers rose to prominence within the Methodist churches that were established in that area. In the 1860s and 1870s things began to change. The British missionaries began to return home, and white settlers started to move into this area and across the prairies. The Methodist Church of Upper Canada followed this westward expansion. The UCC brief to the Royal Commission admits that Native churches were marginalized within the decision-making structures of the church and that the denomination operated under the assumption that "assimilation [later the word became *integration*] was the destiny of Indians in Canada." From the early 1900s until the 1960s, church-run residential schools were central instruments of this assimilation.[7]

Beginning in the early 1970s the UCC began to rethink the place of Native members and congregations within the denomination. Participants in these congregations were asking questions about their role in the church. Some Native elders completed a training program leading to ordination and full-time ministry. In 1977 the General Council (the highest court of the UCC, which meets every two to three years) initiated a thorough evaluation of the church's Native work. This evaluation process, including several Native-organized national consultations, produced two especially significant developments. The first was a formal apology by the denomination to its Native congregations. The second was a system of self-government for Natives within the UCC.

In the periods between the meetings of the General Council, the UCC is guided by the General Council Executive. In the mid-1980s a Native representative to that body, Alberta Billy, concluded the presentation of a report to the executive by saying, "It is time you apologized to Native people."[8] The agenda for the meeting was suspended, and the executive took the time needed seriously to discuss the proposal. It was decided that the National Native Council work on a process. Pamphlets were sent to all UCC congregations informing them of the request for an apology and asking them to reflect on it. The matter was brought before the 1986 General Council in Sudbury, Ontario. Native leaders requested the apology and then all First Nations commissioners left the assembly to wait at the sacred fire outside. They waited for two hours while the rest of the commissioners discussed the matter. In the end, only twelve of the three hundred commissioners voted against the proposal. The assembly joined the Native commissioners at the fire, and the moderator of the UCC offered these words:

Long before my people journeyed to this land your people were here, and you received from your elders an understanding of creation, and of the Mystery that surrounds us all that was deep, and rich and to be treasured. We did not hear you when you shared your vision. In our zeal to tell you of the good news of Jesus Christ we were closed to the value of your spirituality. We confused western ways and culture with the depth and breadth and length and height of the gospel of Christ. We imposed our civilization as a condition of accepting the Gospel. We tried to make you be like us and in so doing we helped to destroy the vision that made you what you were. As a result you, and we, are poorer and the image of the Creator in us is twisted, blurred and we are not what we are meant by God to be. We ask you to forgive us and to walk together with us in the spirit of Christ so that our peoples may be blessed and God's creation healed.[9]

The Native elders' only response was to say "We must go back to the people." But there was a celebration and dancing with a drum. Some of the elders were very happy and responded positively as individuals; others were less sure that the apology signaled a real change of heart and policy by the church. They exhibited a wait-and-see attitude.

The formal response came two years later at the 1988 General Council in Victoria, British Columbia. Representatives of the newly formed All-Native Circle Conference (ANCC) acknowledged the apology, but did not accept it.[10] Rev. Alf Dumont, the speaker of the ANCC, explained: "In the native way, apologies are not 'accepted', they are acknowledged. [This is because] an apology must be lived out if it's to be a real apology. The church is being asked to live out its real apology." He pointed out that the church had been instrumental in the oppression of First Nations.[11]

We might ask why the church did not perceive its need to apologize until 1986—or how it could have allowed itself to become an instrument of oppression in the first place. Whole nations of people were denied basic rights to perpetuate their way of life and their culture, to have a voice in the education of their children, to provide leadership in the institutions that served them. How could this go unnoticed for so long? The clue lies in Tavuchis's notion of moral community. Like Canadian society at large, church members did not see Native people as belonging to the same moral community as themselves until they were assimilated into the growing "European" society that was becoming Canada.[12] There was no felt need to justify the norms of the moral community when dealing with aboriginal people because they were perceived to be standing outside of that community. For the churches, Native conversion to Christianity was a necessary step toward inclusion. It is difficult to say whether it would have been sufficient. In any case, conversion to Christianity was understood to include the adoption of a whole host of "European" cultural values, mores, and manners that are now recognized by the majority of UCC members as extraneous to the religious core of the Christian faith. Until those values, mores, and customs were adopted by Natives, they were not perceived to be in possession of rights provided by membership in the larger moral community.

By the 1970s and 1980s the membership and leadership of the UCC had made significant progress in abandoning this culture-laden understanding of the faith. Also, there was a growing acceptance that non-Christians were also children of God and as such had a place in a global moral community. With this change in perspective came the realization that the rights and integrity of First Nations had been violated in a whole host of ways. Significantly, the apology by the UCC was not only an action aimed at restoring the church's place in a global moral community but an important public acknowledgment of the place of aboriginal people, culture, and nations in that moral community.

Unlike accounts, explanations, or appeals to special circumstances, which rationalize the offender's actions and seek to distance the offender from them, an apology requires an unqualified acknowledgment and a painful embracing of the deed(s). Tavuchis describes a successful apology as the middle term in a "moral syllogism" that begins with a call and ends with forgiveness. The process begins with the naming of the offense and its mutual identification as an "apologizable" action. Second is the apology itself. The offender stands unprotected; accepts responsibility for his or her actions; forgoes recourse to account, explanation, or mitigating circumstances; and expresses sorrow and regret. The sincere expression of sorrow is of central import. Finally, there is the response of the injured party. The one injured may accept the apology and release the offender through forgiveness, refuse to accept the apology, or acknowledge it while deferring a decision on forgiveness. According to Tavuchis, the act of apology itself is crucial, not the offering of symbolic or material restitution.[13]

Apology's bedrock structure is always binary (offender-offended), but apology between groups, institutions, or segments of society is not just a larger-scale version of private apology. Tavuchis explains that the sequence of steps remains the same, as does the appeal to a larger moral order, but at the center of public apology the importance of the expression of sorrow gives way to the "compulsion to generate unambiguous speech," to place the wrongdoing "on the record." In an apology "from the many to the many," such as the UCC apology, individuals do not figure as principals but as official attendants or representatives. The weight of their words comes from their position of speaking and acting on behalf of a larger body. There is a move into a formal, official, and public discursive world. The wording of apologies has little room for spontaneity, elaboration, or qualification. Ambiguity carries too much danger. Institutionally licensed apology is scripted and tends to be composed of language that is abstract, remote, and emotionally neutral. Does the lessened import of sorrow in public apology mean that it is less powerful or transformative than private apology? Tavuchis says no. Public apology gains reparative capability through the symbolic import of putting things on the record, of documentation as a prelude to reconciliation.[14] While he does not use the term, Tavuchis appears to be evoking the power of public truth-telling.

When Tavuchis examines the UCC apology, his interest is not primarily to discover the extent to which it fostered reconciliation between the parties, but rather to flush out the dynamics of apology from the many to the many. Despite this, his analysis does provide some clues to the former concern. He states that the apology discourse between the UCC and its Native constituency was the culmination of complex historical circumstances that served to both bind and estrange the two groups. He juxtaposes the emotional and intimate setting for the apology and the personal responses offered by Native leaders with the formal and official text of the apology itself and asserts that there is a tension generated by an attempt to satisfy the requirements of both personal and collective discourse. He calls the acknowledgment without acceptance of the apology a "nice touch" that served to credit its good will without releasing the church from the consequences of what it had participated in. Finally, he says there is little doubt that the apology vented the source of mutual "disquietude" and paved the way for structural changes in the relations between the denomination and its Native members.[15]

This is a good analysis of the apology, and it highlights some of the important dynamics of the reconciliation process as a whole. First, the legacy of UCC interaction with First Nations has bound its Native congregations to the denomination in a way that produces great ambivalence. Native members have gratitude for exposure to the gospel, and many hold in high esteem the missionaries who first enabled that exposure, but there is anger and grief over the role of the church in the colonization of their physical territory and world of meaning. Second, the reconciliation process bounces back and forth between the macro-dynamics of relations between the UCC and Canada's First Nations, on the one hand, and the micro-dynamics of interaction between individuals and small communities, on the other. Despite its geography, the world of the UCC can be quite small. At times the reconciliation process looks like a matter internal to the denomination. At other times it seems to carry all the weight of the intercourse between Canada and its First Nations. At times the process needs to be carried forward by formal, official discourse and action. At other times it can only move forward through the expression and healing of deep emotions such as sorrow, remorse, rage, and grief. Third, the apology was an event of deep meaning for many Natives and non-Natives, a watershed for the denomination, but it was not a time of closure. The structural and spiritual place of Natives within the church has shifted and grown, but, echoing the words of some of the elders at the time of the acknowledgment, they are waiting for the church to "get real," to give up power and control, and to enter fully—with risk—into the struggle for aboriginal justice in Canada.

The apology to Native congregations was a formative event for the UCC, marking a significant shift in the role of Native people and congregations within the denomination. Native leaders became important leaders for the entire denomination, and Native spirituality and wisdom with regard to decision-making and community building began to inform the life of the denomination in a variety of ways. All of this led church members to believe in ever-increasing goodwill between Natives and non-Natives. The UCC was coming to see itself as an important organization in solidarity with aboriginal peoples as they pursued justice within Canadian society. Perhaps this perception was more common among non-aboriginal members of the church; it is difficult to know. What is clearer is that this positive momentum was slowed by developments in the mid-1990s pertaining to an important aspect of the UCC's historical interaction with indigenous Canadians: residential schools.

Both the Methodist and Presbyterian forbears of the UCC were running residential schools by the end of the nineteenth century. After the turn of the century the residential school network greatly expanded under a system of government and church cooperation. In 1923, two years before church union, the Methodist church was operating five residential schools for Native children, and the Presbyterians were operating seven. At the same time the Anglican church was operating twenty such schools and the Roman Catholics forty. In the 1930s the UCC reached its peak of thirteen schools. The numbers slowly dwindled over the following decades until 1969, when the denomination was no longer overseeing any Native residential schools.

These schools played a central role in the efforts of Canadian society, governments, and religious institutions to assimilate aboriginal peoples and destroy their culture. In many cases officials from the federal Department of Indian Affairs and representatives of the churches worked together to force reluctant Native families to release their children for education in these schools, where the children were usually not allowed to keep their language, their dressing and grooming habits, or their customs. Most suffered emotional, spiritual, and cultural abuse. Many suffered physical abuse, and some became victims of sexual abuse. Native resistance to the schools was unrelenting. It was expressed in the form of parent boycotts, chronic absenteeism, runaways, dropouts, and the burning of school buildings. The UCC's brief to the Royal Commission confesses that "the residential Schools were premised on a racist understanding of the superiority of European civilization" and that they contributed to "a rapid and often brutal disintegration of the Aboriginal way of life."[16]

In recent years the denomination has been forced to come to terms with this legacy. By the late 1990s lawsuits involving hundreds of former students had been launched. Some of these arose from cases of physical or sexual abuse; others focused more on the loss of language, culture, and living skills. It was becoming clear that church liability could potentially run into many millions of dollars. The British Columbia Conference of the UCC formally petitioned the 1997 General Council to apologize for the church's role in Native residential schools. The request was not fully granted. On the suggestion of church lawyers, General Council decided to "repent" of the church's role in residential schools but not to apologize, because an apology would jeopardize insurance coverage. While some Native commissioners to the

General Council agreed with the choice to repent, others were upset, feeling that the church had chosen a path of sophistry and obfuscation.[17]

The decision to "repent" instead of apologize became a symbol of the denomination's overall approach to the lawsuits. It did not deny responsibility and started to take measures to foster healing for individuals and communities that were suffering from the legacy of the schools, but it also went to great lengths to defend itself in court—even when that meant forcing former students who had been sexually abused to undergo difficult cross-examination. This approach caused much controversy across the denomination.

A group called the Task Force on Residential Schools of British Columbia Conference decided to respond when the national church appealed the judge's ruling in the first lawsuit. It circulated a brief document called "Reflections on the Decision by the General Council Executive of the UCC to Appeal." It was written by one of the task force's members, Terry Anderson, and provided a helpful analysis of the church's dilemma. In it, he asserted that within the church there had been two predominant reactions to the revelations of abuse at UCC residential schools and to the legal implications associated with those revelations. For one group of church members, the overriding feeling upon hearing the revelations was remorse—shame and regret over the sins of commission and omission for which the church stood guilty. Out of this complex of feelings came a goal: "The prime goal of the church's response to its wrong-doing should be to acknowledge its responsibility, express sorrow, repent, and seek forgiveness from and reconciliation with God and native peoples—especially those most directly affected. We might call this the 'repentance/reconciliation' goal."

For another group of church members, the predominant reaction was alarm that the denomination was under attack. This sense of alarm was heightened by a general consensus that the number of suits would grow and by a perception that the church might ultimately have to pay a crippling financial cost. Out of this reaction came a different goal: "The prime goal of the church's response to attack should be a defense that will minimize damage to the church. We might call this the 'defense' goal."

Anderson's straightforward analysis strikes to the heart of the dilemma faced by those who realize that they have done wrong. On the one hand is the urge to come clean, to purge the taint of wrongdoing by confessing the offense and seeking forgiveness. On the other hand, there is a fear of the vulnerability that such an act requires. A full and unqualified apology requires that offenders stand unprotected before those they have harmed. This predicament becomes more complicated at the level of community or institutional relations. The choice to stand unprotected could have serious consequences for structures and resources in which many people have vested interests.

With this in mind, one can see why F. W. de Klerk felt unable to come fully clean. Perhaps he would have been willing to suffer the vulnerability himself (or perhaps not), but this would have opened the door to making all or at least senior apartheid officials liable for human rights violations. In a subsequent chapter we will examine the way dynamics such as these influenced many decisions over whether or not to seek amnesty.

Anderson acknowledged that both reactions—defense and repentance— were natural and appropriate, but he criticized the position that the General Council was taking in relation to the two goals. Its position was that the two goals could be held together, that there was no fundamental incompatibility between the goals, and that both could be pursued at the same time. Anderson saw this perspective as flawed and outlined a number of ways in which the goals were incompatible. His most convincing and evocative passage looked at power relations between the church and those who suffered as a result of the residential school system:

> Regarding the church's power vis a vis the victims and native peoples: the two goals lead in opposite directions. The defense goal entails seeking to maintain power over the victims—we must control or at least influence as much as possible the decision as to what is "owed" to whom, and remain as much as possible masters of our own destiny. The object is to minimize the church's vulnerability. This sets us as protagonists against the victims and their relatives. Of course, we pledge to use any such power we may obtain for good. As champions of the poor, we will help native people to get the government to confess, be an instrument to clarify the law regarding "vicarious liability," be generous toward the victims once our security is reestablished, and the like. But this tends to blind us to the central issue. Do we not see how absurd this must sound to the plaintiffs who are victims of the misuse of such power over them by those pledged to pursue their well-being?

Anderson asserted that the church must ultimately choose which of the two goals would be given a greater priority, and argued that the General Council Executive's policy of holding the two goals together had led to a course of action that displayed a de facto prioritizing of the defense goal. Speaking on behalf of the entire task force, he called for the reversal of these priorities and voiced strong frustration with the national church.

Again, this resonates with de Klerk's incomplete apology. He actually said many of the things that needed to be said, things that other apartheid leaders such as P. W. Botha have not even come close to stating, but his unwillingness to go all the way and totally abandon protective armor left observers feeling frustrated and contemptuous. His clinging to the defense goal poisoned the whole series of speech acts.

It was not long before there was a broad perception in the UCC that the choice to make a statement of repentance instead of an apology had similarly poisoned an opportunity to "come clean." An act of repentance can be powerful, and it is not always necessary to use the word *apologize,* but the knowledge that this word had been avoided for legal purposes generated a lot of cynicism among Natives and non-Natives alike.

In October 1998 the General Council Executive met to continue its work on the residential schools situation. After a two-day process of reflecting on the meaning of repentance, it finally decided to apologize for the church's role in the residential schools. The apology, issued by the moderator, began in this way:

> I am here today as Moderator of The United Church of Canada to speak the words that many people have wanted to hear for a very long time. On behalf of The United Church of Canada I apologize for the pain and suffering that our church's involvement in the Indian Residential School system has caused. We are aware of some of the damage that this cruel and ill-conceived system of assimilation has perpetrated on Canada's First Nations peoples. For this we are truly and most humbly sorry.[18]

This apology did not serve as the same kind of watershed as the 1986 one. Once again, the Native leadership within the denomination was being careful with its reactions. It waited to see if words would be followed by meaningful actions, and if the church would be willing to become vulnerable in its relations with First Nations—and with survivors of a school system that all too often took advantage of its students' vulnerability. Since the time of the apology, however, there has been a shift in the tone of dialogue over residential schools. The pessimism within the denomination has moderated, and some steps have been taken toward out of court settlements, alternate dispute resolution, and the work of reconciliation. Not all of this can be attributed to the apology, of course, but it can be credibly argued that it removed an important barrier.

PERSONAL AND PUBLIC APOLOGY AT THE TRC

The tension between personal and public discourse experienced by the UCC was not unique; it could be witnessed repeatedly during the proceedings of the TRC. The hearings of the commission—both HRV hearings and amnesty hearings—were set up so that interpersonal interactions were given a special place as moments of import in the transformation of the nation. Hearings in which a perpetrator or two faced a cluster of victims were given the status of a parable in the text of the nation's reconstitution.

When observing such a moment at an amnesty hearing, time and space take on strange dimensions. At times the dialogue is intensely personal, especially when victims or survivors recount their suffering in front of its agent. At other times a lawyer or a commissioner will insert legal or bureaucratic logic between them. And one cannot help but notice the cameras and tape recorders. During one hearing I moved back and forth between a feeling that I was witnessing a sacred ritual and disgust over the voyeurism of it all.

Placing this kind of political import on unrehearsed conversation among private citizens involves a considerable amount of risk. Private apologies take on political import. When they are uttered, there is no assurance that they will be sincere or skillful. In the case of apartheid security policemen there was good reason to think that they would not be. Through their training and experience, these men had stunted the very empathic faculties that are so important in this kind of dialogue. One televised apology, which took place not during a hearing but when a security policeman visited the family of one of his victims, serves as a good example.[19]

The encounter took place in the main room of the family's modest house. The policeman was white, and the family was African. The policeman sat in an armchair and faced the now-elderly father and mother. In the 1980s their son, Siphiwo Mtimkulu, had been taken into police custody on suspicion of political activity. He was in his early twenties at the time and had an infant son. As a result of his treatment in custody, he died. The policeman had taken part in his interrogation and had been present when the young man's body was disposed of. He was welcomed into the house, the mother being especially gracious. After offering an apology for the death of the young man, he asked for forgiveness. His words seemed sincere. Again, the mother responded with grace and stated her willingness to forgive. First, however, there were details to be uncovered. She and her husband wanted to know what kind of torture their son had suffered and how he had met his death. The policeman responded that he had neither participated in nor witnessed any torture and had not been present at the death. He was pressed on this point and became confused.

It became clear that his insight into the dynamics of apology and forgiveness was severely restricted, as was his ability to empathize with the family. In a banal tone he explained that he had come to apologize and to seek forgiveness and the appropriate next step was for it to be offered. One had the sense that he was unable to grasp the emotional power of the situation, and that he had learned about forgiveness in a rote fashion. Perhaps he had been encouraged to seek forgiveness in support of his amnesty application. It is possible that he had repressed his memory of what had actually happened to the young man and was recounting what he believed to be true. Such repression might partially explain his banality. Whatever the reason, his attitude was starting to undo this opportunity for reconciliation. Pressed again, he was unwilling or unable to offer any more details or to claim any more responsibility. Out of view of the camera, the son of the young man who had disappeared almost twenty years ago was listening and filling up with anger. Now approaching the age at which his father had disappeared, he did not possess the patience of his grandmother. The televised visit was brought to an end when he picked up a vase (or a bottle) and smashed it over the policeman's head, fracturing his skull. The policeman survived the incident and pursued his amnesty application.

This was only one of the hundreds of interactions between perpetrator and victim(s) fostered by the TRC, but it was witnessed by hundreds of thousands if not millions of South Africans. What impressions endured for those viewers? The grace of the mother? The original sincerity of the policeman? The picture of a former agent of the apartheid order coming to an African township hat in hand? Or only the quick burst of violence at the end, symbolizing the failure of this essay in bridge-building?

This episode was certainly more physically dramatic than most of what happened at the TRC hearings, but it was not wholly anomalous. The grace of the old African woman and her surprising willingness to forgive were matched time and again. So was the ineptitude of the policeman, which was surpassed during the amnesty hearings by many agents of apartheid who clumsily tried to do just enough to receive pardon while losing as little face as possible. Fortunately, there were also adroit and heartfelt acts of contrition from former lieutenants of apartheid and of the organizations that had combated it.

The architects of the TRC made a decision not to follow the route of the German commission. There, researchers had chased the truth and then served it up in academic and emotionally tempered language. During the deliberations of the TRC, a tableau was painted with all the beauty and ugliness of the human soul. Such a backdrop is necessarily ambiguous and highlights the need for unequivocal speech from public figures. In its institutional hearings, the HRV committee gave government, business, church, and other leaders opportunities to reflect on the activities of their institutions during the apartheid era. These opportunities to make apologies met with limited success because speakers were asked to make just the kinds of reflections that can serve as qualifiers: explanations of why individuals and organizations acted the way they did. Of course, apologies or statements of contrition in any context are usually followed by explanations. It is human nature to want to know why things happened the way they did. The trick of skillful speech is to offer repentance and explanation in such a way that neither undoes the other.

One piece of testimony at the business sector hearing serves as an interesting example of the search for this kind of balance. It came from a Desmond Smith, the managing director of SANLAM (a large financial services company that was mostly Afrikaner-managed and flourished during the National Party reign).

With regards to our submission, we, the individuals constituting the present board and management of SANLAM, acknowledge that in conducting its business, SANLAM functioned in a political and social environment which violated human rights on enormous scale and was fundamentally wrong, immoral and unjust. We furthermore acknowledge that this environment caused untold hardship, suffering and grief to the people of colour and further that SANLAM as a member of a privileged group benefitted from Apartheid in one way or another, relative to members of disadvantaged groups.

Chairperson, this unjust system which I have just described and the suffering it caused people of colour, leave us with a deep sense of sadness and regret. Regret and sadness that we, the enfranchised citizens of the country, allowed the system of hurtful, institutionalised violations of human rights to be established and developed in this country.[20]

If Mr. Smith's intention was to apologize, he made a good start. But he quickly moved from what Anderson would call the goal of repentance to the goal of defense.

In our submission we refer to a specific issue which I should like to address. Steve Biko was tortured in a SANLAM building in Port Elizabeth. I refer to paragraph 13 of our submission. In cases where the security police of the former Government were tenants of SANLAM property, we had no access to such offices.

As is the case with the current Government, our leases specified in respect of such properties and I quote: "The lessor is aware of the lessees prescribed security measures which will at all time be adhered to. No access to the premises will be allowed unless the lessees prior permission is obtained." The end of the quote. SANLAM thus had no prior knowledge of cases of violation of human rights on its properties and like the general public we had to rely on available public information through media reports on that time—at that time the allegations against security police actions.[21]

Reading the text of Mr. Smith's statement, one feels pained by the speed with which he moved from repentance to defense. It may well be that SANLAM was not culpable, but this was not the time to assert that fact. There was a sinking feeling that the opportunity was lost. But almost as quickly, he switched back to a confession of the complicity of SANLAM and its employees in the unjust system of apartheid. He then entered, with apparent sincerity, into the task of seeking to understand how and why this happened. With a nod to the dynamics of a good apology, he said, "May I stress we advance these prospectives [sic], not as an explanation—as an explanation for inaction, not as an excuse or a justification."[22]

Most of the businessmen and women, church leaders, media representatives, and so on who spoke at the institutional hearings would have been given limited freedom to speak on behalf of their constituencies. It is rare enough that an individual comes to the place of surrender and courage that enables him to stand naked in the light of his wrongdoing. It is almost impossible for a board of directors to reach that place. Even with these fetters, however, some speakers were able to bend their presentations toward the grammar of apology. To the extent that they were able to do this, they nudged forward reconciliation. Some did better than Mr. Smith, some worse. His offering provides an instructive example because it contains elements both of the kind of rhetoric that advanced the work of reconciliation through taking responsibility and of the kind of rhetoric that falls short.

APOLOGY AND MORAL COMMUNITY

Even when it was clumsy, or clumsily communicated, the work by institutional leaders to reassess the past behavior of their organizations made a valuable contribution toward changing the mindset of South Africa's elite. It also opened dialogue among representatives of different constituencies. This raises once again the issue of moral community. Before the early 1990s, what was said earlier in this chapter about Canadians of European origin could also be said of South Africans of European origin: Most of them did not consider the indigenous people of their country to belong to the same moral community as themselves.

Mr. Smith's expressions of remorse for the hardship that apartheid caused "people of colour" not only signal a change in perspective for white leaders, but they also draw upon a new nomenclature of race relations. While the new phraseology is far from ubiquitous, it is spreading with some force. Some in South Africa protest that this development represents a post-1994 political correctness, but this complaint seems to come most often from those who stand to lose relative status from a deconstruction of the old social hierarchy. Can this linguistic reformation be explained solely by a shift in power relations since the election of the ANC, as the cynics suggest, or does it signal the integration of previously alienated moral communities into a larger whole? Many "Mr. Smiths" have had to rethink the relations of their institutions and communities with Africans, Indians, and people of mixed race. They have also been forced to deal on an everyday basis with an increasing number of "people of colour." Have these reflections and encounters redrawn for them the boundaries of moral community?

As a case in point, in examining the exclusion of blacks from the European moral community, we might look to the respective liberation philosophies of the PAC and the ANC. The PAC was explicitly anti-white in its rhetoric and actions. Its members envisioned no place for Europeans in South Africa. This philosophy evolved to the point that a "one settler, one bullet" approach had been adopted by the early 1990s, leading to some of the most infamous acts of violence by anti-apartheid organizations.

The ANC lived a different philosophy. Its belief and teaching were that whites were not the problem, systemic racism was. Under Nelson Mandela's leadership in the 1960s the ANC followed other anti-apartheid groups into the sphere of violent action. The organization turned to armed conflict, but its policy of striking infrastructure and non-civilian targets was largely followed. Some ANC lieutenants did commit gross human rights violations—many of them against Zulus in the IFP—but the organization did not adopt a racist policy or succumb to a racist philosophy. It held up an ideal of a racially inclusive moral community and fought to have it become a reality. A number of whites rose to places of leadership within the ANC, most notably Joe Slovo, a prominent Communist who became commander of MK.

This raises an issue addressed in the previous chapter by Kader Asmal: the distinction between violence in support of the apartheid regime and violence oriented toward its overthrow. One may quarrel with the decision to turn to violence at all, or with operational decisions made by the ANC, but Asmal and others are correct in arguing that the violence employed by the ANC was of a different order ethically than that employed by the police, the military, and such bodies as the Civil Cooperation Bureau.[23]

Although this discussion wanders somewhat from the topic of apology, let us consider the issue of moral community a little further. In general, I take the term to mean a fellowship of persons who believe that they owe one another "good treatment" or behavior guided by accepted human standards. There is an assumption of shared and symmetrical rights and duties. To a great extent South Africa's racial groups have lived as separate moral communities throughout that country's history. There was certainly conflation of these moral communities, but not in such a way that rights and duties were symmetrical and shared.

This leads us back to the discussion of apology. Apologies from members of one racial group to members of another have a special power to advance the integration of moral communities. This is especially true for apologies offered for actions that arose out of a belief that the recipients of those actions were not worthy of the good treatment reserved for one's fellows. Such apologies contain a subtext that says, "I was wrong to believe that we were not members of the same moral community. I now realize that we have the same rights and responsibilities in relation to one another." These speech acts advance the integration of moral community "from below"—from a position of humility. This is very different from attempts to integrate moral community by shaping those outside one's community to resemble those inside. As mentioned earlier, during much of the twentieth century this was the approach of "white" Canadians toward members of First Nations—an attempt at integration from above.

The receivers of such apologies are being granted a measure of power to determine future relations. A number of options are available to them. They can refuse to accept the apology. Such a rejection could serve as a refutation of the perspective that the two parties should become members of one moral community. It is, of course, possible that a rejection would arise from other issues or contingencies, but let us set these aside for the moment. The receivers can acknowledge the apology without accepting it, as did the Native leaders within the UCC. This action could serve as a statement that there is an interest in integrating moral community but that more concrete changes are needed first, especially on the part of the party offering the apology. The receivers can accept the apology without offering further gestures of reconciliation. This response could convey the following message: "We acknowledge that we owe one another a measure of good treatment, but there are limits to the extent that we are willing to recognize you as fellows." Finally, the receivers can accept the apology and offer further gestures of reconciliation. It is quite likely that a statement of forgiveness would accompany this response. Once the recipients of the apology articulate their response, the "ball is back in the court" of the apologizing party, so to speak.

ACCEPTING RESPONSIBILITY: A STEP BEYOND TRUTH-TELLING

Apologies certainly function as a part of the larger process of truth-telling. This was true during the HRV hearings, the institutional hearings, and the amnesty hearings of the TRC. But, beyond the recounting of past events, apologies take an extra step toward political forgiveness: the claiming of responsibility. This is another reason why apologies advance the work of reconciliation and the integration of moral communities. When people accept responsibility for past actions, it becomes easier to trust them.

Unfortunately, there is a broad perception in South Africa that former supporters of the apartheid system are not taking this step. When I visited in 2000, I heard dozens of people make the wry observation that for forty years there were enough supporters of apartheid to elect the National Party every time, but now none of these people could be found. By 1997 Kader Asmal was commenting that "it is already fashionable amongst privileged South Africans to concede apartheid's moral and political weaknesses. Few can be found to admit that they supported apartheid in the past."[24] A lamentably high proportion of the people who benefited from and supported apartheid seems to have chosen Anderson's defense goal.[25]

Before the peaceful transition of the early 1990s, economically advantaged South Africans—almost all of whom were white—were very afraid that an ANC victory would mean a turbulent reversal of the economic order as well as the political order. Adding to their psychological stress was the knowledge that, in the eyes of the majority population and much of the world, they were living a morally indefensible life. People living under this kind of pressure rarely find it easy to be self-critical; this is true of their thinking and even more so of their speech. They tend to build psychic defense mechanisms, as individuals and as communities. Given this, it should not come as a surprise that the more privileged citizens have been and are slow to acknowledge and accept responsibility for their role in South Africa's past. Most observers know this, but many of us are still dismayed with the durability of the denial. The worst fears of the advantaged have not come true.

Instead, Nelson Mandela and other leaders of the new government went to considerable lengths to assuage them.

Why, then, are the beneficiaries of the old order not more willing to acknowledge their roles and to apologize? It is true that a number of "Mr. Smiths" (and the organizations they represented) agreed to make statements of accountability to the institutional hearings, but there were many who did not. Not one judge could be convinced to attend and participate in the legal hearings, for example. Even if more sector leaders had participated in the hearings, there would still be a need for statements and gestures of accountability to be made in many other forums. Citizens with good intentions cannot easily find such forums.

One of the positive acts of the TRC was to establish a register of reconciliation. Mary Burton, the commissioner who proposed the register, explains:

The register has been established in response to a deep wish for reconciliation in the hearts of many South Africans—people who did not perhaps commit gross violations of human rights but nevertheless wish to indicate their regret for failures in the past to do all they could have done to prevent such violations; people who want to demonstrate in some symbolic way their commitment to a new kind of future in which human rights abuses will not take place.[26]

The register is available on-line for people to peruse or to add their own statement. The following statements reproduce common sentiments. The first comes from a fifty-three-year-old white male.

Throughout my life I have consistently held the view that our society was un-Christian, wrong and unfair—it is my single biggest regret, that although vocal, I was not more "active" in making my views take a more practical form. An armchair critic cannot be vindicated if one doesn't produce change in the face of opposition! For this inactivity I am truly sorry. The opportunity was there, I had the motivation—and in many small ways tried to address the balance—but failed to make a significant contribution.

—Peter French, East London, SA

To all South Africans of colour and other people who suffered under the injustices of the apartheid system, I say I am truly sorry. The lifestyle I now live has been made possible because others were disadvantaged.

I pledge to be positive and support the New South Africa not only to make up for past inaction but also in gratitude for having been fortunate enough to have experienced the birth of this wonderful new society.

—Don Lindsay, Henley on Klip, SA

I'm sorry that through all the years of "knowing" what was going on, I, like many other South Africans, was too scared in the knowledge of the draconian rule of the Nationalists, to do something constructive to end the curse on our people.

—Peter Davis, Cape Town, SA

Perhaps these sentiments are more common than we know. The Register of Reconciliation contains hundreds of such declarations. A sad reality is that most of the people who were marginalized by apartheid are not in a position to "surf the Web" and read documents like the Register of Reconciliation. But some of these people have found their way to the register and have left offerings of their own.

As a non-white being hurt by the injustices of the past I wish to apologise to my fellow white South-Africans for hating them for what they have done during the time of apartheid. As many whites were brainwashed about the evils associated with blacks I was brainwashed to hate whites. Until about 5 moths [sic] ago I found it quite difficult to forgive whites for the hurt they caused our people. But in the spirit of reconciliation and as a result of the work done by the TRC I believe I have made the paradigm shift. I do forgive you. We are all brothers and sisters in Christ. God bless Africa!

—Andre Damon, Elsies River, SA

One wants to believe that there are many millions of South Africans who carry the sentiments of Andre Damon, Peter Davis, and company. Vicious circles of resentment certainly color South Africa. Comments like those above give hope that virtuous circles of good will exist as well. An important task for the builders of interracial community will be to get the Andre Damons and the Peter Davises together in dialogues that spin virtuous circles.

Once apologies have been offered or accountability has been verbalized in other ways, the work of accepting responsibility is not over. Quite the opposite. As the Native leaders within the UCC have said, an apology must be lived out to be real. In the next two chapters we will explore, among other concerns, the question of restorative justice and take a look at the reparations component of the TRC. We will also consider retributive justice. Some of the apologies given at the TRC were for horrendous acts. Should the people who offered these confessions be left to walk away "scott free," or is a greater sacrifice required of them? There is a temptation to offer answers to these questions based on a visceral understanding of justice. Our gut feelings about what is right and true are important, but in countries making the fragile transition from oppression to democracy, they must be balanced against other considerations. Every context has its own contingencies, and it is only with these in view that a society can articulate its own definition of transitional justice.

6

Act Three: Building
a Transitional-Justice Framework
Part One: The Amnesty Option

This chapter and the next one will function as companions and will together compose our discussion of the third act in our drama of political forgiveness. The task of this chapter is to describe the South African amnesty process, which was built into the TRC, and to examine some of the debates and discussions that surrounded it and informed it. A number of challenges, dilemmas, and issues related to justice in transitional democracies will come up. They include dignity for victims, accountability for perpetrators, the need to build a human rights culture, distributive justice, the threat of vengeance, and the connection between justice and reconciliation. Here we will examine these issues in a fairly practical fashion, with reference to the work of the TRC's Committee on Amnesty. In the next chapter the same issues will be revisited with a view to the entire TRC process. Our aim in that chapter will be to flesh out the demands and contours of *transitional justice*. The debate between proponents of restorative justice and defenders of retributive justice will be of particular pertinence.

George Bizos is a South African lawyer famous for his defense of Nelson Mandela and many other leaders of the anti-apartheid movement over a period lasting more than three decades. He is widely considered to be a brilliant attorney and is believed to have participated in more political trials than any other lawyer in the world. He recounts the following episode:

In 1988 Bizos was asked to chair an optimistically organized conference on the constitution of a post-apartheid South Africa. During the discussions between academics and leaders of the liberation movements, the question of what would happen to violators of human rights was raised. A member of the ANC Executive in exile eagerly related his feelings on the issue. He recounted some of his own experiences at the hands of the apartheid state and reminded the group of other well-known violations. He insisted that the only acceptable option was to hold Nuremberg-style tribunals. Those who had murdered, bombed, tortured, and committed other horrible acts in the defense of state racism could not be pardoned. Referring to them derogatorily as "Boers," he insisted that they be tried and convicted for crimes against humanity. No compromise was acceptable.

Among those invited was Albie Sachs. A lawyer who had vigorously opposed apartheid, Sachs later became a judge with South Africa's (post-apartheid) Constitutional Court. While teaching in Mozambique, his car had been bombed, and he had suffered serious injuries across his upper body, losing one arm above the elbow. Mr. Bizos chose to recognize advocate Sachs's surviving hand among the many that had shot up after the ANC executive member finished his comments. Sachs argued that calls for vengeance would delay the dawn of freedom. Looking directly at the previous speaker, he said, "Comrade, if I can forgive them, I am sure many more will do so."

Laurie Ackerman, an Afrikaner human rights professor, was the next to speak. He had earlier served as a judge but had become disillusioned with the apartheid legal system and had given up his post. While on the bench he had been respected by Bizos and others for his rulings and light sentences during political trials. With his voice cracking, he said that as an Afrikaner he knew what oppression was. His grandmother had died in a British concentration camp during the Second Boer War. He ended his remarks there, but all understood the implication: Not all Afrikaners should be tarred with the same brush.[1]

The arguments of all three of these men are moving and convincing. In them we see some of the important, and often conflicting, imperatives of societies struggling to make the transition from an oppressive regime to one that is broadly respectful of human rights. There is the imperative to try and to punish those leaders and foot soldiers responsible for atrocious acts, but it is also essential to do what is necessary to bring about "the dawn of freedom." There is an imperative to name the architects and the agents of oppression, but this must be done in a prudent and exacting fashion. Condemning whole segments of society for the actions of some of their members (even if they are numerous) would itself be a violation. Once the day of freedom has come, those responsible for formulating transitional-justice arrangements for a nation are between a rock and a hard place, especially when it comes to retributive justice. Too much punishment for past actions would constitute a new injustice, but so would too little. The first two speakers quoted above give voice to two different kinds of justice, which need not always be in conflict. The ANC Executive member called for a form of *retributive* justice, and advocate Sachs asserted the legitimacy of *restorative* justice. In transitional democracies there is often hot debate about the legitimacy and appropriate expressions of these two forms of justice. In the next chapter we will entertain some theoretical reflections on retribution and restoration. In this chapter we will take a look at the judicial arrangement that sparked what may well be the greatest incarnation of this debate so far: South Africa's amnesty process.

THE INDIVIDUAL AMNESTY ADJUDICATED BY THE TRC

From reunified Germany to Chile, from Uganda to the Philippines, successor regimes have had to decide what to do about the unlawful actions of leaders and agents of the former government. Of course, it is rare that human rights have been violated only by those on one side of a conflict, even in countries like Zimbabwe (formerly Rhodesia), where there was a clear difference in terms of the moral credibility of the parties. This is especially true where change has come through armed struggle. When the struggle ends, one of the most urgent, and dangerous, tasks for those left holding power is to decide what to do with perpetrators of political crimes. In Chile, not much could be done about the horrendous crimes of General Augusto Pinochet and his minions because they retained control of the armed forces. In Zimbabwe, supporters of Ian Smith's white regime feared reprisal after they lost the civil war, but Robert Mugabe, the new president, showed surprising restraint and concern for reconciliation.[2] The current government of Rwanda has held trials and executions for Hutus implicated in the genocide of 1994; international agencies, however, have criticized these trials for not observing due process.

A number of factors influence decisions regarding redress for wrongdoing. They include the strength of judicial and law enforcement institutions; the presence or absence of a culture of respect for human rights; the measure of power retained by members of the old regime; the vigor of civil society; ethical/religious traditions; other cultural resources and traditions; the level of interest that the international community holds in the country; and the dispositions, efficacy, and magnitude of power of the new leaders. These and other factors combine to produce responses that range from impunity to orgies of revenge.

In an effort to find an ethic of just vengeance, Donald Shriver asks the question, "What measure of punitive response is due a wrongdoer?" Shriver outlines a spectrum of possible answers, arguing that both the strongest and the weakest answers constitute lawless responses (quotations in the following list are from Shriver):[3]

- *Terror* is the response of amoral, autocratic powers to actions that they oppose. The motto of terrorism is "For damage to one of our eyes, we put out all the eyes we wish." This response was frequently employed in South Africa by the state security forces. The Sharpeville massacre of 1960 and the killing of student protesters in Soweto in 1976 are prominent examples. Attacks on civilian targets like St. James Church and the Heidelburg Tavern by guerrilla groups associated with the PAC can be called incidents of terror.

- *Vindictiveness* is a "first cousin to terror." It gives a nod to the idea of proportion but still has a motto of "two eyes for one, or a few more for good measure." Again this response was often employed by South African security forces. It was also in evidence during the ANC-IFP conflicts of the early 1990s.
- *Retaliation* is response in kind: "An eye for an eye, a tooth for a tooth." There is a long, well-honored tradition of retaliation referred to in Latin as *lex talionis*. While this practice can have real value in the prevention of vengeance, it is difficult to put into practice because exact retribution is elusive.
- *Punishment* describes a variety of social disciplines. Its motto is, "For your hurt, we hurt in return, but not necessarily in kind. Above all we must reassert the standards which you have defied; our punishment must not defy them either."[4] The official courts and the people's courts in South Africa strove to employ this response. They often failed, the former because of unjust legislation, and the latter by succumbing to the temptation of vindictiveness.
- *Restitution*, or restorative justice, moves by the motto, "Restore what was lost." It follows the imperative to "put it all back," but this can be almost impossible given that many of the things destroyed by unjust action cannot be put back together again. Yet there are ways that restitution can diminish tragedy where retaliation would add to it. The TRC has been struggling to employ this response. Some South African businesses claim that their social investments amount to restitution.
- *Protest* is the response of those who say, "Let us live with the loss, but let us at least name its injustice." This response was widely employed in South Africa by anti-apartheid groups, spontaneous gatherings of people, and organizations like churches.
- *"Passivity*, like terror, belongs to the moral-political spectrum only as a boundary."[5] While both are lawless, passivity is often the iniquity of the powerless. This response was widespread among whites and blacks in South Africa and was preached by some churches.

During the final years of apartheid, its opponents enacted each of these responses to wrongdoing. Granted, most of those who espoused passivity had been supporters rather than opponents of apartheid. Fortunately, the leaders of the post-apartheid government rejected both this logic and its polar opposite—the calculus of terror. During the period of transition and the early days of the new government, the character of Nelson Mandela was formative for the nation. He possessed an extraordinary combination of unshakable strength and unbroken compassion. There would be a reckoning with the past, an ample and arduous one, but it would be conducted with fairness and a view to rapprochement. Archbishop Desmond Tutu, a South African whose moral force was second only to Mandela's, explains in his Chairman's Foreword to the *Final Report* of the TRC why a process of adjudicated, individual amnesty was chosen. He begins with a response to those who had called for Nuremberg-style tribunals.

There were those who believed that we should follow the post World War II example of putting those guilty of gross violations of human rights on trial as the allies did at Nuremberg. In South Africa, where we had a military stalemate, that was clearly an impossible option. Neither side in the struggle (the state or the liberation movements) had defeated the other and hence nobody was in a position to enforce so-called victor's justice.

However, there were even more compelling reasons for avoiding the Nuremberg option. There is no doubt that members of the security establishment would have scuppered the negotiated settlement had they thought they were going to run the gauntlet of trials for their involvement in past violations. It is certain that we would not, in such circumstances, have experienced a reasonably peaceful transition from repression to democracy. We need to bear this in mind when we criticise the amnesty provisions in the Commission's founding Act. We have the luxury of being able to complain because we are now reaping the benefits of a stable and democratic dispensation. Had the miracle of the negotiated settlement not occurred, we would have been overwhelmed by the bloodbath that virtually everyone predicted as the inevitable ending for South Africa.

Another reason why Nuremberg was not a viable option was because our country simply could not afford the resources in time, money and personnel that we would have had to invest in such an operation. Judging from what happened in the De Kock and so-called Malan trials, the route of trials would have stretched an already hard-pressed judicial system beyond reasonable limits. It would also have been counterproductive to devote years to hearing about events that, by their nature, arouse very strong feelings. It would have rocked the boat massively and for too long.[6]

In these paragraphs and the ones that follow, Tutu makes a number of important and defensible points relevant to the decision to allow perpetrators to avoid prosecution and civil suit by participating in an amnesty program. First, amnesty was entrenched in the Interim Constitution, which served as the negotiated agreement ending apartheid and the armed struggle. Two of the three major parties to that agreement—the National Party and the IFP—wanted a blanket amnesty and may have assumed that there would be one when the agreement was made. The third party, the ANC, also had proponents of amnesty among its leadership, which is not surprising, given that ANC deputies were responsible for a significant number of human rights violations, but the organization was opposed to a blanket amnesty. Even though the form of the amnesty had not been determined when the ANC won national elections in 1994, refusal to have an amnesty was not an option.

Second, Tutu is quite right in asserting that the security forces, or at least elements within them, would probably have rebelled if there had been no reprieve for past actions. It is easy to forget the danger of renewed fighting now, given South Africa's relative political stability, but when newly elected president Mandela was presented on a Cape Town dais with white generals standing behind him and air force jets flying overhead, observers understood the ambiguity in the show of support. Those jets, along with the rest of the country's military might, were still under the authority of the officers who had garrisoned apartheid and commanded the men who committed many of its most abhorrent acts. Some of them made it clear that obedience to their new political masters depended on clemency for past acts.

Third, a broad process of criminal prosecution of apartheid perpetrators was not realistic. It would be too expensive, would stretch an already strained criminal justice system beyond the snapping point, and, if due process were followed, would probably result in few convictions—especially of those who had held senior positions. This was demonstrated by the trial of Defense Minister Magnus Malan for authorizing hit squads and assassinations. The trial lasted a year and a half, cost the government twelve million rand (roughly US$3 million at the time), and ended with an acquittal.[7] One thing learned during the trial and the amnesty process was that National Party politicians and senior military and police officials had insulated themselves from legal culpability for the atrocities committed by those under their command. Direct orders to commit such and such an act were never given. Instead, in vague but surely decipherable language, underlings were instructed to "deal with" certain individuals and groups. When, in the late 1980s and 1990s, a few of the soldiers and policemen who committed these acts were apprehended and charged, their seniors hid behind these veils of doublespeak. This stands as an enduring testimony to not only the ruthlessness but also the cowardice of the men who ran apartheid's enforcement machine. In his testimony to the TRC, F. W. de Klerk made recourse to this kind of sophistry.[8]

Fourth, criminal trials are not a very good way to facilitate a broad process of truth-telling. Rules of evidence limit the amount and form of testimony, and the threat of punishment discourages defendants from being forthcoming. They are also harrowing experiences for victims, sometimes to the point of preventing their coming forward.

After replying to calls for Nuremberg-style tribunals, Tutu turns his attention to those who hold the opposite position: that actions before 1994, even horrible ones, should be left alone and that there should be a blanket amnesty. To make his point, he recounts the experience of the central character in Ariel

Dorfmann's play *Death and the Maiden*, which is set in a South American country that has endured the oppression of a dictatorial regime and is now conducting a truth commission. A woman ties up the official who has devastated her. She is ready to kill him for repeating the lie that he did not rape or torture her. Only after he confesses is she willing to let him go. Tutu's interpretation is that "his admission restores her dignity and her identity. Her experience is confirmed as real and not illusory and her sense of self is affirmed." Tutu's reference to this dramatic representation implies both that many South Africans have the same needs as Dorfmann's protagonist and that they might turn to violence, as she did, until these needs are met through truth-telling. He believes that "the past will not lie down quietly"; if its wounds are not attended to, they will putrefy and burst open in further violence. Cleaning the wounds requires a knowledge of what happened and why. Once the details and motivations of trauma-inducing actions are uncovered, steps can be taken to assuage the trauma.[9]

Remembering that a mother at one of the hearings cried out, "Please, can't you bring back even just a bone of my child so that I can bury him?" Tutu explains:

> For all these reasons, our nation, through those who negotiated the transition from apartheid to democracy, chose the option of individual and not blanket amnesty. And we believe that this individual amnesty has demonstrated its value. One of the criteria to be satisfied before amnesty could be granted was full disclosure of the truth. Freedom was granted in exchange for truth. We have, through these means, been able to uncover much of what happened in the past. We know now what happened to Steve Biko, to the PEBCO Three, to the Cradock Four. We now know who ordered the Church Street bomb attack and who was responsible for the St James' Church massacre. We have been able to exhume the remains of about fifty activists who were abducted, killed and buried secretly.[10]

He is right to assert that many more details are known than would have been if perpetrators had not been forced to meet the criterion of full disclosure before receiving amnesty for any given violation. The HRV hearings and investigations uncovered a wealth of evidence about killings, beatings, acts of torture, and other violations, but a lot more information came out, often about the same events, when amnesty applicants gave written and verbal testimony. There was a snowball effect. When one applicant named an accomplice or a superior who had given orders, that individual was informed by the TRC and invited to apply for amnesty himself. A good example of this is the application of five army officers who killed unarmed demonstrators. They identified General Johan van der Merwe as the one who had ordered them to fire; the latter then saw the wisdom of making an application himself, introducing a senior officer into the truth-telling process. Van der Merwe then implicated two of *his* seniors. In the end, over seven thousand applicants sought protection from prosecution and civil suit, astounding those who had estimated that only about two hundred would apply.[11]

It is important to be clear about the fact that the South African amnesty process was not designed by Chairman Tutu and the other commissioners of the TRC. As with other aspects of the commission's work, the framework for the amnesty process was delineated in the Promotion of National Unity and Reconciliation Act of 1995, which in turn was constrained by the provisions of the Interim Constitution. Like all pieces of parliamentary legislation, this act was the product of negotiation, lobbying, party power relations, and the other factors that come into play in the arena of national politics. It is also important to remember that the cabinet which approved this legislation was not made up entirely of ANC politicians. After Nelson Mandela was elected president in 1994, he formed a government of national unity and invited opponents like F. W. de Klerk, Mangosuthu Buthelezi (the leader of the IFP), and representatives of several parties to serve in the cabinet. As such, the Act and the amnesty processes outlined within emerged from a passage through the waters of debate and compromise.

Those who designed and approved the amnesty provisions had several options before them:

- They could have mandated a blanket amnesty of the kind that de Klerk and Buthelezi supported. This option was not acceptable to the ANC leadership, which, like Tutu, was committed to a format that would produce truth-telling and clarify accountability.
- They could have mandated an adjudicated amnesty format that required applications, testimony, and even hearings, but which occurred behind closed doors. In fact, this format was originally chosen by the cabinet as a compromise between its National Party and ANC members, but when this decision was made known, human rights organizations and NGOs successfully contested it.[12] Such a format could have included semi-private hearings, akin to court hearings, with photo taking and audio taping excluded. The conclusions of such hearings could have been made part of the public record.
- They could have mandated an adjudicated amnesty format that included public hearings, forcing applicants to undergo the strain of confessing their culpability in front of victims and observers but requiring no other sacrifices of them. Essentially, this was the format chosen.
- They could have mandated an adjudicated amnesty process (behind closed doors or in open view) that required applicants to accept *lustration*, the surrender of positions within the government or any of its agencies as well as the right to hold such positions in the future. This option may have been rejected because of fears that it would discourage

applications, thereby reducing the number of perpetrators who would participate in the truth-telling, or because the advocates of amnesty in the cabinet and elsewhere considered it an unacceptable truncation of the immunity sought. Certainly, there would have been an element of unfairness in having those human rights violators who cooperated with the truth-seeking of the TRC lose their positions, while violators who refused to participate kept theirs. Such a sifting would also have had detrimental effects on government agencies and would have removed their most experienced employees.

- They could have mandated an adjudicated amnesty process (behind closed doors or in open view) that required applicants to make restitution to their victims or to society at large. Again, this may have been rejected because of the likelihood of deterring applications and the unfairness of having cooperative individuals suffer consequences that non-cooperators avoided. Unfortunately, the lack of a restitutional element caused the amnesty process to have a fundamental moral imbalance. Victims lost something, the right to sue or prosecute their oppressors, without gaining compensation for this loss. The reparations component of the TRC was designed to redress this imbalance, but it has failed quite badly, vindicating in some measure the predictions of the TRC's critics who argued that it would prove to be a "perpetrator friendly" undertaking.

In the end, the cabinet and Parliament approved an amnesty process with the following characteristics:

- Amnesty was offered only for "the violation of human rights through (a) the killing, abduction, torture, or severe ill treatment of any person; or (b) any attempt, conspiracy, incitement, instigation, command or procurement to commit an act referred to in paragraph (a)."[13]
- Amnesty was offered only for those violations "which emanated from conflicts of the past and which [were] committed during the period 1 March 1960 to 10 May 1994 within or outside the Republic."[14]
- Amnesty was offered only for violations "the commission of which [were] advised, planned, directed, commanded or ordered, by any person acting with *a political motive.*"[15] Human rights violations that were motivated by personal gain, personal vengeance or other nonpolitical ends, even racist ones, were excluded. The onus was on the applicant to prove his or her attachment to a political organization or cause.
- Amnesty would be granted only if the members of the Committee on Amnesty, who were charged with making the decisions to grant or withhold amnesty, were satisfied that applicants had *fully disclosed* their role in and knowledge of the act or event for which they were making application. This imperative forced applicants to name collaborators, accomplices, and superiors.

To help determine whether an act was political, and to include the yardstick of *proportionality*, the Norgaard principles were adopted.[16] According to these guidelines, the following factors are to be taken into account:

- The motive of the person who committed the act, omission or offense;
- the context of the act;
- the legal and factual nature of the act, as well as the gravity of the act;
- the objective of the act;
- whether the act was executed in response to an order or on behalf of or with the approval of a political organization or the state;
- the relationship between the act and the political objective pursued, and in particular the directness and proximity of the relationship and the proportionality of the act to the objective pursued.[17]

President Mandela, after a thorough nomination and interview process, named the seventeen commissioners to the TRC in December 1995. Shortly afterward, this group began meeting. One of the first orders of business was to assign each commissioner to one of the TRC's three committees. The Committee on Human Rights Violations was given eight commissioners, the Committee on Reparation and Rehabilitation five commissioners, and the Committee on Amnesty three commissioners. Two individuals who were not commissioners were added to the Committee on Amnesty. Three of the five members were judges, and a fourth an advocate. It is not clear why so few members were initially assigned to the Committee on Amnesty. Perhaps it was felt that the committee would not be able to reach decisions on cases if it were too large. Perhaps the explanation lies in the fact that early predictions were for only a few hundred applications, which would have left the committee with less work than the others.

In any case, the workload of the committee—as well as the political and administrative challenges facing the TRC over amnesty-related issues—grew to proportions far beyond original expectations. The snowball effect of amnesty applications gained momentum throughout 1996, leading to calls for an extension of the deadline for applications, which had originally been set for December 14, 1996. At midnight on May 10, 1997, the revised deadline for amnesty applications, the committee had received over seven thousand applications. It was estimated that about twenty-five hundred of those would warrant a public hearing. All of the applications would have to be screened and judged by members of the committee, who were also responsible for convening, three members at a time, each of the public hearings. It soon became clear that this was too much work for five people. By November 1997 the committee was expanded to include seven new members. Again, most of these were judges or advocates. Even with the new members, it was clear that the committee would not complete its work in the originally envisioned time-frame. When the *Final Report* (to be expanded and revised at a later date) of the TRC was presented in the fall of 1998, amnesty hearings were in full swing. Amnesty decisions were still being made as late as June 2001.

It is difficult to imagine what life must have been like for members of the Committee on Amnesty and for the other officials of the commission—such as Chairman Tutu, Vice Chairman Alex Boraine, the directors of the research department, and Dumisa Ntsebeza, the head of the Investigative Unit—who were involved in the amnesty process. The controversy over the granting of amnesty and over the selection of the method of adjudicating it reached red-hot intensity at home and garnered a lot of attention around the world. None of the political parties represented in the cabinet that had approved the amnesty process ended up acting in a very helpful fashion in relation to it (more on this below). The commission had to face a number of court challenges over the amnesty design and some of the committee's decisions.

South African poet and journalist Antjie Krog gained unique insight into the functioning of the TRC as she covered its work for the radio service of the South African Broadcasting Company. Her book, *Country of My Skull: Guilt, Sorrow, and the Limits of Forgiveness in the New South Africa*, provides a succession of stirring accounts, including these two about the Committee on Amnesty:

Three days before the [original] amnesty deadline. I'm sitting in one of the passages at the Truth Commission offices, studying the amnesty rulings on twelve applicants. The Amnesty Committee has made its findings public under pressure from the Truth Commission itself: desperate lawyers and advocates have been complaining to the commission that only two amnesty rulings have been made so far. As a result, legal representatives cannot fathom how the Amnesty Committee is interpreting the law and don't know how to advise their clients or prepare their cases. And the committee offers them no guidance.

As I'm writing down the names in my notebook, I hear Alex Boraine roaring down the hallway: "Bring it all to my office—I don't understand these people."

I crane my neck: Boraine never raises his voice. I grab a staff member who comes running by. "What's going on?"

"Actually, you're not supposed to be here yet. Please don't report about the amnesty rulings, we still have to add some names to the list."

I do some calculations. Of the twelve amnesty applications, seven were awarded. All seven are black ANC members. Of the five who were refused, four were white. This will not go down well among the people who are being encouraged to apply for amnesty.

When the list is eventually released, it includes the names of another four successful applicants. All four are white right-wingers.

Now where is this coming from?

When Boraine saw the initial list, I hear later, he was furious. He phoned one of the judges: "Have you not given amnesty to any white people?"

"No. Well, we have. . . . Where are those names?. . . They must be somewhere."

"Send them through," Boraine hissed.[18]

Just before midnight (on the day of the final deadline), six black youths walk into the Truth Commission offices in Cape Town. They insist on filling out the forms and taking the oath. Their application simply says: "Amnesty for apathy." They have been having a festive Saturday evening in a township bar when they started talking about the amnesty deadline and how millions of people had simply turned a blind eye to what was happening. It had been left to a few individuals to make the sacrifice for the freedom everyone enjoys today.

"And that's when we decided to ask for amnesty because we had done nothing." They went to a nearby shop, asked the owner if they could use his computer, and typed out their "Amnesty for apathy" statement.

"But where does apathy fit into the act?" a Truth Commission official asks.

"The act says that an omission can also be a human rights violation," one of them quickly explains. "And that's what we did: we neglected to take part in the liberation struggle. So, here we stand as a small group representative of millions of apathetic people who didn't do the right thing."

With applications like this, the amnesty process has become more than what was required by law. It has become the only forum where South Africans can say: We may not have committed a human rights abuse, but we want to say that what we did—or didn't do—was wrong and that we're sorry.[19]

The amnesty process was marked by a number of highly politicized developments, each of which had an enduring effect on the way South Africans of various backgrounds felt about the TRC. The first of these occurred shortly after the design of the amnesty format was made public. The APLA and the Biko, Mxenge, and Ribeiro families, all of whom had had members killed in the anti-apartheid struggle, challenged the amnesty provisions of the Promotion of National Unity and Reconciliation Act before the Cape Supreme Court. If their challenge had been successful, the TRC design would have been struck a crippling blow. The court acknowledged the righteous indignation toward impunity felt by those who had suffered the most during apartheid, but it sided with the TRC, saying that the amnesty component of the Interim Constitution had been an integral part of the negotiated cessation of fighting, and that it could be expected that the commission would make other provisions for reparations.[20] The commission had dodged a bullet but had been grazed. How could it find credibility when it was being contested by the families of heroes like Steve Biko?

Another landmark was the application by the senior leadership of the ANC for a general amnesty that would cover thirty-seven individuals. Both the act of making the application and the content of the submission acknowledged that the ANC was responsible for gross violations of human rights, even if they were committed in service to a just cause. Despite this, the application was seen by many as problematic in that, if it was successful, the thirty-seven ANC leaders would be treated by standards different from those applied to the thousands of others seeking individual, adjudicated amnesty. When the Committee on Amnesty decided to grant the general amnesty, there were strong reactions from within the Afrikaner community, the defense forces, and even the TRC itself. It was reported that commissioners were split over what to do. The commissioners settled the issue during a retreat on Robben Island, which had served as Nelson Mandela's prison home for so many years. They decided to ask South Africa's High Court for a declaratory order on the ANC amnesty. In the end the amnesty decision was overturned, leaving the thirty-seven individuals theoretically open to prosecution or suit. Some of them had also made individual applications, however.

Mary Burton, one of the commissioners with a substantial public profile for her work before, during, and after the commission, says that the autonomy given the Committee on Amnesty in the Promotion of National Unity and Reconciliation Act was unhelpful and was partially responsible for the confusion over amnesty for the ANC:

> The considerable autonomy bestowed on the Committee by the legislation, in retrospect, is a significant weakness in the legislation. The fact that the majority of its members were not commissioners meant that they were not exposed to the often intense debates on these matters that took place in the Commission. Although the legislators may have intended the autonomy of the Amnesty Committee to ensure the impartiality of the Amnesty Committee, this separation created some difficulties and confusion that might otherwise have been avoided.[21]

Even now the issue of blanket amnesty is not settled. In 1998 a working group of ANC representatives and generals from the apartheid-era defense forces was formed under the initiative of Thabo Mbeki (the current president of South Africa) to work out the details of a proposed blanket amnesty for both senior apartheid generals and ANC leaders. The generals had refused to apply for the individual amnesty adjudicated by the TRC, saying that they committed nothing beyond legitimate acts of warfare. In March 2001 the report of the working group was completed and was to be taken under consideration by the cabinet.[22]

I do not know what kind of consideration has been given, but as late as mid-2002 it was still being reported in the South African media that such a clemency was being negotiated between the Justice Department and "right-wingers," and that Archbishop Tutu was objecting strongly.[23] Tutu was also very upset that thirty-three persons had been pardoned (by the Justice Department, using 1990 indemnity laws passed by the National Party government) in May 2002 for what President Mbeki described as "their role in the liberation struggle." The archbishop claimed it was the thin edge of the wedge of blanket amnesty and made a mockery of the TRC's amnesty process.

It is bitterly ironic that the ANC, the very political party that championed a truth and reconciliation commission, turned in such a short time to contemplating a sweeping clemency of the kind that civil society struggled so hard to prevent. This may be due to the deterioration of relations between the TRC and the ANC as Thabo Mbeki's star rose within the latter. He never did seem to embrace the commission as Mandela had. Under his leadership the ANC even sued to block the release of the commission's *Final Report*.

Some of the hearings held by the Committee on Amnesty also served as landmark moments for the TRC. This is true of the hearing for the first applicant to receive amnesty. He may have been carefully chosen for the role. Brian Mitchell was a police officer attached to a riot-control unit in Kwazulu-Natal. As he revealed in his testimony, these units were involved in work other than riot control, much of it related to the countering of anti-apartheid organizations. One of their jobs was to combat the growth and political action of the UDF, an organization closely linked to the ANC. The ANC was banned inside South Africa until 1990; during the mid- to late-1980s, while much of its leadership served from neighboring nations or other places of exile, the UDF was in many ways its in-country subsidiary. In Kwazulu-Natal the police frequently fought the UDF by providing tactical and logistical support to IFP groups, who were sworn enemies of the UDF.

One of these operations was particularly bloody. Police officers, including Mitchell, planned an operation against a house where a number of UDF members were believed to be holed up. The house was located in an area called Trust Feed. The plan was for members of the Inkatha Youth Brigade, with support from special (i.e., African) police constables, to attack the house, burning it down and killing the individuals inside. The operation took place on the designated night, but the attackers went to the wrong house. Inside were a group of mourners who were actually supporters of Inkatha. Eleven of them were killed.

For his role in this operation, Officer Mitchell was convicted of eleven counts of murder and eight counts of attempted murder. He was sentenced to death, but before he could be executed all death sentences in South Africa were commuted. He ended up spending five and one-half years in prison before being granted amnesty and set free.

Ironically, one of the three Committee on Amnesty members who sat for Mitchell's hearing was the judge who had presided at his original trial.

Mitchell provided everything for which the TRC could have hoped. His testimony significantly advanced the truth-telling process regarding conspiracy between South African police and the IFP in Kwazulu-Natal. This was an especially hot topic because the IFP-ANC fighting had become the most bloody conflict in the country, claiming very large numbers of casualties. Proof of complicity with the apartheid security forces undermined the moral credibility of the IFP as an anti-apartheid organization. Mitchell's testimony and cooperation with the TRC outside of his amnesty application also provided many details about the methods and policies of the police forces. Equally compelling were his statements of remorse and pleas for forgiveness at his hearing and elsewhere. He claimed to have been converted to Christianity, to have come to appreciate the legitimacy of the anti-apartheid struggle, and to have understood the tragic consequences of his actions. When he was released, he approached the Pietermaritzburg Agency for Christian Social Awareness in order to become involved in community service in the area where he had worked as a police officer. He also arranged to meet the Trust Feed community so that he could apologize directly.

Despite Mitchell's being a "perfect" candidate for amnesty, reaction to his release was mixed. It was difficult for people who had suffered so long under apartheid to see that its agents, even its killers, were in fact going to receive immunity. Mitchell was one of the few oppressors who was actually receiving punishment for his crimes. The PAC released a statement condemning the release of this apartheid policeman while many of its soldiers were still in jail. There were few statements of forgiveness from the Trust Feed community. Some family members of the victims called for compensation; others explained how painful it was to relive the experience; and at least one asserted that Mitchell should have been hanged. Other groups seemed to accept the value of Mitchell's testimony, acts of contrition, and overtures of reconciliation. Even as it was opposing the extension of the amnesty application deadline and criticizing the TRC for "bending over backward" to accommodate perpetrators who were being less than cooperative themselves, the South African Prisoners' Organisation for Human Rights welcomed the granting of amnesty to Mitchell. The president of SAPOHR praised the decision as a "tribute to the progress the TRC had made towards securing peace, reconciliation, reconstruction and democracy through confession."[24]

Amnesty hearings gained a progressively greater share of the public attention as the HRV and institutional hearings petered out and ended after 1996. None was more controversial than that of police captain Jeffrey Benzien.

Jeff Benzien is a notorious interrogator of political prisoners, who employed the infamous "wet bag" method and other brutal tactics.[25] The confrontation, at his amnesty hearing, between Benzien and his torture victims is one of the most enduring images of the commission for many South Africans. "Initially, the body language of the tortured was clear: 'No one else counts, not the Committee on Amnesty, not the lawyers, not the audience—what counts today is you and me. And we sit opposite each other, just like ten years ago. Except that I am not at your mercy—you are at mine. And I will ask you the questions that have haunted me ever since.'"

One of the victims who confronts Benzien is Tony Yengeni, a member of Parliament known for his confidence—some would say arrogance. But when he faces his tormentor, the confidence is gone. His voice choked, he asks "What kind of a man . . . uhm . . . that uses a method like this one with the wet bag to people . . . to other human beings . . . repeatedly . . . and listening to those moans and cries and groans . . . and taking those people very near to their deaths . . . what kind of a man are you, what kind of a man is that, that can do . . . I'm talking now about the man behind the wet bag." Yengeni demands that the policeman demonstrate the wet bag method. As the Committee on Amnesty members, Benzien's former prisoners, and the TV cameras look on, this stocky white man sits on the back of a black victim, pulling a blue bag over his head. In the police station the victim would have been suffocated almost to the point of death before being given a sip of air. And again . . .

Despite this demonstration, or perhaps because of it—because he has now cast off the garments of the penitent in favor of the long-honed role of all-powerful inquisitor—Benzien does not lose his self-possession in the hearing. In his years as a torturer he became a master of manipulation. During the hearing, as he faces his former victims, he quickly works most of them back into the roles of their previous relationship: He has the power, and they have the frailty.

He turns the tables on Yegeni with a revelation that destroys the latter's political profile. He asks the M.P. if he remembers "breaking" after only thirty minutes of interrogation and betraying a comrade named Jennifer Schreiner. Does he remember pointing out Bongani Jonas on the highway?

Benzien received amnesty and continues to serve as a policeman, now as a captain of the air division. Among his senior officers are some of his former victims.

The amnesty hearings continued far beyond the national threshold of emotional fatigue. There were many highs and lows. A good number of the lows were provided by applicants from the defense forces and from security branches such as the CCB. Speaking in clipped, authoritative phrases and justifying their actions as normal in the everyday give and take of warfare, they showed too much contempt and too little remorse. One wonders if, in the depth of the soul, they are not among apartheid's worst victims. Fortunately, there were a few exceptions, and the *askaris* (members of the anti-apartheid organizations who were "turned" and cooperated with the police) generally demonstrated more humanity. Some of the better moments were provided by African applicants from such organizations as MK and the APLA. The commandos who attacked the Heidelberg Tavern (whom I discuss in the Introduction) are such an example.

In the end, the majority of the applications were rejected for failing to meet one or more of the criteria. As of November 2000, of the 7,112 applications processed, 5,392 were refused. The vast majority of unsuccessful applications were refused because of a failure to meet the criterion of "political objective."[26]

In the next chapter, after some theoretical explorations, we will endeavor to offer a moral evaluation of the TRC's amnesty process. What follows here are some evaluative reflections on the practical effects of the process. By practical effects I mean the extent to which the process advanced or blocked the two central goals of the TRC: truth-telling and reconciliation.

In terms of truth-telling, did the amnesty process provide more and better information than would have been gleaned from a series of criminal trials? Prior to the South African format, amnesties added little to public knowledge about the past beyond the vague and general acknowledgment of accountability that is inherent in the constituting of an amnesty. One of the great innovations of the TRC was the constitution of an amnesty that had revelation as one of its byproducts. The requirement that individuals identify themselves and make full disclosure, often in a public forum, made the South African amnesty a creature of a very different kind from those in Chile, Argentina, and El Salvador. But the question remains: Would a series of criminal trials have provided more and better revelations? Outside of the concerns of retributive justice, with a view limited to truth-telling and reconciliation, criminal trials for political crimes have their champions. Ronald C. Slye explains:

> Proponents of criminal trials over truth commissions argue that the former actively includes the accused perpetrator in the search for truth and accountability. The argument is that a trial forces the defendant to confront his or her accusers and to engage them in a search for the truth. Conversely, trials provide a safe place in which victims may confront their perpetrators. The trial creates a rule-governed space within which a formal dialogue takes place among victims, the accused, and society (represented by the government). . . .
>
> There are two important claims about the utility of trials over commissions. The first claim is based on the participation of the accused in their trial. Such participation has two important effects: it contributes to the rehabilitation and societal reintegration of the accused by including them in the national deliberative process; and it allows the accused to explain, and even justify their actions, and thus provides an important perspective on the truth and context of past events. . . .

The second claim for trials concerns the quality of the information produced. The claim is that trials produce better quality information because they not only provide direct testimony from the accused, but also produce information that has been subjected to the rigors of legal process and the rules of evidence.[27]

By now, it is clear that the TRC successfully countered some of these arguments by providing forums that actively included the "accused perpetrator in the search for truth and accountability." In fact, it can be credibly argued that TRC hearings were *better* forums for such participation. In the HRV hearings there was no imperative for perpetrators to fend off the threat of legal punishment by denying their actions (or those of their accomplices and superiors). In the amnesty hearings there was actually an incentive to forgo such denial. It is also important to keep in mind that in South Africa it was the human rights *violators* who initiated the amnesty hearings. They came seeking something very valuable: immunity from prosecution and civil suit. Surely this made for more cooperative truth-telling than would have been received from defendants at criminal trials. Slye concurs, saying that "in South Africa it seems clear that the amnesty hearings have resulted in substantially more participation by the accused than one finds in a typical trial."[28] In terms of the rehabilitation and reintegration of violators into society, amnesty hearings, again, are probably more helpful than trials. Key to their social reintegration is the acceptance of accountability. Surely hearings where the perpetrators show up and acknowledge their culpability (or at least their actions) serve this end more thoroughly than court proceedings in which defendants maintain their innocence.

TRC hearings were also better, and safer, forums for the participation of victims than trials. The kind of cross-examination victims had to undergo was much less confrontational than that often seen in criminal trials or even civil suits. Also, there were fewer restrictions on the kind of evidence that could be presented.

But does this lack of evidentiary constraint not lead to the gathering of information of a poorer quality? This is a legitimate concern. TRC amnesty hearings were conducted before panels of judges and advocates (mostly) from the Committee on Amnesty. There was legal representation for applicants, the commission, victims, and intervening groups. All of these people functioned with a view to due process for their clients or constituencies, but the rules of evidence and procedure were less fixed and more loose than in either criminal or civil courts. Slye recognizes this concern but points out that the issue cuts both ways. Making rules of evidence and procedure more flexible may have removed a measure of protection for amnesty applicants ("the accused"). This, however, was not as serious a concern in the amnesty process as it is in a trial because the Committee on Amnesty had no power to punish. On the other hand, the loosening of rules also gave the committee freedom to consider a broader range of evidence. This may well have decreased the chances of wrong decisions.[29]

On the other hand, it is important not to overstate this protection. In any judicial or quasi-judicial hearings, participants will have self-interested concerns that serve as motivations to hide or distort the truth. The loosening of rules of conduct will give them more space to act on these motivations. In the case of TRC amnesty hearings, one of those motivations was to construe human rights violations as acts committed for a political purpose. When one examines the cases of amnesty denied, it becomes clear that many individuals sought immunity for what they claimed were political acts but which were really acts motivated by the desire for personal gain or revenge.

When all the factors are weighed, there can be no doubt that South Africa has more information about its past, and of a better quality, than it would have if the new government had decided to go the route of trials or tribunals rather than amnesty hearings. The amnesty process may have been unhelpfully drawn out, but this is nothing compared to the time it would have taken to investigate and try all, or even a significant portion, of the human rights violators.

But what of reconciliation? Has justice been done to this cause as well? To reply to this question a number of issues need to be addressed: the extent to which the truth-telling during the amnesty process advanced reconciliation; the ways in which the amnesty process curbed and generated resentment; the extent to which it facilitated the acceptance of accountability and responsibility; and the extent to which it fostered the growth of a culture of respect for human rights.

Some commentators argue that truth-telling *by nature* advances the cause of reconciliation, because any rapprochement based on the suppression of information or on false perspectives is doomed to fail. They assert that there is an inverse relationship between the achievement of long-lasting reconciliation and the quantity of information remaining secret. Slye does not fully accept this position. Instead, he argues that successful post-conflict reconciliations can only bear so much fact and that there is a necessary element of myth-making as well. He points to the myth of the clean hands of the French resistance and to the suppression of information regarding the complicity of other governments and institutions with the Nazis as abridgments of truth that served stability and cohesion in postwar Europe. "It may be that the de facto path taken by Europe—a combination of the two paths with a temporal dimension: short-term myth-making combined with periodic revelations in the future—is the best one for moving forward and adequately confronting the past."[30] Slye has a point. While it is almost always proper to champion truth-telling, attention must be given to the temporal dimension. During the second half of the 1990s, South Africa was continually awash in stories of violence whites and blacks had done to each other and of atrocities different African organizations committed against one another. Even though Tutu and others were preaching forgiveness and reconciliation, the combined effect of these revelations tainted the soil in which the myth of the Rainbow Nation was meant to grow. On the other hand, one could argue, it is better to deal with this toxin now than to have visions of the new South Africa periodically cut down over the next half century with successive waves of revelation. I suspect that we will be arguing over this issue on the golden jubilee of the liberated South Africa.

With regard to resentment, it is quite clear that the amnesty process has produced its share. Again, this has to do with the amount of revelation during the period between 1996 and 2000. It would be foolishly optimistic to expect that the many South Africans who endured the humiliation of pass laws, who had (and have) access to inferior education and health-care systems, and who will suffer the effects of economic apartheid for generations to come would respond well to the granting of immunity to people like Jeff Benzien, leaving them free, gainfully employed, and financially secure. It would be even less realistic to expect this of torture victims or the families of anti-apartheid martyrs.

Inevitably, there were a number of high-profile cases in which some of apartheid's most brutal killers and devious evildoers were granted amnesty. Craig Williamson, one of the security forces' most nefarious plotters, was responsible for "the remote-controlled murders" of a number of individuals, including a mother and daughter. The South African *Weekly Mail and Guardian* wrote that his amnesty "put into sharp focus the extent to which icons of apartheid-era atrocities have got away with it." Like a number of other apartheid agents, he now earns his living through skills and contacts acquired in service to the old regime. Some, like Slang van Zyl, one of the employees of the CCB,[31] now own and run lucrative businesses that were originally set up as fronts for the operations of the security police. As commander of the nationally infamous Vlakplaas unit, a murder and torture squad, Dirk Coetzee was one of the security forces' most visible and hated officers. He was granted amnesty and went to work for the National Intelligence Agency, where he served for a number of years before leaving to take employment with a Cape Town Mafia boss. The granting of amnesty to men like these has, understandably, not gone over well with millions of citizens.[32]

These developments might have generated a lot less bitterness among South Africa's majority population if they had occurred during a time in which a comprehensive reparations program was being implemented, but this was not to be. Large-scale reparations were promised but not delivered—perhaps the worst of all possible developments. Fortunately, a different byproduct of the TRC's HRV and amnesty hearings has served to moderate resentment and should have important long-term effects. This is the restoration of the dignity of blacks and other groups relegated to the margins by state racism.

During the apartheid era sanctioned criminals like Dirk Coetzee not only enjoyed full citizenship but received commendations for their service. At the same time, more than three-quarters of South Africans were portrayed as less than fully human and were granted a corresponding set of rights. Now the tables are turned. While President Mbeki proclaims his dream of an African renaissance, and the courage and resilience of blacks are being celebrated in the country's burgeoning arts culture, the inhumanity of the old regime is widely exposed and condemned. None of the often brilliant and compelling theater pieces offers more drama than the encounters between perpetrators and victims at amnesty hearings. While the nation watched, leaders and lieutenants of the old regime lost face while their victims became objects of celebration and empathy.[33] Life is not easy for men like Dirk Coetzee and Brian Mitchell. Widely portrayed as monsters, many of them have lost their friends and families.

The amnesty process was only one forum in which judgment was passed on perpetrators and sympathy expressed for victims, but it was an extremely important one. Besides being highly visible, the amnesty hearings carried the weight of formal, officially sanctioned public discourse. They were places where past wrongdoing could be "put on the record" and new attitudes toward it given public sanction. As Tavuchis points out in his sociology of apology, such consultations are extremely important for the formation or alteration of moral community. This reconstitution of moral community not only provides for the inclusion of Africans, Indians, and mixed-race people, but it also moves concern for their well-being to the center of consideration. In the short term, this restoration of citizenship may only partially soothe the foul taste of amnesty granted to people like Jeff Benzien, but it is a powerful assertion of the dignity of blacks.

Related to the reconstitution of moral community is the construction of a culture of human rights. During the National Party reign, human rights were more than simply ignored. Their perpetual violation was built into the structure of institutional life in all sectors. Ideologies that justified violence and exploitation were systematically employed. One could say that a culture of "anti-human rights" flourished. It is also true that resistance movements, even those with right on their side, usually become infected in some measure with the sins of the powers they oppose. Given this legacy, the building of a human rights culture into the foundation of the new South Africa is a daunting challenge of unsurpassed import. How did the amnesty process advance or fetter this work? One thing is clear: Like the HRV hearings, the amnesty process made and kept human rights language prominent in public dialogue. This, in itself, is an important accomplishment that should not be underestimated. By itself, however, it is not enough. For decades, if not centuries, one of the hallmarks of public life in South Africa was a political morality that was observed in speech and ignored in action. A repetition of this duality by calling for but not living a respect for human rights would generate further cynicism and perpetuate the schizophrenia of public ethics.

One of the ways respect for human rights can be strengthened is by establishing measures to ensure accountability. There is some debate over the

extent to which the amnesty process made human rights violators accountable for past actions. On the surface it appears that it did the opposite: By
granting immunity from prosecution and civil suit it freed perpetrators from
being made accountable. Yazir Henry argues that this is not just a surface
reality, but that it reflects a continuation of the deeply entrenched impunity
enjoyed by political criminals during the old regime, and that it is having
troublesome consequences in terms of the actions of the current security
forces.[34] He points to the violent ways police and the military responded to
protest marches that took place in the Western Cape in 1999:

> The manner in which the South African National Defense Force and
> the South African Police Service have chosen to deal with conflict poses
> the question why the new order is so similar to the old. It makes one
> wonder whether the lessons of our recent past have been integrated
> into post-apartheid reality. This, in turn, raises the question of the ex-
> tent to which the TRC and the new South African state has held the
> former institutions of the apartheid state, especially those of the armed
> forces, accountable for past abuses.[35]

What about the loss of face and the public confessions of those who applied for amnesty? Does this not constitute at least a soft form of the punishment that evinces accountability? Henry Yazir, who himself was a victim
of the brutal interrogation techniques employed by policemen like Jeffrey
Benzien, believes that even the small measure of accountability built into the
amnesty process was transgressed in the Benzien case. He argues that
Benzien failed to meet two of the criteria for amnesty: full disclosure and
actions consonant with political motive. On top of this, he asserts, Benzien's
treatment of Tony Yengeni and other victims at his amnesty hearing constituted a continuation of their torture.

> I remember asking myself how a process that was supposed to be
> holding him accountable for his brutal and systematic torture of people
> could go so horribly wrong. I struggled with my anger and resolved not
> to participate in any further amnesty proceedings—even though I knew
> that the people responsible for torturing and nearly killing me would
> apply for amnesty. I realized that the amnesty process was hampering
> my own efforts to deal with the trauma of capture, detention and the
> obligation to watch a comrade and friend die in front of me as a re-
> sult of the police opening fire with guns and hand grenades.[36]

Henry also raises the issue of the accountability of the many South African whites who did not commit gross human rights violations but did contribute to oppression through their support for the apartheid government.
He criticizes the TRC and the government that designed it, saying that there
is "no conducive public space available to whites in which to admit that they

benefited from apartheid and were caught up in a vicious system that also deprived and traumatised them."[37] This oversight, Henry believes, makes it almost impossible for whites to take responsibility for the past as a basis for creating a new society.

Slye takes a different perspective on accountability and the amnesty process. He argues that the TRC amnesty process provided more accountability than any other truth commission or amnesty format. He describes the stipulation that applicants identify themselves and describe their acts, the worst of them in public hearings, as providing an effective calling to account. Through their submissions and participation in public hearings, applicants accepted responsibility for their offenses (at times defiantly). Is this measure of accountability enough to foster reconciliation? Slye says it is too early to tell. He is correct in this but may be a little too optimistic in the tone of his writing. I do not see how the TRC could have built more accountability for offenders into the amnesty process, and therefore I am free to celebrate its many achievements. The many South Africans who suffered under apartheid and still live compromised lives because of its legacy may not have this same freedom. Many have a legitimate need to witness a more thorough form of accountability, and the punishment that evinces it, than that provided by the amnesty process. The fact that the TRC was not able to deliver this, largely because of the political reality in which it operated, is a misfortune of history. Time will reveal the proportions of this misfortune.

This examination of the TRC amnesty process will serve us well in the following chapters. In the next chapter, which serves as scene two in the third act of our drama of forgiveness, we will keep the South African amnesty in mind as we discuss different forms of justice and their role (or lack thereof) in the TRC. In the final chapter the amnesty will be revisited to see how it has affected forgiveness and reconciliation.

7

Act Three: Building a Transitional-Justice Framework

PART TWO: REVENGE AND RESTORATION

Many of the issues raised in the previous chapter will be revisited in this one—especially the ones we identified in our "practical" evaluation of the amnesty process. At the risk of repetition, they are examined again for two reasons: (1) this discussion will broaden our view to include aspects of the TRC beyond the amnesty process, and aspects of the transitional-justice framework beyond the TRC; and (2) our discussion in this chapter is more concerned with theoretical aspects of justice while the previous one was more focused on pragmatic issues. Granted, it is very difficult to separate the two types of concerns when examining transitional democracy.[1]

Lynn, the young English woman whom we met in Chapter 4, the one whose mother was a Communist and whose father was an apartheid soldier, related a story about an ANC organizer who reached the breaking point. This man's neighbor was an eighty-seven-year-old woman. She had a son who was serving as a soldier with MK. One day the security police came to search her house. Finding that the son was not there, they took out their frustrations on the elderly woman, beating her to death. The ANC organizer got up the next morning and went to a busy road where people of all races would be traveling to work. He gathered a crowd of blacks together and worked them to a fury. He urged them to kill the first whites they encountered. Two white laborers came down the road on foot. They were stoned and then set alight. The ANC man then turned himself in to the police. He did not want to hide from his actions. He was proud of them.

OUR AMBIVALENT RELATIONSHIP WITH REVENGE

So far in our discussions of forgiveness we have considered resentment, but what of retributive emotions that burn so hot that they must be given

102

other names? What passion can lead a person to such a white-hot intensity of purpose that he would trade his future for one act of bloodletting? If resentment is a response to insult or injury intended to defend one's psychic integrity, an emotional attempt to reestablish balance, is bloodlust simply a more extreme version?[2] Is it resentment made combustible by the addition of hate? Or is it a passion of another order? Does bloodlust rise when there is no longer a possibility of equilibrium, when the only perceived option is to "blow up the whole damn thing"?

The passions that stir us to vengeance have long been a source of human fascination—and literary imagination. The Athenian playwrights, the writers and redactors of both the Hebrew Bible and the New Testament, Shakespeare, nineteenth-century novelists from Bronte to Melville, and the producers of contemporary "pulp fiction," among many others, have used revenge and the human taste for it as central themes in their work.[3] Despite all this attention, we do not understand the motivations that lie behind vengeance very well. Perhaps they were better understood in other times.

In *Wild Justice* Susan Jacoby argues that the taming of vengeance in systems of justice has been a major, if slow, achievement of the evolution of human civilization. This has happened with an awareness, and an acceptance, that there is an element of revenge in legitimate retributive justice. As civilization evolved, human beings did not stop desiring retribution; rather, we were convinced to accept a certain "distance between aggrieved individuals and the administration of revenge."[4] Society has achieved a balance between the restraint needed to live together with a measure of harmony and the impulse to strike back when one is harmed, but this balance is fragile. It is lost when people cease to believe that, if they are wronged, a legitimate institution will act on their behalf and punish the wrongdoer. When this confidence is lost, actions such as those of the ANC organizer become more likely.[5]

Jacoby fears that our awareness of this balance and our acceptance of desires for retribution are being lost in contemporary Western society. She says that they have been submerged by a psychic split that amounts to a *revenge taboo*:

> The taboo attached to revenge in our culture today is not unlike the illegitimate aura associated with sex in the Victorian world. The personal and social price we pay for the pretense that revenge and justice have nothing to do with each other is as high as the one paid by the Victorians for their conviction that lust was totally alien to the marital love sanctioned by church and state. The struggle to contain revenge has been conducted at the highest level of moral and civic awareness attained at each stage in the development of civilization. The self-conscious nature of the effort is expectable in view of the persistent state of tension between uncontrolled vengeance as destroyer and controlled vengeance as an unavoidable component of justice. The replacement

of this rigorously attained awareness by taboo is a curious development
in a century that has experienced its own full measure of revenge, expanded beyond old limits by modern science and technology. Like all
prohibitions honored mainly in the breach, the revenge taboo contains
a disturbing potential for social regression. It is an enemy of the restraint it is mistakenly thought to encourage.[6]

I think Jacoby is right about our current qualms regarding "retributive
emotions." In our next section we will further examine these emotions and
ask whether they have a legitimate place not only in the administration of
justice but also in the pursuit of reconciliation.

*In 1988 a group of the South African Defense Forces' [SADF] best
trained soldiers, men hardened from years of combating anti-apartheid
forces inside and outside the country, joined together to form a special unit. Two imperatives were to guide the unit's life and work. First,
it was to strike against a broader range of targets than the ANC and
other formally organized and armed groups. "The enemy" was also to
include any people inside the Republic who supported "leftist" causes
or struggled for a nonracial society. Second, it was to be so secretive
that it could never be exposed. It was to function with complete independence from the SADF.[7]*

*The organization, which was given the horribly ironic name of Civil
Cooperation Bureau, was formed along the lines of a private corpo-
ration in which the government had a controlling trust. Using government funds secretly diverted from other budgets, businesses were established to serve as both a front and a source of revenue for the CCB.
Chains of command and communication were structured so that members of the unit didn't know each other. Even the top echelon did not
know all those in their employ, and agents didn't know most of their
bosses.*

*Attending amnesty hearings for members of the CCB a dozen years
later, one could not help but feel that this covert organization had
fallen into the firm grasp of evil. The men attracted to its employ were
the most cold-hearted and devious of soldiers and policemen. The violence they committed for the CCB was secretive, cowardly, and often
directed toward the weak or vulnerable. They hired a gangster to bomb
a township day-care center because a youth group met there. They
hired the same fellow to replace the heart pills of a prominent lawyer
with poison. (The gangster didn't carry out the mission, and the lawyer, Dullah Omar, survived to become justice minister and one of the
architects of the TRC after the 1994 elections.) They hung up a mon-
key fetus at Archbishop Tutu's residence in Cape Town. They shot
university lecturer and anti-apartheid activist David Webster with a*

sawed-off shotgun. They have been implicated in several other poison-ings and mail bombings.

Joe Verster was the director of the CCB. He is infamous not only for his work there, but also for an appearance at a 1990 hearing of the Harms Commission's investigation into death squads. Fearing avengers, Verster showed up wearing a wig and long, false beard. His disguise became a darkly comic symbol of the stealth and cowardice of apartheid's killers.

He was equally furtive at the TRC amnesty hearings on the CCB in 2000, applying for amnesty only for operations that had already been uncovered—making him vulnerable to prosecution. In his writ-ten statement and answers to questions, he revealed as little as pos-sible about the CCB and his role there. He also refused to show con-trition for his acts or sympathy for victims, although repeatedly invited to do so. Unfortunately for Verster, George Bizos was one of the law-yers to question him on behalf of victims' groups.[8] It took no time for Bizos to reveal that the CCB chief was continually lying and withhold-ing information.

Other CCB applicants, such as Slang van Zyl, the man who had hung the fetus in Tutu's yard, followed Verster's example, exhibiting no remorse and blocking truth-telling wherever possible. Even worse, van Zyl and some other CCB lieutenants and the gangsters they hired would cluster in the hallway during breaks, laughing and joking in plain site of their former victims.

In June of 2001 Verster, van Zyl, Botha, and the other CCB appli-cants were denied amnesty. The country waits to see if they will be prosecuted for their crimes.

RETRIBUTIVE EMOTIONS AND RETRIBUTIVE JUSTICE

Until I began to study retributive justice, I assumed that the human urge to retaliate was an instinctive product of our evolutionary history. J. L. Mackie has been thinking along similar lines and has outlined a theory of retribution as a feeling that has evolved in our species, one that is akin to the "bite back" response seen in dogs and other animals.[9] As dogs bite and cats scratch those who attack them, humans have an urge to "hit" those who hurt us. This urge is unreasoned. It is, of course, acted out verbally or sym-bolically more often than physically. While Jean Hampton acknowledges that there is an instinctual element in human retributive emotions, she rejects Mackie's theory.[10] Her rejection is based on the conviction that there is a *cognitive* element in retributive emotions. This conviction arises both out of her understanding of human emotion and out of a concern that retribution would be unjustifiable if it were not *reasoned:*

Appealing though it is, I would argue that this approach to retribution is at best incomplete. Mackie's theory implicitly denies to retribution any cognitive content. (Note that his referring to it as a 'sentiment' presupposes a non-cognitivist approach to the emotions, with which both Murphy and I disagree.) But cognitive content is precisely what those who defend retribution must understand the response to have if retribution is to justify the infliction of harm on wrongdoers. A primitive urge, which is all the bite-back response could be in other mammals, cannot by itself justify anything.[11]

Like Jacoby, Hampton believes that retribution is justifiable. For her, both its validity and its "irresistible character" arise from its "being the conjunction of two basic ideas mandating the harm of the wrongdoer as means to an end."[12] The first of these ideas is *that punishment is a defeat*.

In Chapter 2 we examined the theory of resentment offered by Jeffrie G. Murphy, Hampton's dialogue partner in *Forgiveness and Mercy*. Murphy justifies resentment because, in his view, it protects and bolsters self-respect. When a person willfully and wrongfully injures another, there is a double harm. The first harm is the injury itself. The second is the implicit statement by the wrongdoer that "I am essentially more important than you are. It is acceptable for me to trample your dignity or rights because I am a more important person than you." The generation of resentment within the injured person is a rejection of that claim. It is a counter-assertion of one's worth.[13] As Hampton describes retribution, it is akin to an enforcement of this rejection.[14] It defeats the wrongdoer's original statement about his or her relative value vis-à-vis the victim. Those who wrong others demean them, while operating on the incorrect belief or assumption that their own value is high enough to warrant this treatment. Punishment serves as an enlargement of the relative value of the victim by diminishing the value of the offender. The defeat of the wrongdoer can be directly at the hands of the victim or through an agent, such as the state.[15] In either case, it is not just an instinctual response, but rather a rational assertion about the relative value of human beings.

So far we have considered only the first of the two ideas that, according to Hampton, combine to give retribution its "irresistible character." This is the notion that punishment is a defeat. The second idea expands her treatment of retribution to include its deterrent value. According to Hampton, punishment has *vindicating value through protection*. Punishment is analogous to a nettle's sting. Just as nettles protect a plant through chemicals that produce pain in animals, punishment protects human beings through the activation of unpleasant experiences.

A note may be in order here about the relevance of this discussion to our larger task of building a model of political forgiveness. Even if retribution and the emotions that fuel it are legitimate in modern society and its administration of justice, as Hampton and Jacoby assert, must not this legitimacy be compromised in a post-conflict situation where *reconciliation* is being sought? Many people would say yes.

Those who criticize the pursuit of retributive justice in post-conflict situations usually do so from a place of concern for restorative ends like the stopping of cycles of vengeance, the rehabilitation of both victims and offenders, the creation of respect for human rights, and the healing of the fabric of society.[16] These are legitimate concerns, but they are all jeopardized by *impunity*, and, while retributive justice is not the only medicine for impunity, it is a very powerful one.

Alex Boraine, the vice-chairman of the TRC, outlined the ills of impunity when delineating his argument against blanket amnesty for South Africa:

- Impunity threatens belief in a democratic society. The fact that those responsible for violations are not put on trial and submitted to criminal justice creates doubts and fears about democratic ideas and ideals.
- Impunity confuses and creates ambiguous social, moral, and psychological limits. A society that does not investigate or punish serious crimes blurs the norms of right and wrong.
- The lies and denials are institutionalized and are defended by the laws of the country. One law prohibits violence and force while another protects wrongdoers against fair trial and punishment.
- Impunity tempts people to take the law into their own hands.
- Impunity invalidates and denies what has happened and thereby limits the possibility of effective communication between fellow citizens. This hampers collective mourning and the collective working through of what has happened.
- Impunity strengthens powerlessness, guilt, and shame.
- Impunity affects belief in the future and may leave a historical "no man's land" in which there is both an official and an unofficial version of events—something that may give rise to historical stagnation, limiting the possibility of moving ahead and creating a common just society.[17]

Amnesty International has been a vocal opponent of moves by successor regimes, such as blanket amnesties, that advance impunity. In a statement given before the United Nations Commission on Human Rights, Sub-Committee on Prevention of Discrimination and Protection of Minorities, the organization condemned impunity as negating the value of truth and justice and leading to further violations. It insisted that transitional governments undertake three responsibilities: (1) the investigation of human rights violations; (2) the bringing to justice of human rights violators, even those who served with the past (or current) regime; and (3) the avoidance of amnesty laws that have the effect of preventing the emergence of truth and responsibility.[18]

Unfortunately, but perhaps unavoidably, discussions about transitional justice often are reduced to retribution versus reconciliation debates, with those upholding reconciliation assuming that champions of rehabilitation, restorative justice, and forgiveness will naturally join their side. It is especially common to hear it said that retribution and forgiveness are incompatible by nature, and, on the surface, this seems to be the case. There is another way to see it, however. Remember that the surrender of resentment is key to forgiveness. If retribution (punishment) offers a certain "balancing of the scales" for the offended party, that party may be more likely to surrender his or her resentment after it is administered. Each case will unfold differently, and the movement toward forgiveness will take time, if it occurs at all, but it is certainly legitimate to argue that in many if not most cases there can be a place for retribution on the journey to forgiveness without bringing a premature end to that journey.

In the townships on the edge of Cape Town, there exists a mothers' group of about ten women. The common element that brings these mothers together is not the fact that they all have children but that they have all lost children—to political violence administered by the apartheid state. Several of the mothers of the murdered Guguletu Seven belong to this group, as does at least one woman who is not African but a mixed-race person. They meet to support each other emotionally, to help each other cope with conditions of poverty, and to seek community improvement consistent with the vision of a just society for which their sons died.

For most of them, the poverty they suffer is exacerbated by the death of their sons. Their boys died just as they were reaching adulthood and becoming breadwinners. This new source of income would have benefited the mothers and their families for some time to come, as is the norm in African families. Also, the trauma of losing a child to violence severely affected the women's husbands. Several of them suffered early deaths or debilitating illnesses, pushing their families further into poverty.

These mothers, like thousands of other victims of political violence, were promised a significant amount of compensation under a reparations plan proposed by the TRC. Unfortunately, the ANC government has not seen fit to implement the plan, leaving the mothers exasperated. The ones who participated in the HRV hearings and received a promise of reparation payments feel abandoned.

George Bizos points out that the plight of these mothers is a story repeated throughout South Africa. He says the security forces targeted intelligent and hardworking individuals for "elimination." Those who disappeared are the very individuals who "would have made something of their lives." Their absence leaves their families in financial poverty, and often in a poverty of meaning.

When I met the mothers' group, the women had just received a modest amount of money from a private donor and were discussing what to do with it. The temptation to simply split up the money and use it for household purposes would be very understandable, but this was not contemplated. After considering the possibility of establishing an educational bursary with the funds, they decided to save that project for another time and to use the donation to create a memorial for their children and other youths who were lost to apartheid violence. For them, the most important first step of restoration is restoration of meaning.

RESTORATIVE JUSTICE

In the previous section I argued for the compatibility of retributive and restorative justice. Indeed, to the extent that Hampton's theory is correct, restoration (of human worth) can be seen as the very purpose of retribution; but understanding the relationship between the two categories of justice also requires clarity about their differences. In a very helpful article entitled "Moral Ambition within and beyond Political Constraints," Elizabeth Kiss treats the similarities and differences in a fashion that highlights the essential concerns of restorative justice:

Restorative justice includes a threefold commitment (1) to affirm and restore the dignity of those whose human rights have been violated; (2) to hold perpetrators accountable, emphasizing the harm that they have done to individual human beings; and (3) to create social conditions in which human rights will be respected. As yet, all of these features are perfectly compatible with retributive justice. To be sure, trials rarely do justice to victims' voices in the way truth commissions have the capacity to do, and traditional conceptions of retributive justice place relatively little emphasis on restoring victims' dignity. Nevertheless, legal punishment of rights violators remains a powerful way of affirming the dignity of victims. Thus far, the difference between retributive and restorative justice appears to be one in emphasis and degree rather than in kind. It becomes much sharper when we consider a fourth aspect of restorative justice, its commitment to reconciliation. For while retributive justice demands that the guilty be punished, restorative justice, in Tutu's words, "is concerned not so much with punishment as with correcting imbalances, restoring broken relationships—with healing, harmony and reconciliation." Thus, a key defining element of restorative justice is its privileging of reconciliation over retribution.[19]

We might say that Kiss sees an essential compatibility between the two forms of justice, while acknowledging that they tend to be pursued with different orientations or lived out in different spirits.

Jennifer J. Llewellyn and Robert Howse believe that the difference is more profound. They argue that one is fundamentally oriented toward integration, while the other reestablishes social equilibrium through the employment of *isolation*. Like retributive justice, restorative justice is based on the moral intuition that "something must be done" in response to the offense. But this "something" has the opposite orientation. Retributive measures are designed to isolate people (offenders) from society; restorative measures are designed to reintegrate both victims and offenders into society. Llewellyn and Howse are especially concerned about the repair of social equality in post-conflict societies, and they argue that restorative measures do a better job of this because of their orientation toward reintegration.[20]

They also point to another fundamental difference between restorative and retributive justice that is particularly relevant for societies that have not been fundamentally just. They argue that "criminal justice" (that is, retributive or punitive justice) seeks to return offenders and victims to a *preexisting* state of just equilibrium. In other words, it makes the assumption that before the conflict society was just. On the other hand, they argue, restorative justice does not function with this assumption, but instead opens the question of which set of judicial practices are best for any particular society in transition. Instead of having authorities impose measures designed to return to a pre-existing state of justice, restorative justice functions with the understanding that "restoration will ultimately depend on a broader social transformation to create full equality in society among victims and perpetrators, while at the same time addressing particular offences such as gross human rights violations."[21] This social transformation will require dialogue among, and the participation of, victims, perpetrators, and others. It will also have to employ many devices beyond punishment.

Both the dialogue concerning transformation and the strategies chosen will be influenced by contextual and cultural factors. These factors should give transformative measures much of their dynamism. The recourse to the African philosophy and theology of ubuntu by Archbishop Tutu and a number of others during the proceedings of the TRC serves as an example of contextual vitality.

Rashied Omar is the imam of the Claremont Main Road Mosque in Cape Town, a faith community that is known in South Africa for its progressive views and practices. I have been told that it is the only mosque in the country that will allow women to preach during religious services. In the Western Cape a radically "conservative" Muslim movement has evolved and has shown a willingness to employ violence against those to whose social or religious practices it takes exception. Omar is seen by many as a courageous figure because of his willingness to risk personal harm as he supports progressive and ecumenical causes.

Perhaps this courage was first developed during his student days. Omar was somewhat of a prodigy as an adolescent. Under the guidance of religious instructors, he memorized the entire Qur'an. But it was Islam's teachings on justice that helped him understand the links between his faith and the political aspirations of blacks. Moved by a powerful theology of liberation, he became a leader in national Muslim youth organizations and student organizations at the University of Cape Town.

While Omar does have some praise for the ANC leadership that supported the creation of the TRC, saying that it salvaged something for victims from an amnesty process imposed by the "sunset clauses" of the Interim Constitution, he has strong criticism for the commission itself. He has trouble with the forgiveness rhetoric, saying that it is not a natural outgrowth of the inner transformation of people, but rather a product of both political pressures and the Western Christian theology of Chairman Tutu, Vice-Chairman Boraine, and others. Islam teaches him that it is always better to forgive, "but if the perpetrators do not ask for forgiveness, how can we offer it?" In Islam, he argues, there is a connection between forgiveness and justice that does more to empower victims. Forgiveness is offered when the offender does three things: one, shows remorse; two, reforms; and three, makes restitution or diyah. In this process victims or their families have some power to decide the fate of the person who has harmed them. Omar feels that the amnesty process of the TRC would have been more fair if it had included some of these requirements and therefore given more power to victims.

He is disheartened by the lack of remorse and willingness to offer restitution on the part of whites, both those who participated in the TRC hearings and the community at large. The economic transformation of his country is a major concern for Omar: "True reconciliation will come about only with a fundamental redistribution of wealth and power." Repeating the call of a rabbi at the TRC's faith hearings, he urges the business community to set up funds for the rebuilding of black communities. "We must bring together our best economic minds and find the most compassionate way to bridge the gap between the wealthy and the poor. Otherwise this might be done later through vengeance."

Omar, like so many others, laments the failure of the government to pay out reparations recommended by the Committee on Reparations and Rehabilitation, but he says that even these measures would not correct a fundamental imbalance at the heart of the truth commission. For him, the TRC arrangements, which offered clemency for perpetrators and reparations for victims, were a "patriarchal marriage—with the perpetrators being the male partner."[22]

TRANSITIONAL JUSTICE IN SOUTH AFRICA

One of the great challenges facing successor regimes is the delineation of transitional-justice measures. The difficulty of this task is often compounded by institutional weakness resulting from years of civil war, or by institutional illegitimacy arising from years of oppression, or both. Often the civil sector has been decimated by attacks from governments or other power bases that felt threatened by any form of community organization. Where the civil sector is strong, it may be largely molded and motivated by a liberation paradigm that is inherently suspicious of government initiatives. Where there has been civil war, public-sector institutions are often starved from the diversion of funds to the military. Physical and human resource infrastructures will be reeling. Where there has been state-sponsored oppression, the bureaucracy will be corrupt in some measure and burdened by deformed patterns of operation. Significant elements of the private sector will have blood on their hands and will have developed corporate cultures that are short on respect for the rule of law.

Chilean lawyer and former truth commissioner José Zalaquett is a leading expert on the challenges faced by transitional democracies. His preference is clearly for restorative over retributive measures. Despite this view, Zalaquett accepts both kinds of measures as legitimate contents of a comprehensive transitional-justice policy. For him, such a policy should be oriented to two overriding goals: (1) the reparation of society; and (2) the prevention of the recurrence of human rights violations. Measures that are just and that advance these goals, even punitive ones, are acceptable.[23]

The goals named by Zalaquett further round out Kiss's list of restorative justice's commitments. Her list includes the affirmation and restoration of the dignity of victims; the accountability of perpetrators; the creation of social conditions in which human rights will be respected; and reconciliation. Zalaquett's goal of the repair of society resonates with my highlighting of distributive justice. He speaks of reparation in broad terms that include psychological healing and the memorializing of loss, but that also give economic compensation an important place.[24] The breadth of Zalaquett's concern reminds us that distributive justice is not just about economics. The distribution of life chances, educational opportunities, and recreational and cultural resources is also relevant.

Zalaquett's second goal, the prevention of further human rights abuses, repeats Kiss's commitment to the fostering of social conditions in which human rights will be respected. Actually, there are two objectives contained within these statements; they are related but can be identified individually. The first is the need for sociocultural systems that uphold and protect human rights, and the second is the imperative to prevent or break cycles of vengeance.

In his essay, "Justice without Punishment: Guaranteeing Human Rights in Transitional Societies," Paul van Zyl offers a list of requirements that successor regimes are compelled to meet by international law.[25] Van Zyl gives special attention to the decisions of the Inter-American Commission on Human Rights and the Inter-American Court of Human Rights regarding Latin American countries that have passed through periods of extreme oppression of human rights and have implemented amnesties. Having examined the offerings of Kiss and Zalaquett, his list will seem familiar to us. According to his reading of international law, a state must fulfill five obligations regarding gross human rights violations committed by a previous regime: (1) investigate the identity, fate, and whereabouts of victims; (2) investigate the identity of perpetrators; (3) provide compensation to victims; (4) take affirmative steps to ensure that human rights abuse does not recur; and (5) prosecute and punish those guilty of human rights violations.[26]

Drawing upon Kiss, Zalaquett, and van Zyl, as well as the field research in South Africa, we are now in a position to offer a list of objectives for a program or systematic policy of transitional justice:

1. *The restoration and celebration of the dignity of victims.* It is important to do this in a fashion that does not make victimization the single defining characteristic of their identity. This is why I say their dignity must be celebrated. The courage and sacrificial gift of martyrs can be held up, as can the endurance of those who survived. It is also important to recognize a body of people larger than those who suffered gross human rights violations like murder, kidnapping, or torture. Generally, a much larger number will have suffered economic loss, restricted legal protection, and inferior government services in areas such as education and health care; they may have suffered other injuries as well. As Murphy and Hampton recognize, these are double affronts; there is the concrete loss, and there is the accompanying statement about the inherent value of those who suffer it.

2. *The implementation of measures to ensure accountability.* These measures can lead to accountability for perpetrators that is either weak or strong. A simple naming of perpetrators would fall at one end of that spectrum. The administering of criminal punishments would fall at the other. Only under extreme and rare circumstances would it be acceptable to forgo all such measures.

   There is another kind of accountability as well. This belongs to all those who supported and/or benefited from illegitimate governments, policies, or practices. In South Africa, for example, responsibility for apartheid is shared among those millions who voted for the National Party, benefited from economic exploitation, or simply refused to voice opposition. Almost all whites own a measure of this.

3. *The entrenchment, upholding, and protection of human rights.* This involves the passing of laws that acknowledge international human rights, the fostering of a culture of respect for those rights, and behavior on the part of the government that is consistent with such respect.

4. *The implementation of measures to advance distributive justice.* Here we are talking about policies and practices that redistribute society's wealth, both in terms of financial and physical resources and of life opportunities. This work goes beyond the transitional-justice policy of a successor regime, being a consideration in broad areas of public policy, but it is important that transitional arrangements take distributive justice concerns into account, especially where amnesty is granted. Where perpetrators receive clemency, there is a visible good to them. It is essential that this good be balanced by the granting of something of substantial benefit to victims.

5. *The prevention of revenge-taking and other forms of violence.* This is a more complicated task than it might appear if we accept the perspective of people, like Eric Harper, who believe that the high violent-crime levels in South Africa represent a kind of sublimated vengeance.[27] Even black-on-black violence, they claim, can be understood as partially arising from this dynamic.

6. *The pursuit of reconciliation.* As mentioned earlier, not everyone agrees that this is an appropriate objective of transitional-justice measures. Some feel that it is too "soft" a goal to be incorporated within a justice schema (this opinion does not seem to be held by many proponents of restorative justice); others feel that it is too ambitious. It is true that substantial reconciliation will usually belong to a temporal horizon that is more distant than that of transitional arrangements, but this does not mean it should be ignored. Developments in the years immediately after transition will set a tone for relations between former enemies; if transitional arrangements can make this tone more conciliatory, seeds may be planted that will blossom into forgiveness and rapprochement in the future.

We now turn to a reporting on and evaluation of the transitional-justice arrangements put in place by South Africa's post-apartheid government, including the TRC. Our examination will cover each item on our list of transitional-justice objectives except one: The discussion of "the pursuit of reconciliation" will be reserved for later chapters in which this is a central focus. Here it suffices to repeat that the TRC's commitment to restorative justice incorporated the goals of reconciliation and forgiveness to an extent unmatched by any other truth commission.

THE RESTORATION AND CELEBRATION OF THE DIGNITY OF VICTIMS

It is surprising to remember that for the earliest truth commissions, established two decades ago, the restoration of the dignity of victims was not an important goal.[28] The fact that such restoration was at the very heart of the philosophy and founding principles of the TRC shows us just how far we have come. The truth-telling process, especially the part guided by the Committee on Human Rights Violations, was the part of the TRC's work that was most successful in restoring and celebrating the dignity of those wounded by apartheid. Part of the reason for this was the willingness by commissioners who convened HRV hearings to move out of a stiff, judicial mode of leadership. Following the lead of Archbishop Tutu, who was by far the most dynamic in this kind of facilitation, commissioners sang, prayed, cried, and engaged in other nonjudicial rituals with participants. The deep empathy shown to victims by commissioners, whose membership was representative of South Africa's ethnic and cultural diversity, augmented the power of the revelations about past violations.

The most forceful and oft-repeated criticism of the TRC has come from advocates of retributive justice who feel that the best way to restore the dignity of victims would have been to criminally prosecute human rights violators, and the best way to restore the dignity of South Africa's majority population would have been to try apartheid's leaders for crimes against humanity. In the chapter on amnesty we discuss at some length the reasons, both practical and philosophical, why such trials were not held, but we are still left with the question, Was the amnesty just? We will revisit this question and the larger issue of the defensibility of the TRC from the point of view of justice at the end of this chapter.

Here I will simply say that the victims of human rights violations that I interviewed were not in agreement on this issue. Some clearly felt that the amnesty process was justified because it helped the country move on and it advanced truth-telling. Others felt that amnesty for those perpetrators who made full disclosure without hesitation, offered statements of remorse, and asked for forgiveness was appropriate; but it was not appropriate for those who begrudgingly disclosed as little as possible and showed no regret. Others felt that the whole process was flawed and were angry that they could not prosecute or sue those who had harmed them or taken loved ones from them. Yazir Henry, for one, felt that the amnesty hearings prolonged and intensified the pain of victims while giving offenders a gift of clemency—surely an unjust configuration. On the other hand, some victims did report that the revisiting of pain during amnesty hearings advanced their healing process.

THE IMPLEMENTATION OF MEASURES TO ENSURE ACCOUNTABILITY

This has already been discussed at some length. As a review, we can point out that several kinds of accountability were clarified by the TRC. First, the HRV hearings not only recognized the everyday indignities and injustices of apartheid, but they also sought to name the people, systems, and attitudes that were responsible for them. Those representatives of public-sector and private-sector bodies who were willing to testify at these hearings often voiced responsibility for supporting or being complicit with unjust systems. Others were pushed to do so. An unfortunate aspect of these hearings arose out of the fact that participation was voluntary (for the most part); many of the people who were complicit in systemic oppression did not show up, and many of the organizations with behaviors or policies to account for were not represented. Perhaps the most flagrant example was the failure of even one judge to attend the legal hearings. The TRC was given fairly strong powers to subpoena persons, but they were rarely used—the case of former president P. W. Botha being the most prominent exception.

A second kind of accountability was that accepted by amnesty applicants who confessed their offenses. As mentioned earlier, the very act of application amounted to an admission of responsibility. The suffering of moral judgment and of public shaming can be seen as a soft form of retribution.

A third kind of accountability was that imposed on individuals and organizations by the *Final Report*. In our chapter on apology we discussed former president F. W. de Klerk's refusal to accept responsibility for the actions of security forces under his control. In the *Final Report* he is designated such responsibility and criticized for his justifications. Former president Botha and other leaders are also judged for their roles in systematic programs of oppression.

A controversy that arose out of the TRC and its *Final Report* focused on whether the commission adequately distinguished between the kind of accountability that must be accepted by those who committed violations in support of apartheid and the kind that belongs to those who committed violations in an effort to end apartheid. This is an important issue. Those who hold that the TRC was just offer its value for truth-telling as their strongest argument; if the commission proved unable to make such fundamentally important distinctions, then this argument loses much of its power. The ANC leadership felt strongly that this distinction was not being satisfactorily made and even sued to prevent the release of the *Final Report*. The suit was unsuccessful. To outsiders, this controversy can be perplexing because the *Final Report* clearly distinguishes between violence in support of and in opposition to state racism, and judges apartheid itself as a crime against humanity.

THE ENTRENCHMENT, UPHOLDING, AND PROTECTION OF HUMAN RIGHTS

The two objectives considered already, dignity for victims and accountability for perpetrators, can be seen as two sides of the same coin and are essential to the creation of a culture of respect for human rights. The hearings held by the Committee on Human Rights Violations of the TRC were a stellar example of a process that employs both corrective activities. What is more, as indicated by the name of the committee, the whole orientation of the process was toward human rights. The educational value of this for a country that had experienced such a long period of disdain for fundamental rights cannot be easily overstated. While the HRV process may have given greater attention to empathy for victims than to censure of violators, the balance was shifted back the other way by the amnesty process.

Even the debates and controversies had (and continue to have) educational value—including the one that arose from perceptions that the TRC failed to label apartheid itself as a human rights violation. In order to take a side in these debates and to make credible arguments, people were forced to consider definitions and theories of human rights. These definitions and theories became a part of common knowledge and everyday public discourse in some sectors.

It is easy to see how the TRC, in its hearings and its *Final Report*, underscored the importance of human rights through the *deconstruction* of apartheid. But it also advanced the cause of human rights through the *construction* of a social good that has long been in short supply in South Africa. Amy Gutmann and Dennis Thompson call this good "democratic reciprocity" and link it closely with "deliberative democracy." According to these authors, the strongest argument that can be offered by those who would justify truth commissions is their value for the building of democracy that is deliberative and reciprocal. In other words, the kind of dialogue and debate that takes place at a truth commission, which brings together former enemies and people from different sectors of society, teaches members of society to perceive one another as co-citizens with whom it is best to work out differences through debate and democratic process. Such a process is reciprocal because each social group understands the other groups to possess the same rights, responsibilities, and worthiness of respect.[29]

It is certain that South African society will be subject to extreme disagreements, moral and otherwise, for some time to come. The potential danger of these disputes to catalyze further human rights violations is increased by the legacy of problem-solving through violent means—a legacy shared by whites and blacks. Any forums in which citizens, especially those of different racial and cultural backgrounds, learn to handle disagreements by other means will be extremely helpful. If these forums are highly visible, thereby providing modeling for large numbers of people, all the better. Over the course of several years the TRC provided a continual succession of such forums. Whites and blacks served as commissioners and conveners. Whites and blacks served as witnesses. Whites and blacks served as advocates, amnesty applicants, and affected parties who were given standing to speak. It is true that the proceedings sometimes became strained or confrontational, but all parties were protected by, and expected to act in accordance with, a common set of standards for debate and deliberation. Some have argued that blacks or whites or perpetrators or victims were given preference or greater leeway. This may have happened on isolated occasions, given that the commissioners who presided over the hearings were allowed broad sway in which to exercise their judgment, but there is no evidence that there was a general tendency to treat some groups with preference over others. Certainly victims were recipients of greater displays of empathy than were perpetrators, but one could hardly argue that this was inappropriate.

THE IMPLEMENTATION OF MEASURES TO ADVANCE DISTRIBUTIVE JUSTICE

The greatest social ill in South Africa, one that is responsible in significant measure for other problems like AIDS and violent crime that receive more international attention, is relative poverty.[30] In 1994, when the first democratic government came to power and was charged with building the country's transitional-justice framework, there was no more pressing concern than distributive justice. The architects of the TRC recognized this and included a Committee on Reparations and Rehabilitation as one of the commission's three core councils. Despite what could be seen as a good beginning, the reparations component of the TRC has been its greatest and most bitter failure. Ironically, most of the blame does not lie at the feet of the commission but rather with the ANC-led government that designed it, or at least approved the design. For reasons discussed elsewhere, relations between the TRC and the ANC leadership deteriorated badly. As a result of these tensions, plus apparent financial and administrative difficulties, the payment of reparations has been severely delayed and the amount that the ANC has agreed to issue to survivors of human rights abuses is only a small fraction of what the TRC originally recommended. Many of the other recommendations made by the Committee on Reparations and Rehabilitation await action as well.

There was to be a trade-off in the truth commission arrangements: clemency for human rights violators, reparations for victims. The fact that perpetrators have received their good but victims have not is simply unjust. It has extended the injustice of the original violations.

This failing has been tempered by some successes of the new regime. The implementation of affirmative-action policies, support programs for black businesses, the vast improvement of water distribution systems, and a measure of land reform serve as examples. If we understand these measures to be part of the government's comprehensive transitional-justice policy, which seems reasonable, then we can say that the overall transitional-justice framework incorporates economic reparations more successfully than did the TRC. However, these successes themselves are overshadowed by stubborn poverty, very high unemployment, excruciatingly slow rates of reform in the education and health-care sectors, and a host of other socioeconomic problems. The enduring lack of distributive justice threatens to reverse progress made toward the fostering of respect for human rights and the boosting of democratic reciprocity. How can whites and blacks be expected to meet and deliberate as equals when their socioeconomic situations are so radically different? Gutmann and Thompson recognize this problem:

> Reciprocity also calls for establishing social and economic conditions that enable adults to engage with each other as civic equals. To the extent that those socioeconomic conditions are absent, as they are to varying extents from all existing democracies, a conception of deliberative democracy offers a critical perspective on socioeconomic as well as political institutions.[31]

The damage that relative poverty threatens to cause goes beyond sociopolitical erosion. Untreated, it may spark criminal violence even worse than that currently being experienced or bring about a return to political violence.

THE PREVENTION OF REVENGE-TAKING AND OTHER FORMS OF VIOLENCE

It would not be an overstatement to say that the society over which the government of national unity assumed responsibility in 1994 was awash in vengeful emotions. If we have a rudimentary knowledge of South African history, then we will not be surprised by the pervasive nature of retaliatory feelings during this time. Members of the majority population suffered denigration of their humanity on a daily basis—as individuals, communities, and ethnic and cultural groups. How could there not be a flood of resentment and other antipathies?

A sour irony of history is that some of the developments that are tempering black resentment are becoming causes of bitterness among whites; the overwhelming election of the ANC, affirmative-action measures, and the truth-telling process being prominent examples. One of the unfortunate qualities of human nature is a tendency to overestimate the wounds and slights we suffer and to underestimate the ones we inflict. This characteristic is a major contributing factor to cycles of revenge. Visitors to South Africa are often surprised to discover how many whites believe they are hard done by. Jacoby, Hampton, and others describe retributive emotions as affective defenses of a social or moral equilibrium. A major problem in South Africa is that members of different communities have very different perceptions of what would be a just equilibrium. Action to shift economic or political balances in one direction will inevitably cause resentment among those who feel that the scales are already tilted too far in that direction. Given its numbers and its poverty, the African constituency seems most likely to produce acts of vengeance. Thus the greater practical urgency is to improve its socioeconomic lot. Fortunately, the greater moral urgency corresponds. Unfortunately, economic power is so firmly held in white hands that the growing resentment among whites will make balancing the scales all the more difficult. This adversity is compounded by the current economic policies of the ANC, which moved with breathtaking swiftness from a socialist to a neo-capitalist program.

At present the level of political violence in South Africa is fairly low, at least when compared to the situation a dozen years ago. In 2002 there was a number of bombings by a right-wing Afrikaner organization seeking to overthrow the ANC government. In the last few years there has been some violence among supporters of different organizations in KwaZulu-Natal, and there have been racially motivated hate crimes in other areas of the country, some committed by white policemen.

In the Western Cape, which contains Cape Town and African and mixed-race townships populated by millions of people, a form of vigilantism that was both criminal and political arose in the late 1990s. At the heart of this development was a group called People Against Gangsterism and Drugs (PAGAD). It was formed in boroughs that are mostly populated by people of mixed race and that have some of the highest violent-crime rates in the world. These rates were being inflated by the activities of and the wars among criminal gangs, as well as an ineffective criminal justice system. It is difficult to get solid information on PAGAD. What is known is that the organization grew progressively more vigilant and violent in the final years of the 1990s. Several gang leaders and members were killed, and some of PAGAD's leaders were sent to jail.

During the same years a number of seemingly politically motivated bombings occurred in or around Cape Town. Some targets appear to have been picked for their association with the United States. These included a McDonald's, a New York Bagel restaurant, and the local Planet Hollywood. There has been much speculation that Muslim groups connected to PAGAD were involved, but these assertions remain unproved. Whatever the underlying motivations and groupings, the conflation of politics, ideology, and criminal activities has spurred fears of a new wave of terrorism.[32]

Another kind of political-criminal violence is present in rural areas: attacks on white-owned farms and the violence farmers have employed in response. The level of such strife is much lower than in Zimbabwe, however.

Despite these very serious developments, the overall incidence of political crime in South Africa is relatively low, considering how close it was to civil war a little more than a decade ago. We should not be surprised by a rise in political violence in the coming decades if greater distributive justice is not achieved, but, in the meantime, the potential for some other forms of retributive action is equally worrisome.

South Africa's high rates of violent crime are not unrelated to the retributive emotions spawned by apartheid and its legacy. These arise not only from decades of belittlement and economic oppression but also are stimulated by the evident reality that economic apartheid lives on. While black townships suffer from soaring unemployment rates and a dearth of social services, the minority population that supported and benefited from apartheid continues to do quite well. I am unaware of any studies or data that link relative poverty to property crimes by blacks against whites, but how could it be otherwise? And these property crimes, especially car-jackings, are becoming more violent. It is true that most of the crimes committed by blacks have other blacks as their target, but we would be naive to think that retributive emotions are not a causal factor in these acts as well. There is reason to believe that rage arising from political and economic apartheid is very much at play.[33]

Another potential form of vengeance is what Juan J. Linz calls "ressentiment politics":

The new rulers have a tendency, probably based on their feeling of moral superiority, to waste energy in what might be called *ressentiment* politics against persons and institutions identified with the old order. This would consist in petty attacks on their dignity and their sentiments. Such measures are likely to be echoed at lower level [sic], in administration and local government, particularly in the rural societies, and may even be used in settling personal accounts.[34]

Perhaps the most troublesome characteristic of ressentiment politics, outside of the perpetuation of bitterness that they cause, is their tendency to degrade both persons and values—a caustic combination in a country struggling to establish a human rights culture. Their negative effect on institutional performance can hardly be afforded when there is such a great need for socioeconomic reconstruction. Given that most business corporations in the country are still controlled by whites, resentment politics may well be employed against blacks as well. Indeed, there will be many more contexts in which the lion's share of the power is held by whites over blacks than the reverse.

We have already discussed most of the transitional-justice measures that can be expected to contribute to the prevention of vengeance. They are the same ones employed to meet other transitional-justice goals: truth-telling, which vents anger and offers the balms of acknowledgment and empathy to victims, and which enacts the "revenge of memory"; an amnesty process that assigned accountability and soft forms of retribution; reparations, although a clumsy start was made in this area that engendered more resentment than it assuaged; other measures designed to foster distributive justice, including affirmative action policies; and efforts to foster forgiveness and reconciliation. We might also mention the steps toward healing taken by the TRC, to be discussed in Chapter 8.

To date, South Africa has clearly employed more restorative measures than punitive ones. It is a risk. As Jacoby warns, when people do not believe that, should they be victimized, a legitimate third party will exert punitive measures on their behalf, they start to take the law into their own hands. Has the soft punishment included within the amnesty process been strong enough to discourage this kind of vigilantism? Has the commitment to human rights voiced by the new government and embodied in the TRC assured citizens that they will be protected in the future? It is too early to tell. The lack of political violence is a good sign. The crime rates are a bad sign.

If the ANC government decides to prosecute senior officials of the apartheid regime, the retributive component of the transitional-justice framework could be augmented. A strong case can be made that human rights violators who decided not to apply for amnesty, as well as those who failed to meet the requirement of full disclosure, should be prosecuted where possible. In the amnesty process there was a trade-off: freedom from prosecution and suit for those who aided the causes of truth-telling and reconciliation. It seems fair that perpetrators who refused to help those causes not be granted immunity, even by default. On the other hand, if the contemplated amnesty for senior ANC officials and apartheid-era generals is legislated, the soft form of retributive justice achieved to date will be further weakened.

CONCLUSION

Having surveyed the transitional-justice measures implemented in the new South Africa, we are left with the question, Are they just? In other words, from the point of view of justice, are the TRC and the other measures that form the overall policy morally defensible?

The first point that should be made is that the *manner* in which these policies were selected was fair and democratic. South Africa did not have an amnesty or any other program imposed by the military, or even by presidential decree. The truth commission and other policies were approved by a democratically elected parliament, after due debate and consideration. In fact, the political parties represented in the cabinet that approved the TRC earned well over two-thirds of the vote in the 1994 election.

In order to answer our question regarding the moral defensibility of the transitional measures, we will have to address a number of sub-questions. The first one we should ask is, Was the South African experiment with a framework heavily tilted toward restorative justice and reconciliation justifiable? Certainly, there was an enormous amount of social-political-economic damage to be undone in South Africa. In a situation like this, restorative justice provides many more options than does retributive justice. Even if many of the restorative measures employed in the TRC and elsewhere had not been previously tested to a very great extent, they needed to be tried. Desperate situations call for some risk-taking. Risk-taking based on a philosophy of rapprochement is a better gamble than risk-taking based on a philosophy of punishment.

The TRC experience has been an invaluable gift of trial-and-error learning for South Africa and for the world. Beyond that, however, the best argument in support of its restorative orientation is simply the availability of a greater range of instruments of transformation. And transformation was what was needed—not back to a preexisting situation of social justice and harmony, but forward toward the envisioned Rainbow Nation. There certainly was no desirable status quo ante in South Africa. If Llewellyn and Howse are right in their assertion that restorative justice is best suited to the creation of a new and just social equilibrium, then the choice for restoration was the correct one.

Our second sub-question is, Was it just to deny victims the right to prosecute or make civil suit? In other words, is the amnesty morally defensible? To this question we can offer several answers of yes, and one no. Yes, because it was necessary in order to employ a broad restorative program, which was needed for the reasons just outlined. Yes, because only those perpetrators who fully and voluntarily participated in one aspect of the restorative program, truth-telling, are protected from prosecution and suit. Yes, because, while the retributive character of the amnesty process was quite soft, it was strong enough, combined with truth-telling, significantly to undercut impunity. No, because the delay and weakening of reparations has broken the balance between immunity for perpetrators and compensation for victims that was to characterize the TRC. The ensuing imbalance can only be seen as unjust. As mentioned earlier, other distributive justice measures being employed by the current ANC government may redress this situation, but, unless there is an implementation of many of the measures recommended by the Committee on Reparations and Rehabilitation, the fact will remain that the TRC was perpetrator-friendly to an extent nobody wanted (except perpetrators, perhaps). Indeed, one of the key reasons given by the court that upheld the amnesty provision of the TRC was that victims could expect compensation in the form of reparations.[35]

Our final sub-question arises from the spectrum of possible responses to wrongdoing.[36] These range from responses, like terror or vindictiveness, which are illegitimate because they are too strong, to passivity, which is illegitimate because it is not strong enough. Thus we might ask, In the wake of such a long period of oppression and such extreme violations of human rights, did the successor regime employ reasonable responses to the wrong done? Through the TRC and other agencies, the new government enacted three clear responses: (1) punishment, albeit a weak form; (2) restitution, the moral form of which was much more comprehensive than the material; and (3) protest, through discourse and documents that continually labeled apartheid and action in support of it as unjust, and which described some of the actions of anti-apartheid groups as wrong. All three of these responses are legitimate in general and can be justified in the specific context of South Africa, given the political and socioeconomic contingencies.

A problem with discussions like ours in this chapter is that they are painted in such broad strokes that many small but important successes and failures receive no attention. In these broad strokes, however, and with the exception of the reparations failure, South Africa's transitional-justice framework comes off looking fairly good in comparison with the measures (or lack thereof) implemented by successor regimes in some other countries. The leaders of the government of national unity, and of the TRC, acted with courage and conviction. They fell short sometimes, they succumbed to petty politics sometimes, but their vision and their resilience in the face of mammoth challenges are worthy of admiration. My interviews with "ordinary" South Africans showed me that they too are reaching deep for vision, resilience, and courage. Some find more in the well than others. In the next chapter we will see how, individually and collectively, they are finding ways to heal.

8

Act Four: Finding Ways to Heal

The opening section of this chapter will be concerned with trauma, a phenomenon that has terror at its core and that was lamentably common in South Africa during the era of apartheid—and still is to a disturbing extent. We will ask how healing takes place for and within a traumatized nation. In section two we will examine the ways the TRC did and did not meet the national need for healing and the individual needs of trauma survivors. The final section will consider the Committee on Reparations and Rehabilitation of the TRC, its recommendations, and the fate of those recommendations.

During one of the early HRV hearings a man named Lucas ("Baba") Sikwepere testified that he was at a community meeting, where twenty to twenty-five people were discussing communal violence in a couple of townships near Cape Town, when some security police drove up and told the group to disperse. Sikwepere recounts: "I was just standing for two minutes next to the window, I found out now—now this white man opened the door and withdraw his gun. Now I wanted to find out what is the story going on, on the other side of this car. I tried to peep and I was looking straight into him, straight to him. When—while I was still looking at him, these people asked him, 'How can you ask us to disperse, and yet we have no aims to do harm to anyone? We are here to stop whoever who is trying to burn this place up.'

"This white man said this in Afrikaans—'You are going to get eventually what you looking for. And I am going to shoot you.' I was shocked at what this white man said to him, to me. He said in Afrikaans, 'I am going to get you.' Now I wanted to find out why is he talking to me like this. And I was just trying to find out, was he referring to me by all these, and one—one of the men behind me ran. I saw this people surrounding this van—I was now wondering when— where do these people come from surrounding this van, all of a sudden.

"After I saw this running men, now I didn't even care about this one I was talking to. After that I heard a loud noise, it sounded like a stone hitting a sink, now it—it ended up looking now I was going to be included among these people surrounding this van. But I decided not to run. I decided to walk. Because I knew that if you run, you were going to be shot, so I decided let me just walk into a safe place where I can just start now running. But during that time shootings were going on, there were two white men in this car. . . .

"When I arrived at the place when I thought now I am safe, I felt something hitting my cheek. I couldn't go any further. I stayed right there only to find out I had been hidden by a corner of a house. I felt my eyes itching. I was just itching my eyes. I was scratching my eyes. I wasn't quite sure what happened to my eyes at that particular time. I felt somebody stepping on my right shoulder. And saying 'I thought this dog has died already.'"

Later, Bapa Sikwepere was taken into custody. . . .

"The same white man still tried to torture me, another night this white man came again. They came to fetch me and I was staying that time with my girl friend. When I got to where the Casspir was going, it was Nyanga East at the police station. That's where they really beat me up so much that they said I was the organizer of all these riots.

"I was worried, tried to think where were they taking me, they emphasized all—they were concentrating on me, most of the time, they took me to the cemetery. I was with Lulama Magoje, and she was the one who was holding my hand. And they pushed me into a hole and they were—I was told to tell the truth even if you could die here now, nobody would know anything."

After finishing his account, Baba Sikwepere is asked by a TRC commissioner about his experience of testifying at the hearing:

Ms. Gobodo-Madikizela: Thank you, Baba.

Mr. Sikwepere: Yes, usually I have a fat body, but after that I lost all my body, now I am thin, as you can see me now.

Ms. Gobodo-Madikizela: How do you feel, Baba, about coming here to tell us your story?

Mr. Sikwepere: I feel what—what has brought my sight back, my eyesight back is to come back here and tell the story. But I feel what has been making me sick all the time is the fact that I couldn't tell my story. But now I—it feels like I got my sight back by coming here and telling you the story.[1]

THE TRAUMATIZED NATION

In her wonderfully lucid and challenging book *Trauma and Recovery*, Judith Herman surveys the history of the psychiatric study and treatment of trauma and outlines her own understanding of traumatic injury, as well as her model for its treatment.[2] One of the things she is careful to point out, and that we need to be mindful of as we examine the vestiges of terror in South Africa, is that traumatic experiences and the psychological conditions they cause are heterogeneous. The psychic wound and healing processes for a person who undergoes one terrifying experience caused by a natural disaster will be very different from the wound and healing of another person, with a different personality and self-understanding, who is subject to extended confinement and repeated torture. We need to be wary of sweeping generalizations. Still, the psychological world of trauma and its repair has a topography that can be interpreted and even codified to a certain degree. Herman will serve as our guide as we proceed into this territory with inexpert steps.

"Psychological trauma is an affliction of the powerless."[3] It occurs when a person is rendered helpless by a force so powerful that it cannot be resisted. Tornadoes and earthquakes constitute such a force; so do rapists, torturers, and military juntas. When people fall prey to them, they become so wounded that they can lose their senses of control, connection, and even meaning. This psychic rupture seems to be connected to the full but unsuccessful employment of our natural defenses. The normal human response to danger involves a complex system of mental and physical reactions. The sympathetic nervous system becomes highly aroused. Attention becomes fiercely concentrated. Fear and anger rise. The person is prepared for intense action, ready to fight or to flee. Trauma occurs when these actions and reactions fail, and neither resistance nor escape is possible. The instruments of self-defense become overwhelmed and disorganized. "Each component of the ordinary response to danger, having lost its utility, tends to persist in an altered and exaggerated state long after the actual danger is over."[4] The overall effect on the victim is a rupture of psychic integrity that leaves lasting changes in physiological arousal, emotion, cognition, and memory. Dysfunction may get worse as traumatic symptoms become disconnected from their source and take on lives of their own.[5]

These symptoms include *hyperarousal,* a permanent alertness of the system of self-preservation arising from the sense that danger may return at any moment; *intrusion,* the reliving of the event as though it were continually recurring, often through daytime flashbacks, nightmares, or reenactments of the trauma scene in disguised forms; and *constriction,* a surrender into numbness and shutting down of self-defenses that resembles a "rabbit caught in the headlights" and that amounts to the opposite of hyperarousal. People suffering from a traumatic disorder often fall into a pattern of alternating between intrusion and constriction. In a desperate attempt at healing, the unconscious tries to re-create and resolve the traumatic event. When this gambit fails, there is a fall into despair.[6]

A key issue is memory. Following the ground-breaking French psychologist Janet, Herman explains that traumatic memories are not encoded like ordinary adult memories in a linear, narrative fashion that is integrated into an ongoing life story. They are instead frozen and wordless. They do not give forth stories but symptoms. The survivor of traumatic experiences retains them as horrible images that burst out in nightmares and can dominate the person as an idée fixe.[7] A major task in healing work is the transformation of these memories into narrative form. This gives the survivor some power over the memories, and it serves as preparation for the incorporation of the traumatic event and its damaging effects into a new self-image and self-understanding. In order to put the painful memories into narrative, however, they have to be verbalized, and this is often resisted both by the victim and by the people around the victim. Herman goes so far as to assert that the "conflict between the will to deny horrible events and the will to proclaim them aloud is the central dialectic of psychological trauma."[8]

The way that Herman characterizes this "central dialectic" is striking in its resemblance to the truth-telling imperative of the TRC (and other truth commissions). It leads us to ask the question of whether a large-scale truth-telling venture such as that initiated in South Africa can be considered therapy for a nation. This is a controversial question. Some of the people who study or work in post-conflict situations feel that it is appropriate to speak of "national therapy," even if this is understood metaphorically. Others oppose this view and argue that nations are not persons; they maintain that it is misguided to apply psychological concepts to them. In this chapter we will not attempt to resolve this debate but will live with it as we examine issues such as the following: How intertwined are the work of personal healing and the work of societal healing? How much can happen in the absence of the other? Is the correlation between the two always positive, or can measures to advance one retard the other?

The worst kind of trauma, that which is prolonged and repeated, occurs in situations of captivity. Traumatic captivity can take place in prisons, concentration camps, situations of enforced prostitution, or the family home. Domestic imprisonment is not enforced with bars and locks, but rather with the invisible instruments of conditioned dependency. In all these contexts the perpetrator becomes the most powerful figure in the life of the victim.

Herman recognizes a personality type common to captors in a wide range of settings. The most remarkable characteristic of the typical perpetrator is apparent normality. Hannah Arendt's characterization of Eichmann as "normal," even banal, seems to be the norm. Somewhere in their makeup, however, torturers and brutalizers have an intense will to power and control. Herman offers this portrait:

> Authoritarian, secretive, sometimes grandiose, and even paranoid, the perpetrator is nevertheless exquisitely sensitive to the realities of power and to social norms. Only rarely does he get into difficulties with the law; rather, he seeks out situations where his tyrannical behavior will be tolerated, condoned, or admired. His demeanor provides an excel-

lent camouflage, for few people believe that extraordinary crimes can be committed by men of such conventional appearance.

The perpetrator's first goal appears to be the enslavement of his victim, and he accomplishes this goal by exercising despotic control over every aspect of the victim's life. But simple compliance rarely satisfies him; he appears to have a psychological need to justify his crimes, and for this he needs the victim's affirmation. Thus he relentlessly demands from his victim professions of respect, gratitude, or even love. His ultimate goal appears to be the creation of a willing victim. Hostages, political prisoners, battered women, and slaves have all remarked upon the captor's curious psychological dependence on his victim.[9]

While reading this passage, I was reminded of Jeffrey Benzien, the apartheid policeman who employed vicious interrogation methods. In attempts to curry his victims' affection, he brought them ice cream and took them outside to play. At second glance, however, an even more disturbing insight arises: This passage not only describes the agents of apartheid, but it also describes apartheid itself, as well as the regime that enforced it. The apartheid regime was authoritarian, secretive, and oriented toward total control. It legislated who could marry (or even have sex with) whom, where people of different skin colors could live, and what types of employment and recreation they could engage in. It went to the ridiculous extremes of measuring people's lips, hips, and the stiffness of their hair in order to provide them with a racial designation. Blacks were not only enslaved by being brutalized, but great efforts were made to make them passive and cheerful participants in a paternalistic relationship with whites. This was the goal of the Bantu education system, labor legislation, and much of Christian missionary activity.

When the carrot did not work, there was little hesitation to employ the stick. Herman describes the method of gaining control universally employed by captors: the "systematic, repetitive, infliction of psychological trauma."[10] Violence need only be employed infrequently and as a last resort. The threat of violence can be used much more frequently, keeping captives in a constant state of fear. This is augmented by measures designed to destroy their sense of autonomy. Again, this is a perfect description of the policies and practices of the apartheid regime. Blacks were not the only targets. Whites who fought or unmasked the system of state racism were imprisoned, tortured, raped, and murdered. Their families were subjected to threats and social ostracizing. Churches weighed in with judgments and condemnations. Soldiers in the SADF were forced to witness or commit atrocities and were subjected to punishment when they refused. Some of them may be among the most traumatized people in South Africa.[11]

By the time the new dispensation was ushered in in 1994, South Africa was undoubtedly a traumatized nation with millions of citizens suffering from stronger and weaker forms of traumatic disorders.[12] Many thousands of citizens had participated in or witnessed warfare, violent demonstrations, vigilante justice, or factional fighting between groups such as the ANC and the IFP. A significant number had been detained and tortured. Many more had been violated by criminal or domestic violence.

It is difficult to know the extent to which nonpolitical violence in South Africa (such as criminal violence and domestic violence) was and is a secondary effect of political violence. I am aware of no studies that have examined the link between these two kinds of strife, but I have been told by psychotherapists that they are convinced such a link exists. Eric Harper, a therapist at The Trauma Centre for Survivors of Violence and Torture in Cape Town asserts that, in large measure, the current crime rates can be attributed to the country's political history. Society was traumatized during apartheid and is now acting out of that trauma and the psychosocial damage it caused. "The violence of apartheid has definitely been internalized and acted out." He points to domestic violence as an example and argues that it can be directly linked to the apartheid regime's attempt to humiliate black males and make them impotent. He also explains that the years of struggle caused many blacks to construct their identities around the ideal of the hero. This introduced an element of mania into a lot of personalities. Now that the struggle is over, the forum in which this mania could be legitimately expressed has disappeared. Gang membership, criminal activity, and domestic strife may all reflect the sublimation of manic energy.[13]

If I had not visited South Africa and witnessed the vitality and resilience of its people firsthand, I would find it disheartening to contemplate the depth and scope of societal healing that is needed. It would have been equally dispiriting to consider the number of individuals who need psychological repair from trauma. Even with South Africa's cultural and spiritual riches in mind, one is daunted by the magnitude of the therapeutic task. What are the parameters of this task?

Herman outlines two principles that are of central importance for the treatment of trauma. They arise from the reality that the core experiences of psychological trauma are disempowerment and disconnection, and are oriented toward recovery from them. The first principle is the *empowerment of the survivor*. "She must be the author and arbiter of her own recovery."[14] Even if a therapist or an intervener understands the healing process better than the survivor, he or she must not take control of that process from the one seeking healing. Advice, support, assistance, and affection are all appropriate, but an intervention that takes power from the survivor will likely founder.

The second principle is that *relationship is essential to recovery*. "In her renewed connections with other people, the survivor re-creates the psychological faculties that were damaged or deformed by the traumatic experience."[15] Rehabilitation of these faculties will restore the survivor's ability to trust, to be autonomous, to take initiative, to construct identity, and to be intimate. The relationship with a therapist will be key. For this relationship to have optimal effectiveness, the therapist will have to honor several imperatives. The first, as already mentioned, is that the therapist must not wrestle control of the healing process from the client. The second is that the sole objective of the relationship must be the recovery of the patient.[16] The third is that, while the therapist will be *technically* neutral, meaning that the therapist will not take sides in the client's inner conflicts, he or she must not be *morally* neutral. The therapist takes a stance of solidarity with the victim and offers judgment of the acts that traumatized the person.[17]

This last point is important for Herman and some others in the field. They insist that trauma and its treatment must be seen as *political* where the traumatic injury was spurred by or even related to sociopolitical factors. The healing of the survivor cannot be disconnected from the transformation of society toward justice, even within the safe bounds of the therapeutic relationship. In fact, the disconnection of traumatic injury from its sociopolitical origin can worsen symptoms and impede recovery.[18] The connection of treatment to societal change or social healing may well improve its chances and/or scope of success.[19]

According to Herman, the healing process for trauma survivors passes through three stages.[20] The first stage begins with the tricky work of diagnosis. Traumatic disorders are often misdiagnosed as other psychological conditions. They are also heterogeneous. Once a traumatic disorder has been identified, the first task is to establish *safety* for the survivor. Patients initially work with the therapist to restore control over their bodies. Survivors feel unsafe in their bodies. Physical strategies like medication, behavioral techniques, and exercise may be employed.

Once this foundation of security is built to a reasonable degree, then there is a shift of focus toward creating a safe environment. Survivors will need safe refuge and a stabilization of relationships. Support from sympathetic relatives or friends can be of great help. Patients work on a plan for future protection, which serves the twin purposes of creating safety and granting them more control over their own life through the exercise of their judgment.

Because the challenges of the first stage are arduous, both the client and the therapist will be tempted to bypass them. Herman calls this error serious and common. Without a proper foundation of security, the recuperative enterprise can collapse in upon itself at a later time.[21]

The primary task of the second stage is to remember and mourn. There should be a shift from dissociated trauma to acknowledged memory. The focus of this stage is on truth-telling about the trauma, not in a coldly analytical manner, but in a narrative fashion that, not unlike the HRV hearings of the TRC, honors the survivor's emotions and subjective "knowing." Again, it is the patient who will choose the pace and the degree to which horrors are confronted. A critical task is the reconstruction of the story of the trauma. This work transforms traumatic memory from a frozen and wordless state (dissociation) into a narrative form, which also includes traumatic images and bodily sensations that can then be integrated into the survivor's life story. This integration seems to be essential for a favorable recovery. The survivor needs to come to a self-understanding as a person whose life has been forever altered by the violation. Good things may actually come from the alteration, but the cost has been enormous and there can never be a complete return to one's old self.

This realization inevitably opens the survivor to strong grief, which necessitates deep mourning. The descent into mourning, while crucial, is often dreaded and resisted; the chasm of pain seems too broad and deep to be traversed. Particularly dangerous at this stage are fantasies of magical resolution through revenge, compensation, or forgiveness.[22]

In stage three the primary task is to reconnect with ordinary life. There is a shift from the past to the future and from isolation to renewed social connection.[23] After facing what has happened and mourning the losses, survivors now develop a new self with new relationships. They may feel like refugees entering a new country. The issue of safety is often revisited at this stage, but now the goal is security in active engagement. Concrete steps are taken to increase the survivor's sense of power and control. A conscious choice to face danger may be taken. Survivors may take self-defense courses or try a wilderness challenge such as canoeing or rock climbing. Such activities provide opportunities to reconstruct normal psychological and physiological responses to fear and danger. The group component of the activities can establish trust and relationship skills.

Mrs. Mekgwe is in her late fifties or early sixties. As a young woman she moved from one of the homelands to a township near Johannesburg. Like most of her neighbors, she and her husband struggled to provide for their family, but they got by and the situation started to improve when her sons reached an age at which they could contribute. While neither Mrs. Mekgwe nor her husband was politically active, one of her sons began to go to meetings of a group connected to the ANC.

She found out that her son had been shot and killed by security policemen when she turned on the evening news and saw his dead body. Her husband never recovered from the shock and the grief, dying of heart ailments three months later.

Mrs. Mekgwe was not able to complete her interview with me. Twice she broke down in tears while speaking of her losses. She is still overwhelmed by the events that happened a decade and a half ago, and by the poverty she fell into with the loss of two breadwinners. After the death of her son, she began attending ANC meetings and gathering with others who lost loved ones. She has found some support there but has never been able to return to her old self or to find her way out from under the weight of her losses.

An askari (traitor) who was involved in her son's murder has come to her seeking forgiveness. She has refused, saying she carries a powerful hate for him.

HEALING AND THE TRC

One of the debates surrounding the TRC has dealt with its therapeutic value. One side of the debate argues that the commission's hearings (and the public dialogue they fostered) have restored the dignity of apartheid's victims, given them an opportunity for catharsis and mourning before sympathetic witnesses, and started the work of constructing a national narrative of empathy for their suffering and respect for their sacrifice. Those on the other side of the debate counter that nobody can be healed in one episode of public testimony, that most victims were never given even that small opportunity, and that the rehashing of traumatic events has actually been detrimental to some victims. Truth can be found in both sets of arguments.

The paragraphs that follow seek to contribute to the debate by identifying some of the needs of trauma survivors that were and were not met by the TRC. It would be foolish, of course, to expect that the thousands of South Africans suffering from traumatic disorders would be healed to any great extent by a process of public hearings that was limited in scope and duration. It is appropriate, however, to ask whether this process contributed to their healing, established conditions that would facilitate it, and/or began the processes of healing the nation as a corporate body. One way to respond to this question is to relate the activities of the TRC to the needs of trauma survivors in each stage of recovery. As for the issue of the healing of the national body, we are not working with a model of national healing, and it would be naive to presuppose that Herman's model of individual healing can simply be applied "as is" to a national psyche. On the other hand, it is not too much of a stretch to assume that many of the needs of traumatized individuals—safety, stability, truth, management of symptoms like manic hyperarousal, reconstruction of identity, and so on—are shared by traumatized societies. There will be heuristic value in considering the ways the TRC responded to those needs.

When viewing the TRC through the lens of Herman's three-stage model, it quickly becomes clear that the commission catered most to the challenges of stage two. The central activity of stage two is truth-telling; this is what the TRC did best. But let us begin with the first stage and move through the steps in order.

The most important tasks of stage one are to establish safety and to foster healing relationships. It cannot be said that the TRC provided lasting aid to survivors of traumatic violation in this regard. Nor did it attempt to. The commission had neither the mandate nor the resources to alter the life circumstances or the relationship web of the thousands of victims who made themselves known. Counseling services were provided to victims who participated in HRV hearings (they were less available to those who testified at amnesty hearings), but these services were not long term. It is possible that counselors facilitated access to longer-term services for some victims, but there was and is a dearth of such services for South Africa's poor. In retrospect, we can see the wisdom of having one component of the reparations package up and running early in the life of a truth commission: a network of counseling and social services for victims of trauma. It seems certain that some of the trauma sufferers who testified would have been entering the work of stage two—remembering and mourning—without having first laid the groundwork of support and security. Such a situation seems primed to increase the woundedness of some survivors.

It can be said that most of the testimony-givers who were asked to describe horrible events were given space to express the grief that accompanied their memories, and were given succor and empathy at the time of their testimony.[24] TRC hearings, especially the HRV hearings, were infinitely more effective than criminal trials in this regard. They were explicitly concerned with upholding the dignity of those whose humanity had been trampled during the events under examination. Anyone who has witnessed the cross-examination of a rape victim during a criminal trial or of a sexual abuse survivor during a civil suit can only be thankful that the TRC was a creature with different stripes. There were exceptions to this protocol, of course, but my impression is that they were infrequent. At least for the time that survivors were testifying, they were accorded safety.

I am less clear about the extent to which the etiquette of sympathetic treatment was extended to perpetrators. During my interviews a small number of anecdotes were shared that suggested that perpetrators, especially members of the apartheid enforcement apparatus, were denied both the solicitous treatment and the offer of counseling services given to victims. On the other hand, successful amnesty applicants were provided with security in the form of freedom from prosecution and civil suit, which may well have helped them get on with their lives and face the work of coming to terms with their involvement in horrible events.

I would argue that the amnesty process was only one element of a gift of security that the TRC gave to agents of the old regime, to the white community at large, and ultimately to the nation as a whole. When the new government was elected in 1994, democracy was green and fragile, there were legitimate fears of a coup or ongoing political violence, and whites were very concerned about the possibility of a backlash against them. The design, tone, and rhetoric of the TRC, combined with other policies of the ANC-led government, made it clear that South Africa's new black leaders were seeking reconciliation instead of revenge, that they saw an important place of full citizenship for whites in South Africa's future, and that the bosses and soldiers of the old regime would be treated with fairness and even generosity.

None of the fears mentioned above have come true to any significant extent; South Africa is enjoying a level of political and social stability today that must be attributed in part to the TRC. This amounts to a significant meeting of the safety needs of the nation.

One matter that came up over and over during my interviews with white South Africans was the role of Desmond Tutu. While many of the interviewees (especially whites) admitted to mistrusting and disliking him during the years of struggle, almost all of them spoke of a change in attitude during the life of the TRC. He made them realize that powerful Africans recognized their humanity and their citizenship. His concern for the forgiveness of white perpetrators and empathy for white victims became a national symbol (leading many blacks to feel some resentment toward him). It can be asserted, credibly if not definitively, that during the years of the TRC's operation South Africa as a whole entered into a therapeutic relationship with the archbishop—and with the TRC through him. It was a relationship with ambivalence, with negative and positive transference, and with its ups and downs, but it was one that fostered healing. The work of healing will have to continue for many decades to come, and others will have to pick up Tutu's mantle, but his charismatic leadership as chairman was a gift to the nation. Even if the commission was unable to accommodate fully the stage-one needs of the individuals it encountered, it was able to advance the stability of South African society and to apply some balm to the national psyche.

The core challenge of stage two of Herman's model is to engage in truth-telling that facilitates transformative remembering as well as mourning. Tina Rosenberg, among others, has recognized the value of truth commissions for both individuals and nations in this regard. The following represents one of her contributions to a dialogue about truth commissions held at Harvard University in 1996:

> I am struck by how many comments outline the parallels between truth commissions and the therapeutic process of dealing with victims of post-traumatic stress disorder. The similarities are striking. People need to tell their story, but this is not all. Two other levels are important. People need to tell their stories to someone who is listening to them seriously and validating them. This is official acknowledgment.
>
> More importantly, victims must be able to reintegrate that narrative into their whole life story. It must not be a separate and shattering incident. This has obvious importance for the victims of human rights abuses who recount their stories. Indeed, if the whole nation is suffering from post-traumatic stress disorder, this process would be appropriate for the whole nation.[25]

A participant who spoke after Rosenberg rightly cautioned the group about "using the analogy of post-traumatic stress disorder [to move] too quickly from the individual's process to the collectivity."[26] He was concerned that such a move would depoliticize their perspective on truth commissions. While such a depoliticization would indeed be unhelpful, it is possible to employ the analogy of post-traumatic stress disorder without falling into this trap. Herman politicizes both the definition and the treatment of post-traumatic stress disorders. Any employment of the analogy that was informed by her model could not be apolitical. With this in mind, it is fair to say that a traumatized nation has a real need for rearticulation of its corporate story such that memory is "unfrozen" and freed to be built into new narratives. These narratives can then be used in identity reconstruction and the building of a new future.

If identity construction is to happen such that former enemies come to understand one another as co-citizens, or even fellows, then the new narratives will have to be true to past experiences, while including empathy for the subjective experiences of all parties—even former oppressors. This does not mean that judgment and punishment of wrongdoing must be abandoned, but rather that empathetic penetration of the motivations that led to the wrongdoing should accompany the judgment. The location of the origins of the myth of apartheid in Afrikaner experiences during the Boer Wars serves as an example. Such balancing of empathy with judgment is an imperative that distinguishes "societal therapy," if you will, from individual therapy.

The TRC struck a helpful balance in this regard, at least from the point of view of national healing. It did not provide as much empathy for supporters of apartheid as many whites would have liked, and it did not offer as much judgment of apartheid as many blacks (and the ANC leaders) would have liked, but it made space for both. Perhaps in the treatment of individual traumatic disorders, empathy for the violator is unnecessary—Herman's model seems to suggest this—but the treatment of national trauma cannot dispense with it. To do so would further fracture the national community, leaving one group (or groups) to retreat into isolation. Such constituencies tend to turn to reified and resentful myths or narratives to guide their self-understanding and their relations with other constituencies—not a good situation for a country worried about future returns to violence and trauma.

Shifting our perspective to the healing of individual trauma sufferers, it can be said that, while the TRC was certainly not a substitute for the prolonged process of remembering and mourning that would take place in therapy, it may have aided survivors in ways related to Herman's second stage. Counseling services are not readily available to South Africans who cannot pay for them, so, for many victims, testifying to a TRC scribe or before a hearing may have been the only opportunity they had to tell their story to sympathetic listeners. It is an open question whether a single episode of such sharing is likely to do more harm or good.

From one perspective these were not *single* episodes. Each person who testified became a part of a national process of transformation, lending credibility to his or her story and bonding the individual to many others. As such, the testimonies of others became each person's testimony in a dramatic way.

Tutu, among others, argues that Africans are more communal and less individualistic than Westerners. Thus, this initiation into "something larger" may have been particularly powerful for Africans.

Herman describes some powerful therapies for traumatic stress disorders that have testimony at their core. Some of the developers of these methods are Chilean psychotherapists working with victims of General Pinochet's terror. At the heart of these methods is a form of testimony that closely resembles that used by the TRC—both at hearings and in individual depositions. The difference is that the therapies take place over lengthy periods of time. Testimonies are offered, reworked, and ritualized in a context where relationships of trust have been carefully built.[27] The truth-telling process at the TRC seems to have tapped into the power of these therapies without including the safeguards. Is this a risk worth taking? To what extent have victims found healing in these encounters? How many accessed psychic material they were unable to handle? Were the risks reduced by the brief nature of the encounter and the availability of counselors? These are fascinating questions for further study.

For now, we can say that these encounters and their national visibility served two purposes. First, they *modeled a process of truth-telling* that was both political and oriented toward healing. The drama of victims telling their stories, displaying strong emotions, and being joined by commissioners in their grieving was repeated many times, often on the airwaves. Many trauma survivors, even those who remained in anonymity, witnessed a pattern for dealing with their pain. Other people—family, friends, neighbors, fellow church members, and so on—were exposed to the same model. It is impossible to know how many families, congregations, and neighborhoods are changing the ways they deal with the hurts of the past in response to this modeling, but some must be.

Second, the TRC and its hearings have *developed a national narrative* of violation and repair that can serve as a tableau against which trauma survivors can interpret their own stories. Herman underscores the importance of the exercise of both moral judgment and sociopolitical analysis in coming to terms with traumatic injuries. The TRC provided judgment and analysis in a form that was not reified and final, but that served as an opening to understanding, an exploration that all citizens were invited to join in their own ways.

The challenge to trauma survivors in stage three of Herman's model is to develop a newly empowered and reconnected self. They accept their wound and its effects, including helplessness and isolation. With a new self-understanding arising from the stage-two process of telling their story, they break out of helplessness by learning ways of facing fear and danger, and they escape isolation by building relationships of greater intimacy. The truth-telling activities of the TRC may have helped South African survivors of political trauma with the stage-two goal of self-understanding, thus laying the groundwork for the labor of stage three, but it offered little in terms of the challenges of stage three proper. Again, if the reparations package had been implemented, things may have been different. One of the measures recommended by the Committee on Reparations and Rehabilitation was the development of community rehabilitation programs. As proposed, these would have provided health care, mental-health services, housing, education, and conflict resolution—all forms of aid that could have helped trauma survivors with the challenges of empowerment and reconnection.

One of the TRC's forms of empowering victims that we have already mentioned may have helped with stage-three needs. I am referring to the repeated, public acts of recognition and expressions of empathy for people who were trampled by apartheid or the struggle that it spawned. Rosenberg referred to the survivors' "need to tell their stories to someone who is listening to them seriously and validating them. This is official acknowledgment." After such acknowledgment, trauma sufferers may feel less helpless.

The flip side of this acknowledgment, however, at least in the case of the TRC, was that individuals who had suffered loss or violation were being acknowledged *as victims*. The bestowing of the status of victim is a tricky business; it involves a confirmation of the harm done and an offering of succor, but it can also reify a characterization (and self-understanding) of that person as helpless. Throughout her book Herman uses the term *survivor* instead of *victim*. This is a more hopeful designation, as it implies strength and endurance.

In terms of the needs of the nation, the TRC may have advanced both empowerment and reconnection. Stage-three empowerment involves facing fear and danger and learning helpful ways of dealing with them. Through the TRC, South Africa faced the danger of revelations about its past. When the design of the commission, with its dominant truth-telling component, was made public, many were concerned that revelations would lead to acts of revenge, to political violence from those being named as perpetrators, and/or to an outpouring of pain and rage that the nation would not be able to handle. While the river of revelation has generated resentment, the fears of destabilization and violence have not been validated. The body politic and the citizenry are learning how to disagree and debate about issues of great emotional attachment and political import. South Africans are feeling less helpless under the weight of their past than they were a decade ago.

In terms of reconnection the TRC has aided the formation of both in-country and international relationships. It was a very large undertaking, which brought together members of almost all political and racial constituencies to work cooperatively. Commissioners, researchers, advocates, therapists, and technicians from a wide variety of communities worked together in intense circumstances that certainly generated conflict but also fostered trust and intimacy. Academics, journalists, and policy-makers from around the world flocked to South Africa to learn from its unprecedented experiment, and they invited South Africans to their countries to share their learning. The global visibility of the TRC has helped change the international image of South Africa from a country in chains to a Rainbow Nation.

Moving to sum up this section of our chapter, we can say that, no, the TRC was not therapy, in full form, for the many South Africans traumatized by political violence. But it did perform some therapeutic tasks: It provided a forum for truth-telling, remembrance, and mourning; it offered this forum to the nation to aid trauma survivors in their quest for self-understanding; and it may have helped some of these survivors in their search for healing models and healing relationships.

Was the TRC therapy for a traumatized nation? This is a more difficult question to answer. It certainly seems to have performed therapeutic tasks related to each of Herman's three stages. On the other hand, a full course of treatment for a nation like South Africa would take decades, not years.

A final word before moving on. It is important to underscore the point that healing takes time and cannot be rushed or programmed. There is an element of grace in healing. Sometimes all of the "right" things are done, all of the appropriate kinds of interventions made, and healing still does not happen—or it happens excruciatingly slowly. At other times it takes place despite the fact that there is minimal (or no) assistance and succor for the wounded person. This point is especially fitting when we are dealing with the healing of peoples. The kinds of interventions we are discussing in this chapter can only foster the possibility of healing, or perhaps augment the probability; they come with no guarantees.

Darby Ackerman is a middle-aged white man. In the early 1990s— during the time of transition after the unbanning of the liberation organizations but before the election of the government of national unity—he lived near Cape Town and was a very active member of St. James Church in one of the suburbs. On a Sunday evening he was attending worship with a number of Russian sailors whom he had befriended through his participation in the congregation's outreach mission. Suddenly, the door to the church burst open, shots were fired, and grenades were thrown. The attack, carried out by APLA commandos, lasted less than a minute, but eleven people were killed and at least fifty-six injured.[28]

Knowing that his son and wife were seated elsewhere in the sanctuary, Mr. Ackerman went looking for them. His son was unharmed, but his wife was badly wounded. He rushed her to the hospital, where she died shortly after arrival. He then returned to the church to check on the fate of the Russian sailors and the rest of the congregation. Upon his return, he was met with TV cameras. Wanting to convey the message that "like Paul, murderers could be forgiven," he was immediately able to hold out forgiveness to the attackers. Both Mr. Ackerman and the congregation as a whole continued to offer the same message of pardon in the weeks that followed the massacre. He attributes this disposition to the grace of God and Christian training.

Nine months after the shooting, he began to slide into depression. A couple of years later, "the wheels really came off." Mr. Ackerman decided to leave his senior post with an important agency and seek healing. He now acknowledges that his choice to offer forgiveness so quickly at the time of his wife's death was a sacrifice that kept him from facing fully his pain and beginning his mending process.

At a TRC hearing he was given an opportunity to confront the commandos who attacked the church. Each apologized in turn and asked for forgiveness. Even though he questions some of their factual statements made regarding the mission to attack the church—he believes they held back information to protect their seniors—Mr. Ackerman offered forgiveness. "If they expressed remorse, we had to forgive them." He also reminded them that he had no power to forgive sins. For him, the meeting with the perpetrators was a tremendous release and a cleansing that coincided with the beginning of the lifting of his depression.

When I met Mr. Ackerman in mid-2000, he was working as a director and fund-raiser for a Christian school near Johannesburg. He has remarried.

REPARATIONS

Following a period of civil war or widespread abuse, many survivors suffer from physical, psychological, and economic injuries. Some require basic medical care, some are in need of psychotherapy, and large numbers need financial help after losing family breadwinners, suffering property damage, or being unable to work as a result of their physical and emotional ailments. International law clearly establishes an obligation on the part of states to provide compensation for these injuries to the extent that they result from state abuses.[29] Even where there is no legal obligation to implement reparations, there is a practical one: Attempts to repair the damage and rebuild a viable future will be hampered without them.

Reparations can take many forms beyond the payment of cash. Hayner points out that *reparations* is a general term encompassing the following forms of redress:

- *restitution* aims to reestablish to the extent possible the situation that existed before the violation took place;
- *compensation* relates to any economically assessable damage resulting from the violations;
- *rehabilitation* includes legal, medical, psychological and other care;

- *satisfaction* and *guarantees of nonrepetition* relate to measures to acknowledge the violations and prevent their recurrence in the future.

A mixture of these is often appropriate.[30]

All of these measures seem like good things to do, and they usually are, but it is important to underscore just how difficult they can be to implement. It is even more of a challenge to announce and then execute a reparations program that does not end up dashing the hopes of potential beneficiaries. Martha Minow offers the following caution.

One danger with any reparations effort is the suggestion that because some amends have been made, the underlying events need not be discussed again. Equally troubling to many survivors are assertions that monetary reparations can remedy nonmonetary harms, such as the death of a child, the loss of an arm, the agony of remembered torture, or the humiliation and shame of being wrongly detained and interned. The amounts of money likely to emerge from political processes, especially in economically depressed societies such as South Africa, can offer only token gestures whose small size underscores their inadequacy. As statements of actual value, they trivialize the harms.[31]

The reparations program in South Africa faced all of these dilemmas and more. Perhaps its largest challenge arose from its association with the amnesty process. As mentioned in earlier chapters, one of the sources of controversy around the TRC was the perception that something concrete—freedom from prosecution and civil suit—was being offered to the perpetrators of crimes while no similar benefit was being offered to victims. In fact, argued critics of the commission, victims were actually having an important right stripped from them (legal redress). These criticisms would have been valid if compensation for victims had not been built into the structure of the commission. The TRC's *Final Report* clearly states that the need to counterbalance amnesty was a large part of the rationale for including reparations in the TRC process as one of the three primary areas of work.[32]

The fact that final individual reparation grants have still not been granted several years after the deadline for application makes the original criticisms that the commission would be unbalanced and perpetrator-friendly more valid than they seemed at the time. Before we delve into this issue, however, let us take a closer look at the work and recommendations of the Committee on Reparations and Rehabilitation.

Designing financial restitution to individuals and communities that were victims of apartheid and the violence that it spawned was the primary task of the Committee on Reparations and Rehabilitation. At an individual level, people who suffered human rights violations were invited to make claims for compensation. The claims were then investigated by the Committee on

Human Rights Violations and lists of people to be compensated were drawn up. The compensation fell into two categories: final reparations, and urgent interim reparations. It was promised that final reparations would be granted after the TRC had finished its work and a comprehensive restoration plan had been designed to accompany individual cash payments. It was recognized, however, that the situations of some victims were so desperate that they could not await the final package.

In response to these needs, a plan for interim compensation was developed. In this plan five categories of urgent interim reparations were outlined: emotional suffering and pain; medical care and assistance; material or financial need and limitations; access to and continuation of education; and the duty and obligation to remember (symbolic measures). The final category was the least concrete, but the plan outlined some possible measures: the clearing of victims' names, especially those with criminal records or considered to be informants; visiting burial sites or places where violations took place; expediting cases and payments; settling legal procedures; issuing death certificates for loved ones; exhumations and reburials; tombstones and shrines; facilitating public acknowledgments and apologies; and mediating between victims and offenders.[33] As it turned out, the interim reparations consisted largely of individual cash payments, the first of which were not released until 1998—a time when it was originally expected that final reparations might begin to be implemented. The emphasis on cash payments arose from a decision by the Committee on Reparations and Rehabilitation not to take a "service approach." More on this below.

In the meantime, the committee continued to work on the framework for final reparations. In October 1997 it released its proposed policy. The committee used several sources in the development of its framework. These included statements of witnesses, the TRC database, and an intensive consultative process. It conducted monthly workshops in each regional office, inviting representatives of NGOs, community-based organizations, faith communities, academic institutions, government departments, and youth organizations. The evolving philosophy and convictions of the committee were tested in communications with bodies such as the American Psychiatric Association, the British Medical Association, the United Nations, and the World Health Organization.

Guidelines for the implementation of the proposals were also articulated. The committee was concerned that the implementation strategy allow for active community participation. It called for the process to be driven from the grassroots, and proposed the following "pillars upon which each service should be founded": it should be development-centered; it should be simple and efficient; measures should be culturally appropriate; services should be community based; measures should aim at building capacity, and they should promote healing and reconciliation.[34]

In the end the reparations and rehabilitation policy was structured into five components. These components and the activities proposed within each were only *recommended* by the Committee on Reparations and Rehabilitation and the TRC. Neither the committee nor the commission had the mandate, or a budget, to implement them. The power of implementation was retained by the federal government. The five components were:

- *Urgent Interim Reparations*
- *Individual Reparation Grants:* It was proposed that individual reparation take the form of a scheme under which survivors of gross human rights violations receive individual, annual monetary grants for a period of six years. People living in rural areas, where it is more difficult and expensive to access services such as health care, and those with many dependents could receive higher grants. The regular payment was to be between seventeen thousand and twenty-three thousand rand per year (in mid-2003 values, approximately US$2,125 to US$2,875).
- *Symbolic Reparation/Legal and Administrative Measures:* Symbolic reparation was designed to facilitate the communal process of commemorating the pain and victories of the past. Among other measures, symbolic reparation was to entail the nomination of a national day of remembrance and reconciliation and the erection of memorials and monuments. On a more individual level, some of the symbolic measures previously outlined under urgent interim reparations were also proposed. The commission further recommended that streets and community facilities should be renamed to remember and honor individuals or events in those communities. It identified a need for culturally appropriate rituals, such as cleansing ceremonies, in certain communities. These were to be arranged by local and provincial authorities in close cooperation with faith communities and cultural and community organizations.
- *Community Rehabilitation Programs:* These were proposals for the establishment of community-based services and activities aimed at promoting the healing and recovery of individuals and communities that have been affected by human rights violations. In order to enable individuals and communities to take control of their own lives, community rehabilitation programs were to be administered on the principle that reparation should be development centered. Their success would depend on the provision of sufficient knowledge and information about available resources to victims through a participatory process. It was recommended that there be rehabilitation programs at community and national levels. These were to include the following initiatives: community health care; mental-health care; education and housing; a program to demilitarize youth who had come to accept violence as a way of resolving conflict; and a multi-ministry program to resettle the thousands of "internal" refugees driven from their homes due to political conflict.
- *Institutional Reform:* These proposals focused on legal, administrative, and institutional measures designed to prevent the recurrence of human

rights abuses. The recommended institutional reform overlapped with the broader aims of the commission and was to be implemented in a wide range of sectors including the judiciary, media, security forces, and business.[35]

For most of the life of the commission the reparations component of the TRC received the least attention from the media. This was surprising, given that the proposals offered by the Committee on Reparations and Rehabilitation, if implemented, would have had a radical impact on South African society. We see in the reports of the committee a growing vision of a broad, deep, and enduring effort to reverse the tide of history. The architects of the TRC saw rehabilitation not only in terms of individual compensation but also in terms of the healing of whole communities. The Committee on Reparations and Rehabilitation, like the other two core committees, clearly felt that its work needed to be oriented toward a mending that was emotional, communal, institutional, and financial. In its view, reconciliation included not only the formation and repair of relationships that crossed ethnic and cultural groups, but also the drawing of marginalized cultural and ethnic groups into the center.

From the beginning the implementation of reparations has been painfully slow and fraught with controversy. By the time of the publication of the final two volumes of the TRC's *Final Report* in early 2003, little had happened except the individual interim payments. Even the administration of these grants was clumsy and contentious. In the late 1990s the government allocated 300 million rand for interim reparations, but by mid-2000 only R30 million had been paid out. Government representatives and TRC officials accused each other of failing to set up the necessary structures for implementation.

As for final reparations, the ANC government finally agreed to pay individual reparations grants but cut the proposed R17,000-23,000 per annum for six years to a one-time offering of R30,000. In April 2003 President Mbeki announced this figure and also accepted the Committee on Reparations and Rehabilitation's proposals for wider group and symbolic reparations but did not offer a detailed plan for their implementation.[36] An inter-ministerial committee led by the Justice Department had been working on a reparations policy, with seemingly little progress. In June 2002 a victims' rights group, frustrated with waiting, filed suit under access to information legislation to see a copy of the government's reparations policy.[37]

It remains to be seen to what extent the government will implement the recommendations of the Committee on Reparations and Rehabilitation and how successful its program will be. The ability of the nation to reverse its vicious circle of history into a virtuous one will depend in significant measure on the pursuit of a vision like the one articulated by the Committee on Reparations and Rehabilitation. Such a reversal will need the participation of all sectors of society.

The effects of the delay in paying out reparations include the growth of strong resentment among victims who participated in the TRC and the generation of widespread cynicism in South Africa regarding the whole reconciliation process. Many voices are saying, "I told you the killers and torturers would get the most from this." So far they are at least partially right. NGOs, churches, and other civil society agencies have expressed outrage, several of them coalescing to pressure the government.

Another issue that generated controversy was the role of the private sector in reparations. Shortly before closing shop in mid-2000, the TRC conducted a workshop on this question. Jubilee South Africa, an NGO that focuses on debt relief, was spearheading a call for every government rand directed toward reparations to be matched by one from the business community. So far businesses have resisted this request, claiming to already be spending large amounts on social investments.[38] This reticence may be one of the reasons for a number of suits launched by victims' rights groups against corporations and banks that did business with the apartheid government. Ford, Crédit Suisse, Citibank Corp., and IBM, among others, have been targeted.

A number of reasons appear to have contributed to the tardy and unsatisfactory nature of the reparations process. The most obvious is the slowness of the entire TRC process. Even though the commission submitted the first five (of seven) volumes of its *Final Report* in 1998, its offices remained open until mid-2002. The largest piece of work carried out after 1998 was the completion of the amnesty proceedings, but the Committee on Reparations and Rehabilitation also continued its labor. Nobody expected the work to drag on that long, and the delay gave the government an excuse for doing little in the way of restitution.

A second impediment to timely and effective reparations was the outbreak of conflict between the TRC and the ANC government. The ANC leadership was so displeased with the *Final Report* released in 1998 that it went to court in an unsuccessful bid to block its publication. The major source of its displeasure appeared to be a perception that the commission and the report did not make a clear enough distinction between violence perpetrated by the forces of apartheid and violence performed by liberation forces.[39] Other issues, including responsibility for delayed compensation and the possibility of a blanket amnesty for ANC leaders, fueled the friction.

A third impediment was the state of South Africa's federal bureaucracy. The ANC could not ask too much of government departments and social service agencies because those bodies were undergoing dramatic change and were severely under-resourced. This situation does not appear to have improved significantly.

Originally, the Committee on Reparations and Rehabilitation envisioned itself designing a comprehensive "service approach" to reparations, but when it surveyed the social health and welfare system upon which this policy would depend, it decided that this approach was untenable:

Closer inspection revealed massive problems with the service approach. Services are not without cost, and we could not expect Government to approve free or low-cost services to victims without an estimate as to what the actual cost would be. Some sort of financial limit would have to be put on the cost of the package per recipient, which would, inevitably, mean that many (if not most) recipients would not receive everything that they felt they needed. There are huge disparities in the provision of services between rural and urban areas and from one province to another. Reparation recipients in poorly resourced areas would thus be prejudiced and would not receive equal reparation to those, for example, in a large urban area. The mere process of needs' assessment costs money. How would the practical process of preparing a suitable 'package' for each and every victim (and his/her dependents) be operationalized? Needs change. A recipient who wants assistance with funding of tertiary education today may receive a bursary from another source tomorrow and may then see counseling as a significant need.[40]

These factors led the committee to make individual cash payments the core of both its interim and final reparations frameworks. However, its recommendations for final reparations still included strong measures in the areas of symbolic gestures, legal reform, community rehabilitation, and institutional reform. In other words, the onus was now on the government to come to terms with the systemic difficulties outlined in the above quotation.

The final impediment to reparations that I will mention may be avoidable for future reconciliation programs in other countries—and perhaps in South Africa. It appears to have been a mistake to give the TRC the responsibility to design the compensation program without giving it the mandate and resources to implement it. In hindsight, it seems inevitable that the commission's work, which included so many controversial elements, would become politicized to the point that its working relationships with political bodies such as the ANC would deteriorate. Perhaps the commission should have been designed and empowered to follow through on reparations. Perhaps another body, unconnected to the controversial truth-telling and amnesty processes, should have been formed. There are no easy answers here, even in hindsight.

9

Act Five: Embracing Forgiveness

Wilhelm Verwoerd, an Afrikaner, is a professor of philosophy and ethics at the University of Stellenbosch. A few years ago, he took a break from university life to work as a researcher for the TRC. Before that, he campaigned for the ANC. This political activity received a lot of attention (and surprise) in South Africa. You see, Wilhelm is the grandson of one of the most notable architects of apartheid. As a cabinet minister and prime minister his grandfather, Hendrik Verwoerd, implemented some of the National Party's most draconian legislation. His time as prime minister ended with his assassination.

Wilhelm Verwoerd daily absorbed National Party politics and Dutch Reform theology in his family and in his hometown of Stellenbosch, which lay in the heart of Afrikaner wine country and served as an intellectual center of apartheid. Considering a career as a pastor, he trained in theology and then went to the Netherlands and Oxford for further study. It was during his period abroad that he began to question the religion and politics of Afrikaner nationalism. He was particularly affected by his meetings with black exiles from his country. Their personal accounts of suffering and humiliation stripped away his layers of denial.

With his future wife, Melanie, also an Afrikaner, Wilhelm embarked on a personal process of intellectual deconstruction and soul searching. For Melanie, this journey led to election to Parliament. For a time she was the youngest female deputy and the only Afrikaner in the ANC caucus. Despite strong opposition, and occasional rough treatment from Stellenbosh farmers, who are known to bully their African farmhands into voting for the National Party, she was elected to a second term in 1999. For Wilhelm, the process of soul searching led to the stage at an ANC rally in May 1993. The posters announcing his joint appearance with internationally known anti-apartheid leader Alan Boesak must have given many pedestrians pause. When he stood before the audience, mixed among such calls as "One President, one

147

Mandela!" and "Viva ANC!" were shouts of "Viva Verwoerd!"—a cry that no one could have envisioned ushering from an ANC rally.[1]

Wilhelm's politics have caused him to be alienated from his father and other members of his family. This is a painful price, but, unlike so many other white South Africans, he is willing to make difficult sacrifices for the sake of reconciliation. The process of absorbing and then deconstructing a philosophy of domination has made Wilhelm acutely aware of "patriarchy." He continually challenges himself to make "creative choices" in family life and in other spheres.

In Chapter 1 I asserted that forgiveness has a core grammar, which is stretched and tested but not broken when we move from the interpersonal to the sociopolitical realm. I employed a model to interpret this grammar, describing a process of forgiveness as a drama that moves through a number of acts. For interpersonal relations, this drama has three acts: (1) the naming and articulation of the harm done; (2) an apology in which the offending party confesses the wrong done and accepts responsibility; and (3) the offering of forgiveness by the victimized party.

My contention is that in political forgiveness, like interpersonal forgiveness, the three acts are played out as we move to the sphere of sociopolitical relations, but more acts need to be scripted. I have added an act concerned with transitional justice and another with psychological and social healing, leaving us with a drama of political forgiveness in five acts:

- Act One: truth-telling
- Act Two: apology and the claiming of responsibility
- Act Three: building a transitional justice framework
- Act Four: finding ways to heal
- Act Five: embracing forgiveness.

Each of the goals that gave shape to one of the first four acts is a sociopolitical good that can be considered an end in itself, but each can also be considered a leg on the journey to forgiveness. Some commentators reject this latter assertion. They argue that forgiveness, like reconciliation, is too ambitious and too difficult a goal. It is more appropriate, they say, for a successor regime or other intervening body to set its sights on peaceful coexistence and the establishment of a liberal democracy in which disagreements are arbitrated through debate or recourse to legitimate adjudicatory institutions. Their fear is that if people are pushed toward too intimate a rapprochement while antipathy lingers, they will rebel or resentment will grow even more powerful, undermining whatever progress toward democratic stability has been achieved. These warnings are certainly appropriate.

Rajeev Bhargava makes the point in reference to truth commissions. He argues that truth commissions are not the right instruments to bring about reconciliation, but instead should focus on the goal of creating a "minimally decent society." For true reconciliation or forgiveness to occur, he argues, wrongdoers must shed their prejudice, own up to the evil they have done, and go through a gut-wrenching self-confrontation:

We might say of such persons that in such moments their souls are punished. This punishment of the soul must necessarily involve a profound change of identity, which must be witnessed by the victims if they are to be convinced that forgiveness is appropriate. Truth commissions that must operate within a compressed time frame, in the immediate aftermath of evil, are simply not equipped to bear the burden of effecting or encompassing this fundamental transformation. Truth commissions can create conditions for reconciliation in the future. But such reconciliation, if and when it comes about, can only be a fortunate by-product of the truth commission.[2]

This is a very good description of the deep transformation required before broad political forgiveness can be manifest in a context like post-apartheid South Africa. Bhargava's warning is well taken and is supported by events in South Africa. The hopes for reconciliation among the designers and leaders of the TRC were too high and too focused on immediate results. After the first heady months of deliberation, commissioners realized that the horizon for comprehensive forgiveness was further off than they had anticipated. A mistake had been made in the original framing of expectations, which, when left unmet, produced a rebound of resentment.

Still, I disagree with Bhargava's assertions that forgiveness and reconciliation can only be byproducts of a truth commission and that such commissions cannot go beyond the creation of conditions for future reconciliation. The best metaphor for political forgiveness is not the building of a structure where groundwork is laid and then built upon piece by piece, each being added in a foreordained sequence. Rather, it can be better understood as seeds that are planted here and there; in some places it immediately flourishes and flowers, sheds its pollen, and spreads; in other places it withers and dies. As the TRC experience has shown, a commission cannot seed a whole country with a forgiveness that will be harvested after a short season. Yet, as it brings enemies together in truth-telling exercises or amnesty hearings, it can try to create conditions that will nurture the occasional blossom. The TRC produced a significant number of blossoms that in turn captured the attention of the nation. It is reasonable to hope that they are being reproduced throughout the country in important, if less publicly visible, forms. It is doubtful that these moments of grace would have occurred, at least in equal number, if Chairman Tutu and other officials had not believed forgiveness could happen and tried to be ready for it.

We have a bit of a paradox. On the one hand, the TRC's expectations of forgiveness and reconciliation were overly optimistic and fostered a disappointed or cynical resentment when they were not met. On the other hand, these same expectations probably made possible a number of extraordinary moments of pardon and rapprochement that have entered the country's collective memory. The lesson for future commissions seems to be to stay open to the possibility of grace, but be careful about promising that it will appear.

I envision political forgiveness in two ways: (1) as a social good, akin to justice or healing or the claiming of responsibility, which can be pursued with tangible policies, even if it will take longer to achieve than these other goods; and (2) as something more mysterious that materializes in crucibles that mix human pain, need, imagination, and good will. The tension between these two characterizations can be frustrating, but it seems unavoidable. Perhaps it is also creative.

It is with this dual characterization in mind that the relationship between act five and the preceding acts in our drama of forgiveness can be clarified. On the one hand, acts one through four can be seen as preparation for act five. While each can stand on its own as a legitimate enterprise or can be seen as contributing to the more immediate goal of establishing democratic coexistence between old enemies, each can also be seen to be preparing the national soil for the future growth of a broad and deep reconciliation that includes the abandonment of resentment and the generation of fellowship among former enemies—in other words, forgiveness.

On the other hand, forgiveness can be seen as a sub-theme in acts one through four, hiding in the background most of the time, but breaking out in special moments to advance the causes of truth-telling, claiming of responsibility, justice, and healing. As an example, we might point to the moments of reconciliation between victims and their former tormentors during the TRC's HRV hearings. The good will generated and antipathy surrendered in these moments liberated perpetrators from stances of psychic self-protection and enabled them to be more truthful about human rights violations they had committed or witnessed. It also freed victims to be more empathetic toward the people who had harmed them and enabled them to better understand the motivations that had led to the offenses. Thus, a manifestation of political forgiveness advanced the cause of truth-telling. Put another way, episodes from act five were acted out in the midst of act one, changing its dynamics.

Rajeev Bhargava is correct to assert that political forgiveness involves soul work and fundamental alterations of identity. For forgiveness to be manifest between Africans and Afrikaners, for example, each group will not only have to alter narratives that characterize the other, but each also will have to alter narratives that define itself. Actually, the two kinds of transformation are inseparable. If this is to happen, myth-makers and other architects of culture will have to reach deep into the symbol systems that give shape to the two cultural/ethnic groups and rework those systems. Forgiveness requires the surrender of resentment and other antipathies; it also involves the embracing of former enemies in a new fellowship. For this to happen, each party has to come to see the other as a *former* enemy. As long as Africans see Afrikaners primarily as oppressors, embrace will be impossible. As long as Afrikaners see Africans primarily as labor, or as a threat, reconciliation is precluded.

The difficulty of inspiring enemies to undertake this kind of collective soul work is surpassed only by its importance. This is one of the reasons why leaders like Nelson Mandela are so rare and so vital. Mandela's ability to rise from his own suffering to a place of generosity toward his oppressors was a remarkable incarnation of the very spirit that can heal the nation. I believe that most of us are capable of embodying such a spirit, but we have deep resistance. We settle more easily into self-defining narratives of victimhood and estrangement. This is true of individuals and of communities, and there is rarely a shortage of power-seeking opportunists willing to ride and guide these feelings of alienation. If we can learn anything from contexts like South Africa, the Balkans, or Northern Ireland, I hope it is the need to confront our appetite for these narratives. We need a corpus of leaders—global and local, spiritual and secular, artistic and technocratic—who can offer us more noble fare. Ultimately, the choice is between a collective self-understanding that keeps us sick from feeding on the poisons of the past and one that nourishes, heals, and offers the strength to chase a liberated future.

As an aside, albeit an extremely important one, I would like to point out that socioeconomic changes are usually necessary before these shifts of constructed identity can take place in a fundamental way. For most of South Africa's majority population today, whites are still economic oppressors. It does not matter how many seeds of forgiveness are dispersed over South African soil; that soil will be too barren to nourish most of them until blacks receive education comparable to whites, until blacks benefit from good health care, until there is fundamental land reform, until equality is achieved in the work place, and until distributive justice is actualized in a host of other ways as well. Forgiveness requires the surrender of resentment. Except for the extraordinary few, this is not possible for people who are forced to survive on what trickles down from their oppressors.

So far in this chapter we have used terms like *soul work* and *mystery*—terms that resonate with spirituality. This marks something of a departure from our discussions in previous chapters, which rarely wandered onto the terrain of religion or theology. The shift is not by chance. While my model of political forgiveness is not a theological one, I intend for it to be applicable to a wide range of contexts, both secular and religious; it moves closer to the realm of spirituality in act five. When we consider the alteration of cultures and identities, we are moving onto "sacred ground." This sanctity holds even for the nonreligious. For most people, nothing is more important than their web of relationships and the symbol systems that inform and animate that web. Act five is about bringing metamorphosis to that web and those systems; it is about altering our most deeply held beliefs.

This is one of the reasons I have chosen two theological examples of cultural creativity to outline in the pages to come. Miroslav Volf and Desmond Tutu, the two theological artists we will be discussing, are both adept at explaining the kinds of changes people will have to make, the things they will have to surrender, and the suffering they will have to accept in order for political forgiveness to become a possibility. One need not be a Christian (or a religious person of any kind) to appreciate their deep understanding of human and communal transformation.

Another reason for choosing the theologies of Volf and Tutu is their applicability to the South African context. A clear majority of South Africans adhere to a faith tradition. Religion was in no small part responsible for the scandal of apartheid. Perhaps religion can help clear it up. While the country is very religious, it is far from exclusively Christian. It would have been equally valid to offer an example from Muslim theology, but I am less qualified to do this. Neither am I qualified to offer examples from African traditional religion, although the discussion of Tutu's *ubuntu* theology will have a certain relevance.

The first example is the theology of Miroslav Volf, in particular his treatment of rending and reconciliation in his book *Exclusion and Embrace*.[3] Volf works within the parameters of traditional European Protestant theology and has been influenced by contemporary evangelicals. He is deeply concerned with nationalism and ethnic conflict. Having grown up in Yugoslavia, he has very personal attachments to the conflicts in the Balkans. All of these characteristics make him a writer of particular relevance to South African Christians, because European Protestantism has been extremely influential in South Africa. Its theology has been reworked to provide an ideational basis for apartheid and to articulate anti-apartheid theologies of liberation. Volf understands the ways Protestant theology has been molded into ideologies of exclusion, but he also sees within it powerful resources for a theology of inclusion. Given the number of South Africans—of all colors—who actively participate in Protestant churches, Volf's theology of inclusion holds strong potential as a resource for reconciliation. South African blacks and whites appear to be gathering together in increasing numbers in evangelical Protestant churches, especially those with a charismatic worship style. Exposure to the ideas and themes of Christian thinkers like Volf could help them extend their interracial fellowship beyond the sanctuary and the Bible study room, and could nudge theologically conservative churches—so often places of resistance to change—toward becoming centers of rapprochement.

My second example will be the *ubuntu* theology of Desmond Tutu. Like Volf's, Tutu's theology is Christian, but it is also very much influenced by the world view and wisdom of traditional African cultures. The concept of *ubuntu* is central to the Xhosa people's understanding of humanity, community, and spirituality. In a fresh and powerful way, Tutu has combined his people's understanding of *ubuntu* with his understanding of the Christian gospel to produce a living theology. This theology first served him as a leader of the anti-apartheid movement. Now it serves him as a prophet of forgiveness and reconciliation. Unlike many theologies of liberation, Tutu's *ubuntu* theology did not require massive revision when the imperatives of social justice changed from overthrowing an unjust regime to reconstruction and reconciliation. The growth of African Initiated Churches is transforming the religious landscape in South Africa.[4] Tutu's combining of traditional African and Western Christian theologies may be appealing to members of those churches and may aid them in developing their own contextual theologies.

The Cape Town house that I lived in while doing the research for this book was located in a comfortable suburb populated mostly by whites. To visit the African townships, I would get into my car, drive through other pleasant boroughs, and cross a major highway that split the city. When I reached the two huge cooling towers of the power plant, I knew that I was entering the townships where Africans were forced to live under apartheid, and where most are still forced to live today because of economic apartheid. This swift passage across symbolic barriers ushered me into a remarkably different world. The first thing that impressed me was the poverty. In minutes I would move from the First World to the Third World. But quickly other impressions would push to the fore: the interactions among people on the streets, the friendliness toward strangers like myself, the groups of children playing in open spaces—all things I had missed in suburbia. Unlike their countrymen living on the other side of the highway, the township residents did not seem to be dominated by fear.

On two of my trips I visited congregations of the Order of Ethiopia, a denomination of African Initiated Churches. The people I met in these churches struggled on a daily basis with poverty, poor heath care, poor education systems, very high crime rates, and a host of other social ills. They were very proud. They were astute commentators on political conditions and developments in their country. Men and women of strong faith, they were willing, some were even eager, to forgive their oppressors. But almost all offered the same message: The whites are not doing what they must to bring about forgiveness. These are the things they require of South African whites before they will be ready to forgive: a profound sharing of economic resources; acknowledgment of what happened in the past; confession and repentance regarding their support of and their benefiting from apartheid; truth-telling on the part of those who committed atrocities; and a surrender of the fear that causes them to hoard their wealth and that keeps them from visiting townships or befriending Africans.

Memories of the many young people who died in or disappeared from their communities prevent the members of the Ethiopian Order churches from settling for cheap forgiveness. Mr. Sipoyo, whose brother spent twenty years on Robben Island, the prison complex where politcal prisoners were kept, expressed his frustration at the refusal of whites to "bow down and apologize." Except for those applying for amnesty, he did not see whites acting penitent.

Melo Mbilini, a young man, said today's youth become filled with anger as they learn of the humiliation of their people. "The people who did these things must be given a serious task to make up for what they did."

Nomfundo, a woman who was detained more than five times and tortured, still suffers from nightmares and other symptoms of post-traumatic stress disorder. When the ANC was unbanned and political prisoners released, she became ready to forgive, but those who mistreated her have never asked for forgiveness. "My soul is not contented with the TRC. We are missing 80 percent of the perpetrators who should come forward and apologize."

Bishop Dwane began to take the issue of national forgiveness seriously in the early nineties and has worked hard at it. "Personally, yes, I think the anger in me has gone, and I have now forgiven." But national forgiveness requires work on both sides. "Whites are not prepared to make gestures of reconciliation. They want us to let bygones be bygones. They are not prepared to acknowledge the hurt or their responsibility."

Having heard the complaints of these people, I became especially attuned to the discourse among whites regarding the reconciliation process. I observed two things. Most of the whites who agreed to an interview with me did speak from a place of repentance, at least some of the time. But, while engaging in or overhearing less formal conversations, I was repeatedly struck by the refusal of whites to search their souls.⁵ Denial was alive and well.

EXCLUSION AND EMBRACE—THE THEOLOGY OF MIROSLAV VOLF

In *Exclusion and Embrace* systematic theologian Miroslav Volf examines the dynamics of rending and rapprochement in contexts of ethnic and cultural conflict. In his thinking, conflict among cultures is best understood as a part of the larger question of identity and "otherness." As a Croatian living in the United States, his perspective on this question is largely shaped by developments in the West, and he uses the history of European contact with the cultures and peoples of other continents as his entree into the topic of identity construction.

Europe's past is full of the worst of violence committed in the name of European identity (and with the goal of European prosperity!). Europe colonized and oppressed, destroyed cultures and imposed its religion, all in the name of its identity with itself—in the name of its absolute religion and superior civilization. Think only of the discovery of America and its genocidal aftermath . . . a sad story of dehumanization, depredation, and destruction of millions. And it was not too long ago that Germany sought to conquer and exterminate in the name of its purity, its identity with itself.[6]

One of history's tragic ironies is that modernity, with its ideal of inclusion, was born in Europe during the era of colonization. The story we tell ourselves in the "modern, democratic West" is one of progressive inclusion. That is why we are shocked when we see ethnic cleansing in Europe. We try to recharacterize the cleansers as non-European and savage. Volf challenges this smug attitude and argues that there has always been "a momentous inner tension in the typically modern narrative of inclusion." Following postmodern critics like Dussel, Nietzsche, Derrida, and Foucault, he describes the birth of modernity as entailing exclusion of colossal proportions. Indeed, this is Europe's history of interaction with non-Europe, whether non-Europe is that which existed on other continents or that which existed on the European continent but was excluded from Europe's formulation of its own identity. Whatever came to be characterized as "not us" was labeled as uncivilized, even barbaric. The modern self is constructed through the exclusion of the other.[7]

When it comes to deciding how to overcome exclusion, however, Volf disagrees with the postmodernists. He rejects what he sees as their push for inclusion to the point that all boundaries are suspect. His quarrel with modernity arises from his theology of creation. God created and continues to create the world through work that involves differentiation and judgment, each of which can be contrasted with exclusion. Creation involves binding *and* separation. Exclusion is the sin of reconfiguring creation by separating what God has bound or binding what God has separated.[8]

In a penetrating section of his book Volf explains that exclusion often arises from an unhealthy desire for purity. He believes that human beings have a legitimate will to purity, but the proper focus of this will is a person's own spiritual life. Problems arise when we engage in a kind of projection in which we shift our aspiration for purity from our inner selves onto others and become concerned with their "cleanliness." There emerges a politics of purity with various kinds of exclusion to exercise against its targets:

- Exclusion by *assimilation* says "You can survive, even flourish, in this society if you abandon your identity and become like us."
- Exclusion by *domination* subjugates the other to a lesser place and makes that person the victim of exploitation.
- Exclusion by *abandonment* is common today in the stance of wealthy classes toward the poor and the developed world toward the developing world. The underprivileged are left to their fate.

At the level of the self, what is at the bottom of this? Why do we exclude? Volf gives several reasons: We exclude because we project hatred of ourselves onto others; we exclude because we resist that which disturbs our identities, boundaries, and cultural maps by mirroring something we do not want to see in ourselves or by challenging our assumptions; we exclude because we want what others have; we exclude because we want to be at the center and be there alone.[9]

Volf's treatment of identity and otherness certainly rings true to race relations in South Africa. South Africans of European descent have consistently constructed their identities by contrasting their own "superiority" against the "backwardness," "helplessness," and "irrationality" of the Africans. Two of the three forms of exclusion he mentions—domination and abandonment—have been extensively employed. Identity construction was so restrictive and reified that assimilation, the third kind of exclusion mentioned by Volf, was rarely employable.

For those of us who recognize that we have been guilty of exclusion and who want to reverse this, Volf describes the essential "moments" in the movement from exclusion to embrace. These are (1) repentance, (2) forgiveness, (3) making space in oneself for the other, and (4) the healing of memory. By passing through these, humans can emulate the self-giving love modeled by Jesus the Christ.

Volf's description of the first "moment," repentance, closely resembles the work of act two in my drama of forgiveness—apology and the claiming of responsibility. Predictably, he calls for aggressors and agents of oppression to repent by taking themselves out of the mesh of large and small evil deeds that characterize so much of social intercourse, to refuse to justify their behavior or accuse others, and to take their wrongdoing upon themselves. What is surprising is that he calls for victims to do the same things. He argues that victims are rarely blameless themselves. Oppression is soul destroying. Very often victims become filled with resentment and a lust for power that makes them want to take the place of their oppressors. Repentance for victims means resisting the seduction of the values and practices of the oppressor. He claims that the revolutionary character of Jesus' message lies in the connection between the hope he offered to victims and the change he required of them. To the extent that oppression has filled them with hatred, they need to repent of what has happened to their souls.[10]

The second "moment," forgiveness, does not come easily.[11] Volf empathizes with victims' frequent reluctance to forgive. He says our "cool sense of justice" tells us that perpetrators do not deserve to be forgiven, that forgiveness would be unjust. We instinctively seek not to forgive but to gain revenge. This is not just pathos but a desire to restore an integrity that has been shattered by violence. But balance cannot really be restored through vengeance. Volf agrees with Arendt's assertions that revenge enslaves us and that forgiveness is the only way out of the "predicament of irreversibility."

"The injustice of oppression must be fought with the creative 'injustice' of forgiveness."[12]

Volf's third "moment" in the progression from exclusion to embrace is the making of space in oneself for the other. This involves emulation of two of the characteristics displayed by Jesus the Christ in his ministry, his teachings, and especially his passion: (1) self-giving love that overcomes enmity, and (2) the creation of space in oneself for estranged humanity. This relates closely to Jesus' teaching to love our enemies. It can be uncomfortable, painful, even risky to make space in oneself for people who are radically different from us, who offend our sensibilities, or with whom we have been in conflict, but this is what the gospel demands of us. For Christians, the celebration of the eucharist is the ritual time in which Christians honor God's making space for humanity. By receiving Christ's body and blood, Christians make space for all those whom Christ embraced through his suffering.[13]

Volf's last "moment" in the movement from exclusion to embrace is the healing of memory. He acknowledges the important role remembering plays in reconciliation but says there must eventually be a forgetting. Remembrance on the part of the victims will protect against future oppression of the same kind. Remembrance on the part of the guilty will change the soil of the past into the more hopeful soil for building a future. But only those who are willing ultimately to forget can remember correctly. This willingness is really eschatological. Forgetting will happen in the "arms of God."[14]

In a "drama of embrace" Volf offers the four structural elements of embrace: opening the arms, waiting, closing the arms, and opening them again. All four must be there in an unbroken time-line. Opening the arms is a sign of discontent with one's own self-enclosed identity and of desire for the other. It is also a sign that one has made space in oneself for the other to come in and has initiated a movement out of oneself so as to enter the space created in the other. As well, it suggests a fissure in oneself through which the other may enter. Finally, it serves as an invitation and a soft knock on the other's door.

After opening the arms, the self rests at the boundary of the other, waiting for desire to arise in the other, and for the other's arms to open. The other cannot be coerced or manipulated into embrace. Closing the arms is the goal of the embrace. It must be reciprocal, each party being active and passive. It must be a soft touch, and boundaries must remain in place. Neither oneself nor the other is denied; the identity of both is preserved and transformed. Preservation of the alterity of the other requires the skill of "not understanding" the other, which opens the possibility for new and better understanding. Finally the other must be let go of so that the "negotiation of difference, which can never produce a final settlement," can continue.[15]

Three aspects of Volf's work can be highlighted as particularly relevant to the dynamics of apartheid and reconciliation in South Africa. The first is his identification of a twisted will to purity as a source of exclusion. The myth of apartheid and the political program that it produced were driven by a vision of the Afrikaner people as a special race, divinely selected and set apart. The Dutch Reform churches can benefit much from Volf's insight as they face the task of theological deconstruction and reconstruction in a new South Africa. Dutch Reform theologians, and other Afrikaner cultural artisans, will be of great service to their people if they can unmask the Afrikaner will to purity and direct it toward more appropriate goals.

The second aspect of Volf's work to be highlighted here is more relevant to English-speaking South Africans and other whites who were more open to liberal or "modern" values than were most Afrikaners. Many English-speaking South Africans took pride in having attitudes toward race that were much more progressive than those of Afrikaners, but the English-speaking communities, their political parties, and the business community that they dominated almost never tackled apartheid head on.[16] Instead, they were marked by a complicity from which great material benefits were gained. Current attitudes have not changed that much. There is a general willingness to condemn apartheid, but few whites are voicing a willingness to accept a substantial redistribution of wealth, for example. Volf's depiction of the "momentous inner tension in the typically modern narrative of inclusion" speaks to these people and can serve as reminder that the adoption of "progressive" values does not guarantee that one is more a part of the solution than the problem of racial inequality.

The third aspect of Volf's work that I would highlight is his call for victims to repent. First, a note of caution. It is important to remember that throughout the apartheid era there was no shortage of white clergy preaching to black South Africans that they had much for which they needed to repent. There is danger in adding another white theologian to the list, even if his writing amounts to a refutation of the theology of apartheid. Despite this danger, Volf's point regarding the tendency of victims to be overcome by resentment and the will to power bears recitation. He does not fall into the trap of blaming the victims and arguing that their misfortune is a punishment for earlier sins. In his eyes they are the sinned against, not the sinners. Perhaps because of his own history in the former Yugoslavia, he understands that oppression very often erodes the inner life of the oppressed, leaving them vulnerable to hatred and malevolent desires.

The history of South Africa is rife with examples of this. It was after having suffered great abuse at the hands of the British that Afrikaner religious politics turned most purposefully toward apartheid. The ANC committed its worst violations during the eighties and early nineties, when South African security forces had reached their apotheosis of repression and the IFP was hunting down ANC members. The PAC split from the ANC and developed an anti-white ideology response to the radical legislation implemented by the National Party during its first mandates.

Given the number of political and economic victims in South Africa today, not to mention the growing number of people who have been hurt by criminal violence, Volf's warning is grave. Most of the measures taken or called for by the TRC can be seen as attempts to curb the danger of victims becoming agents of further rending. But other measures will be needed. The churches and other communities of faith seem particularly well placed to call victims to the soul work of examining and transforming their antipathies and to support them in that work. The Trauma Centre in Cape Town and a number of other agencies around the country have been helping torture survivors and others with this kind of work, but relatively few South Africans have access to this kind of psychotherapy.

Stan Abrahams is a tall, dignified man of mixed race. Now in his early seventies, he has retired from a career as an engineer and works as a lay minister at Central Methodist Mission in Cape Town. Even though the mixed-race District Six was razed by the government in the late 1960s, it still exists in a very vibrant mythology, and Stan continues his love affair with that community. Growing up in District Six, Stan reveled in its street festivals, in the seemingly endless string of colorful personalities one would encounter in a day, and in the rich and supportive relationships his family shared with its neighbors, who came from a wide variety of religious, cultural, and ethnic backgrounds. He also gained a deep sense of peace and spirituality from Table Mountain, which towered over the city.

Although Stan was embittered by the destruction of his community and by prejudice in the work place, which caused less skilled white colleagues to be paid much more than him and to be promoted above him, he emotionally survived these and other humiliations doled out by apartheid. Many of his friends fared worse. The residents of District Six were shipped off to townships that lacked its physical beauty and cultural vitality. Some of his friends turned to alcohol. Some were ground down by poverty. Some succumbed to bitterness. Stan's sadness was palpable as he talked about "the inner light going out" of some of his boyhood friends.

Stan keeps his light alive by visiting the national gardens at the foot of Table Mountain, by serving an interracial congregation in the heart of Cape Town—surely there is no better death knell for apartheid— and by helping to run the District Six Museum, of which he is a founder.

DELICATE NETWORKS OF INTERDEPENDENCE—
THE THEOLOGY OF DESMOND TUTU

Just as South Africa's transition to democracy would have been radically different without the wisdom and charisma of Nelson Mandela, the TRC would have been a very different enterprise without the faith and folly of

Desmond Tutu. By his faith, I mean, of course, his faith in God, but even more so, his faith in the South African people, in their ability to find courage and mercy in their hearts. By his folly, I mean the kind of foolishness of which Paul writes:

> Where is the wise man? Where is the scholar? Where is the philosopher of his age? Has not God made foolish the wisdom of the world? For since in the wisdom of God the world did not know him, God was pleased through the foolishness of what was preached to save those who believe. . . . For the foolishness of God is wiser than man's wisdom, and the weakness of God is stronger than man's strength. (1 Cor 1:20-21, 25, NIV)

According to "the wisdom of the world," especially the skeptical wisdom of the political world, it is folly to risk time, energy, money, and hope on forgiveness in a place like South Africa—where such bitter enmity has developed, and where there are so many other pressing concerns. Tutu rejected this wisdom for another kind.

Holding to his belief that "we all have the capacity to become saints,"[17] he wore his clerical robes to commission hearings and became the confessor of the nation. In doing so, he flouted many of the tenets of political "common sense." By wearing vestments, praying, and singing hymns, he rejected the stipulation that religion and politics must be kept separate. By openly weeping on many occasions, he embodied the opposite of the cool-headed public figure. By accepting the risk of a momentous failure in order to pursue public goals that could only be articulated in spiritual language, he redefined the parameters of success and failure.

To understand Tutu's goals and motivations with regard to the reconciliation process, it is essential to grasp that his leadership was not guided by a political philosophy; it was driven by a theology. To understand his theology, it must be appreciated that it is deeply influenced by both Western and African ideas. At its center there is a convergence of the Christian motif of the *imago Dei* with the African concept of *ubuntu*.

To gain some notion of the meaning of *ubuntu*, it is important to understand how the traditional world view of the Bantu-speaking peoples of Southern Africa differs from that of the modern West.[18] Westerners tend to see persons as independent, solitary entities. We also tend to reject the existence of spirits and the continued existence of dead people—or we at least conceptualize firm boundaries between our realm and theirs. Not so for Africans who hold to their traditional world view; for them, the boundaries are much more porous. Individuals gain their humanity through their deep rootedness in community, and community gains its vitality through its immersion in *umuntu*—"the category of intelligent human force that includes spirits, the human dead, and the living."[19] Tutu uses the phrase "delicate networks of interdependence" to characterize traditional African anthropology-cosmology.

Ubuntu means "humanity" and is related to *umuntu*. The Xhosa people, to whom Tutu belongs, have a proverb: *Ubuntu ungamnutu ngabanye abantu*. Roughly translated it means "A person depends on other people to be a person."[20] Tutu offers this explication of *ubuntu*:

> *Ubuntu* is very difficult to render into a Western language. It speaks of the very essence of being human. When we want to give high praise to someone we say, 'Yu, u nobuntu'; 'Hey, he or she has *ubuntu*.' This means they are generous, hospitable, friendly, caring, and compassionate. They share what they have. It also means my humanity is caught up, is inextricably bound up, in theirs. We belong to a bundle of life. We say, 'a person is a person through other people'. It is not 'I think therefore I am'. It says rather: 'I am human because I belong.' I participate, I share. A person with *ubuntu* is open and available to others, affirming of others, does not feel threatened that others are able and good; for he or she has a proper self-assurance that comes from knowing that he or she belongs in a greater whole and is diminished when others are humiliated or diminished, when others are tortured or oppressed, or treated as if they were less than who they are.[21]

It is possible, I presume, to believe in *ubuntu* but conceptually to restrict its parameters to be coextensive with one's own community and ancestry. Indeed, it must be tempting for South African Africans to envision whites as excluded from the web of relationships that constitutes humanity. Tutu's Christian anthropology prevents him from falling into this trap. For him, all human beings are created in the image of God, the *imago Dei*. This conviction, combined with a belief in *ubuntu*, leads him to see all people as included in the same "delicate networks of interdependence"—a philosophy that could not be more directly opposed to the logic of apartheid. Michael Battle, a former assistant to Archbishop Tutu—now a professor of religion in the United States—puts it this way:

> From this African worldview, *ubuntu* shaped Tutu's subsequent work as the center from which to make racial reconciliation comprehensible in the African culture. Tutu needed to communicate at this level because interdependence is necessary for persons to exercise, develop, and fulfill their potential to be both individuals and a community. Only by means of absolute dependence on God and neighbor—including both blacks and whites—can true human identity be discovered. Indeed, such human interdependence is built into our very creation by our being created in God's image, our common *imago Dei*.[22]

Unlike so many other liberation philosophies, the theology that informed Tutu's resistance to apartheid was also perfectly matched to the pursuit of reconciliation. Again, *umuntu*—the intelligence and vitality that encompasses the living, the dead, and spirits—is relevant. When any part of the network of interdependence is wounded, the life force that sustains all communities and individuals is weakened. When anyone suffers degradation, the humanity of all is tainted. From this point of view, apartheid was bad for everybody, even those who gained some material advantage, and so is nonreconciliation in its wake. It is this perspective that enabled Tutu to empathize with perpetrators. In his view nobody was more diminished by human rights violations than the violators themselves. Tutu holds a special compassion for the agents of apartheid, the men and women who had their humanity leached out of them by their indoctrination and training. He delights when one repents, knowing that the restoration of that person's decency augments the integrity of the whole nation.

Battle identifies four "vectors" in Tutu's *ubuntu* theology: (1) "*ubuntu* theology builds interdependent community"; (2) "*ubuntu* theology recognizes persons as distinctive"; (3) "*ubuntu* theology integrates cultures"; and (4) "*ubuntu* theology can overthrow apartheid." Together, these thrusts point to a future characterized by reconciliation, justice, and vital community at all levels.

The first vector is driven by Tutu's belief that God created humans in a state of interdependence. Human attitudes or systems that encourage selfishness and a high degree of competitiveness defy the divine intention. It is better to accept the fundamental human "vulnerability that builds true community."[23] It is in vulnerable relationships that we recognize how our humanity is bound up in the humanity of others. Given that this is his perspective, it is not surprising to discover that Tutu is critical of the individualism, consumerism, and competitiveness that characterize both Western society and the global economy. True to his African roots, he cherishes community and celebrates the freedom from the difficulties of life that arises in communal cooperation—a different kind of liberty than that which is usually revered in the West.

Nonetheless, Tutu can also be critical of African communalism. He recognizes that there is a danger in *ubuntu*: the tendency to sacrifice the needs and rights of individuals and small minorities in favor of the needs and rights of the many. His corrective comes from his employment of a Christian interpretation of relationship, instead of other forms of communalism, to define *ubuntu*.[24]

Battle's second vector—"*ubuntu* theology recognizes persons as distinctive"—explicates Tutu's take on Christian relationship. The following allegory, offered by Tutu during his address when receiving an honorary doctorate from Columbia University, illustrates his perspective:

There was once a light bulb which shone and shone like no other light bulb had shone before. It captured all the limelight and began to strut about arrogantly quite unmindful of how it was that it could shine so brilliantly, thinking that it was all due to its own merit and skill. Then one day someone disconnected the famous light bulb from the light socket and placed it on a table and try as hard as it could, the light bulb could bring forth no light and brilliance. It lay there looking so disconsolate and dark and cold—and useless. Yes, it had never known that this light came from the power station and that it had been connected to the dynamo by little wires and flexes that lay hidden and unseen and totally unsung.[25]

Tutu's *ubuntu* theology recognizes that persons are distinctive and are ends in themselves, but only through the discovery of their relationship to others in the web of community and ultimately to the divine "power source." There is balance here. As a reflection of the *imago Dei*, every person has value in and of himself or herself. On the other hand, the divinity itself lives in a trinitarian relationship web; all are constituted in relationship. It is this balance that makes the seeking of superiority unnecessary. If I am distinct and can be celebrated as such, then I do not have to be better than anyone else to feel special or important. If the "specialness" of another arises from a grid of relationships of which I am a cherished part, then that "specialness" shouldn't threaten me. Indeed, I should be pleased by the way it makes my life richer.[26]

The third vector in Tutu's *ubuntu* theology—"*ubuntu* theology integrates cultures"—amounts to an extension of the second vector to relations among communities and among nations. Just as each person is unique, so is each nation and each culture. Like persons, they are vulnerable, enmeshed in networks of interdependence. This vulnerability needs to be embraced by a community of nations, each of which celebrates and benefits from the uniqueness of every other one.[27]

The implicit power analysis of *ubuntu* became explicit when Tutu confronted apartheid. He did not adopt an "ends justify the means" approach to liberation. Rather, believing that "*ubuntu* theology can overthrow apartheid" (vector four), Tutu acted as though his oppressors were his fellows—not by excusing them, but by calling out the essential humanity that was hidden beneath their ideology and their actions. This was his attitude:

We will grow in the knowledge that they [white people] too are God's children, even though they may be our oppressors, they may be our enemies. Paradoxically, and more truly, they are our sisters and our brothers, because we have dared, and have the privilege to call God "Abba," Our Father. Therefore, they belong together with us in the family of God, and their humanity is caught up in our humanity, as ours is caught up in theirs.[28]

Given this theology, we can see why Tutu is compelled to seek political forgiveness. As long as "apartness" reigns, God's intentions for humanity and the world are thwarted, the vital force that nourishes all people is weakened, and the delicate networks that sustain all communities are fractured. A stable democracy that adjudicates lingering conflicts, even one that does so justly, is not good enough.

Earlier in this chapter I explained that I see political forgiveness in two ways: (1) as a social good, akin to justice or healing, that can be pursued with tangible policies; and (2) as something more mysterious that materializes in crucibles that mix human pain, need, imagination, and good will. Tutu is politically astute, and sometimes has a lot to say about "tangible policies," but his vision of forgiveness is more about the mysterious, even the mystical. He likes to leave the programming and policy-making to others, preferring to seek God's "foolishness" and to try to live out this folly in the world. To return to a pair of metaphors employed earlier, he is more of a planter than a builder. He scatters seeds of forgiveness with faith that God will provide at least some of them with the nourishment they need to grow. Tutu is not a systematic theologian. He is widely published, but his most powerful theology is that lived in his actions. It comes alive in his confidence that forgiveness is not only essential, but ultimately unstoppable: "There is a movement, not easily discernible, at the heart of things to reverse the awful centrifugal force of alienation, brokenness, division, hostility and disharmony. God has set in motion a centripetal process, a moving towards the Centre, towards unity, harmony, goodness, peace and justice; one that removes barriers."[29]

Like Volf's, Tutu's theology will not appeal to all South African Christians. Some, even some Africans, are too disturbed by any theology that incorporates themes from the pre-Christian beliefs of the Bantu-speaking peoples. Others will see it as too political. But Tutu's collation of Christian and traditional African beliefs such that exclusivism is worked out of each is a gift to the nation and the world. The spirit of his reform can be emulated by people who ascribe to neither of its sources. Thus, by learning from Tutu's adroit technique and his unshakable compassion, Muslims can challenge exclusivism within their own tradition, as can Hindus, Jews, and champions of humanist philosophies.

It is confounding to consider the variety of symbol systems that influence South Africans as they construct identity and spin narratives of inclusion and exclusion. They come from a dramatic plurality of Christian sources, from Islam, from Hinduism, from African wisdom traditions, from Marxist philosophies, from liberal philosophies, and, unfortunately, even from fascist philosophies. Given this pluralism, no one source of cultural reform can pull everyone toward political forgiveness and away from hate and exclusion. The "better angels" of a variety of belief systems will have to come to the fore. If they do, and if they can cooperate to generate "movement at the heart of things to reverse the awful centrifugal force of alienation," then the vicious circles of South Africa's past may slowly be reversed. Volf and Tutu call forth the better angels of their traditions. We can only hope that they are heard and joined by their counterparts in other traditions.

To close this chapter, I would like to return to a debate examined earlier. Some observers of post-conflict contexts like South Africa would undoubtedly respond to my model of political forgiveness by arguing that it should have ended with act four. What we would have, then, would not be a drama of forgiveness but rather a drama of justice and healing, a drama of national restoration, or perhaps a drama of creating a "minimally decent society," to borrow Bhargava's phrase. This would be more to their liking. Among those who hold this perspective, many feel that the imperatives of justice are too strong to fetter their pursuit by mixing in a quest for forgiveness or deep reconciliation. They have a point; the imperatives of justice are of utmost importance—in the long term as well as the short. But who among us wants to live in a "minimally decent society"?

Societies that are more than minimally decent are marked by charity as well as justice; forgiveness can be understood as a form of charity—in other words, something that is not owed but is given because of altruistic impulses, or, more important for our discussion, out of a sense of civic concern. The major institutions of civic charity are established to sustain bonds of community by helping the powerless and marginalized and by maintaining social, cultural, and religious institutions. Forgiveness is also an act that restores or builds community by repairing its fissures. Justice without charity leads to obsession with rules and a wearing down of the fabric of society. A society marked by justice but not by charity would be minimally decent, perhaps, but it would suffer from a dearth of community. Community requires fellowship and bonds of affection. Charitable acts that involve the giving of material goods, time, energy, or empathy build such bonds. So do acts that involve the surrender of well-founded resentment or legitimate claims to retribution. They can be equally charitable.

10

Conclusion

A FINAL WORD ABOUT THE TRC

In Chapter 1, I described the TRC as a national "baptism in tears," an extended ritual that announced the birth of a new nation. It was many other things as well: a communal act of penance; a forensic investigation of the apartheid state, its crimes, and its death throes; a breathtaking venture in restorative justice; a media circus at times; and a forum for political gamesmanship. It will take decades for South Africa and the world to understand the achievements and failures of the commission. As the decades pass, however, the sharpness of immediate experience will recede. With the clarity of hindsight we will learn about the legacy of the TRC, but we will forget its raw power.

In the last few years, when the dramatic impact of the commission was still fresh and the contours of public response were becoming legible, the process of applying history's judgment to the TRC got under way. This judgment has been articulated in countless conversations, news reports, and newspaper articles in South Africa and around the world. A significant number of books and articles concerning the commission have been published and more are undoubtedly on the way. The Institute for Justice and Reconciliation (IJR), an NGO based in Cape Town and headed by the former director of research for the TRC, is making a particularly strong contribution to the clarification of South African public attitudes toward the TRC. In mid-2001 the IJR released a study based on 3,727 interviews with a representative sample of the South African population.[1] Some relatively clear trends can be identified in the findings. In the paragraphs that follow I will make some general evaluative comments based on my interviews, my survey of media and academic reports, and the findings of the IJR study.

The first thing that I would say is that the TRC's truth-telling process was its greatest and least qualified success. The combination of HRV hearings, special hearings, institutional hearings, and an amnesty process that required full disclosure from applicants has led to the release into the public domain of a remarkably extensive body of information regarding human rights

166

violations between 1960 and 1994 and the institutional and communal dynamics that fostered these violations. If truth is an essential component of a foundation upon which to build a new nation, then the TRC has made impressive progress in laying that foundation. Of course, reporting the facts is only one aspect of truth-telling. Sharing experiential narratives and debating interpretations are equally important. The TRC made significant contributions in these areas as well and has spurred a national debate outside its halls.

The IJR data show that South Africans generally agree that truth-telling was what the TRC did best. "The task on which the TRC is most charitably rated is that of helping the families of the victims to find out what happened to their loved ones—uncovering the truth about the past. A majority of South Africans of every race agrees that the TRC has done a very good job on this function."[2] Such a consensus could not be found on any other aspect of the TRC's work. A positive view of truth-telling is one of the very few attitudes concerning the TRC shared among all of South Africa's racial groups. Given earlier surveys that reported that many South Africans believed that the TRC had generated resentment and caused a deterioration of race relations,[3] it is significant that the IJR study shows that citizens of all races supported the revealing of information about the past.

There is certainly no such consensus about the amnesty process. The majority of people surveyed by the IJR felt that the granting of amnesty was unfair to those who died during the apartheid struggle, to other victims, and to South Africans in general. This was true for Africans, whites, mixed-race persons, and Asians. Despite this, the majority of *Africans* approved the giving of amnesty.[4] This approval seems to result from a view that an amnesty was a necessary evil of the negotiated end to hostilities.

Most serious commentators agree that an amnesty was necessary to avoid civil war in South Africa.[5] Assuming that they are correct, it must be said that the designers and facilitators of the TRC's amnesty process wrestled some real benefits out of a political arrangement demanded by the military and the outgoing regime. The greatest benefit was the contribution to truth-telling. Many of the facts regarding policies and activities of the security forces, for example, were uncovered only when members or former members applied for amnesty. This is true to a lesser extent of liberation organizations with armed wings. More was known previously about their activities. Another benefit of the amnesty process arose from the accountability that applicants had to accept, even if this was a soft form.

While celebrating these benefits, we have to be clear about the fact that the amnesty process had very real limitations. Anyone who thought that it would serve as a watershed that would put issues of prosecution and punishment for political crimes behind the nation will be sorely disappointed. Most of the senior members of the apartheid security apparatus refused to apply or cooperate. Many of the senior ANC members who did apply surrendered only sparse information in their applications. Many of the operatives who committed acts of gross violence were reticent about naming their superiors. Now that the commission has ended, the ANC government is faced again with the choice of holding criminal trials. It is contemplating a blanket amnesty for generals of the SADF and senior ANC officials, a move that would generate much cynicism.[6] The debate over retribution for political crimes will likely get hotter in the near future.

I have already mentioned a number of times that the reparations component of the TRC has been a strong disappointment. Primary fault does not lie with TRC officials, except to the extent that the dispersal of urgent interim reparations became mired in inefficiency. Even here, it is not clear where the blame lies. In terms of the larger reparations process, the unwillingness to grant the commission the powers and resources necessary to implement a full reparations program and the hesitance of the ANC government to implement the measures recommended by the Committee on Reparations and Rehabilitation appear to be the main causes of its being a failure to date.

Another failure relates to the fact that organizations like businesses and churches have not been drawn into the reparations process. Corporations claim that they are already making contributions through social investments, but many businesses do little or nothing in this area. The IJR study shows that Africans and whites hold very different viewpoints on this issue. Africans are strongly united in the view that large businesses, the Afrikaans churches, white South Africans, individual companies profiting from apartheid, South African farmers, and the perpetrators themselves should all be forced to pay compensation. It is not surprising that only 10 percent of whites feel that they should be required to offer compensation, but it is remarkable that only one-third of them feel that businesses that directly benefited from apartheid should be forced to pay.[7]

The growing debate in the United States and elsewhere over reparations for African slavery has highlighted an issue relevant to this discussion. While some advocates of reparations for slavery call for cash payments to the descendants of slaves, it is becoming more common to hear suggestions that other, more communal forms of "restitution" would be better. It has been suggested, for example, that the United States could put together a resource package for the fight against AIDS in Africa as a form of compensation. Another idea is that resources be channeled into the education of African American children and the building up of civil society in the neighborhoods where they live.

In South Africa many kinds of community reparations have been recommended, but individual payments have been at the heart of the reparations program. While such payments are certainly deserved, I remain unconvinced that this is the best way to allot resources. It holds potential for dividing communities. All blacks in South Africa are victims of apartheid and economic apartheid. Perhaps it would be better to funnel scarce resources into programs that improve health care, education, and social conditions for all members of the majority population, and that build up civil society. The

Committee on Reparations and Rehabilitation seriously considered a service approach to reparations but rejected it because of administrative difficulties and a disparity of services available in regions of the country. Their logic is convincing. What they considered, however, was a service approach to compensation for *individuals*, not communities. They were forced to do this because the legislation that instituted the TRC had arranged for a reparations package to be offered to individual victims (and families) who were identified by the HRV investigations. Again, the clarity of hindsight seems to suggest that the reparations program originally built into the architecture of the TRC was flawed.

Perhaps the most important question we can ask about the TRC is whether it actually advanced political forgiveness between the races in South Africa. Opinion on this issue is far from homogenous. Among international commentators and observers, most seem to believe that the commission has laid important groundwork for a future society less marked by racial tensions. Many highlight the fact that the commission has forged a collective memory to which South Africans of all backgrounds can accede. The IJR study supports this view.

While there are differences of opinion about the validity of separate development as an idea, a clear majority of South Africans of all races agree that apartheid was a crime against humanity. They also agree that those who struggled for and against apartheid committed horrible abuses. There is less consensus about the extent to which whites were aware of apartheid abuses and whether these abuses are best blamed on individuals or institutions. Debate will continue about the causes of injustice and the proper allocation of accountability, but it will rest upon consensus that pervasive oppression existed and spawned terrible conflict. Even this level of agreement is a gift to a country that was so much at odds only a decade ago.

In their praise for the TRC, international observers also point to its opening of "democratic reciprocity" and "deliberative democracy,"[8] its application of soft but real forms of accountability, its healing value for individuals and society, and its importance for curbing cycles of vengeance, among other goods. In general, South African commentary on the TRC is more mixed.[9]

There are many in South Africa who praise the same aspects of the TRC that have received international commendation, but there are also many who argue that the TRC has not made the races more disposed toward rapprochement. Such criticism comes most often from white quarters. Are they correct in this view? A principal objective of the IJR study was to test the state of race relations. Its authors argue that it would be

> unfair to hold the truth and reconciliation process responsible for creating a reconciled, multi-racial South Africa. What colonialism, apartheid, and racism created over centuries cannot be erased through the activity of a government commission acting over the course of a tiny slice of time. Nonetheless, we would be remiss were we not to consider

the question of the degree to which South Africa has achieved some degree of racial reconciliation at the beginning of the 21st century.[10]

Their findings are mixed:

> How much racial reconciliation is there in contemporary South Africa? Our data are ambivalent on this matter. On the one hand, large majorities of South Africans of every race reject the view that the country would be better off if there were no people of other races in South Africa—an encouraging finding. At the other extreme, most South Africans find it difficult to understand people of the opposite race, and substantial minorities (sometimes majorities) subscribe to negative racial stereotypes. Thus, the evidence of reconciliation is mixed.
>
> One of the most interesting aspects of these data is the tendency among black South Africans to express more racially hostile attitudes than whites, Coloured people, and South Africans of Asian origin. Blacks hold negative views of whites in part due to their lack of interactions with white people, which we find is widespread. Black South Africans do not understand whites, they feel uncomfortable around them, do not trust what they say, and find it difficult to imagine ever being friends with a white person (and in fact few claim to have any white friends).[11]

The authors do not blame the TRC for African attitudes toward whites but rather attribute it to the isolation of most Africans from contact with whites—a dynamic that the TRC may actually have moderated in small measure. They also make the point that the current state of race relations must be put in perspective by imagining how respondents to their questionnaire might have answered their questions a decade ago. It is almost certain that figures indicating racial tension would have been much higher.[12]

Can the reduction of tensions assumed by the authors be attributed to the TRC in any measure? I think it can. Racial groups have less to fear from one another because of the TRC. The unmasking of the apartheid security apparatus during HRV and amnesty hearings freed blacks from having to worry about the perpetuation of hidden cadres waiting for the day when they could retake power. The choice of a truth commission over vengeful measures by the new black-led government assured whites that they would not be persecuted or dispossessed. The humbling of human rights violators from both sides of the conflict and the empathy shown to their victims by people of all races revealed to whites and blacks their mutual humanity and their common pain.

What about forgiveness? Did the TRC advance the surrender of resentment and other antipathies in such a way as to free South Africans for the building of interracial fellowship? It cannot be questioned that many instances of individual victims (or clusters of victims) forgiving their tormentors were facilitated by the commission. Added up, these small dramas amount to an advance in political forgiveness that will influence society as a whole. Perhaps even more important is the modeling offered by the victims involved in these dramas and by commission leaders like Archbishop Tutu. American biblical scholar Walter Wink asserts that victimized Christians are called to be ambassadors of forgiveness, not waiting for the oppressors to take the first step through confession but rather initiating the reconciliation process.[13] Tutu operated out of this understanding of forgiveness as he led the TRC. A number of victims followed his model in their testimony. By offering pardon to their oppressors, sometimes even before it had been asked for, they were *calling out* the humanity of perpetrators and apartheid supporters. The TRC can similarly be seen as an exercise that, through its forgiveness discourse, called out the decency, the empathy, and the moral courage of all South Africans who had become embittered by apartheid and the struggle to end it.

The life and work of the TRC was too controversial, too messy, and too marked by paradox for the enterprise to be called an unqualified success. In the wake of the apartheid struggle anyone who anticipated this from a truth commission would have been naive. Despite the political gamesmanship that tainted the commission and the public response to it, despite the rage that was inevitably voiced, and despite the Herculean task it was given when it was decided that the truth commission would also be a reconciliation commission, the TRC did not implode or cause the country to explode with vengeance—as some had feared. Instead, it cleared away a goodly amount of the psychic rubble left over from apartheid and the war of liberation, leaving the horizon clearer for South Africans to see a future marked by peace and justice. It also recovered some of this rubble to be recycled and used as building material for national reconstruction. Anger has become resolve. Despair has changed into empathy—at least in some measure. These are things to celebrate.

South Africa's baptism in tears was excruciating in many ways. Some of those present abandoned the ritual. But most stayed on and joined the Rainbow Nation whose birth was being announced to the world.

A FINAL WORD ABOUT THE MODEL

In the preceding chapters the explication of my model has been tightly interwoven with commentary on the TRC process. This was a natural way to illustrate the model, given that its character arises in no small measure out of lessons learned from the commission. That said, it should be made clear that my five-act drama is not meant to be restricted to cohesive initiatives like truth commissions. It is equally a model of an extended, less tightly coordinated process that a society might pass through over the course of years or decades. While I have largely focused on South African truth-telling, justice-building, and so on, as overseen by the TRC, the pursuit of these ends outside the parameters of the commission is equally relevant. Hence, the documentation of human rights violations by NGOs or other bodies functioning outside the bounds of the truth commission also belongs to act one of my drama—truth-telling; the prosecution of former defense minister Magnus Malan belongs to act three, and so on.

This being so, this model of political forgiveness does not apply only to post-conflict societies that are embarking upon large, well-coordinated initiatives like truth commissions or national reconciliation programs. It is appropriate for any nation that has experienced a period of civil war or gross persecution and which is moving out of this strife toward a more just and peaceful dispensation. This last point clarifies a limitation to the applicability of the model: it applies, at least in its fullness, only to societies that are *transitional*. By this I mean they have moved out of—or are in the process of moving out of—the period of fighting or oppression toward stability and greater justice. This does not mean that the model has no heuristic value for those studying nations that are still in the midst of open strife. Truth-telling, responsibility-claiming, justice-seeking, and healing are very relevant, and the model's treatment of these matters may be of use, but such societies are rarely ready for the pursuit of political *forgiveness*.

In the paragraphs below, to clarify further the suitability of the model to different situations and to try a couple of tentative applications to societies other than South Africa, I will discuss two contexts of rending. The first is one to which the model does not yet apply but for which it may have heuristic value: Palestine. The second context appears to be on the verge of readiness for the full pursuit of political forgiveness: Northern Ireland.

I should point out that I am writing these reflections in early 2003. In the coming months dynamics in these societies may change considerably. I should also point out that I have no expertise regarding the challenges that face Palestine or Ireland. My knowledge is based on general reading and media reports (with all their flaws). I have chosen to relate my model to these contexts because the general contours of the struggles are so well known that a certain level of reader familiarity can be assumed.

APPLYING THE MODEL TO THE ISRAELI-PALESTINIAN CONFLICT

Let us turn first to Palestine. This is a context very different from current South Africa. A form of apartheid is still being imposed on Palestinians by an occupying power. At the same time, the Palestinian Authority not only condones terrorist action against Israelis, but it also perpetrates horrible human rights violations against its own people. Palestinians suffer a form of double oppression. The situation is made extremely complex by religious militancy and the multifaceted role of "liberation" groups like Hamas, which serves as both a social-service agency and a terrorist organization with broad international links.

Had President Clinton been successful in late 1999 in his efforts to bring about a second Camp David accord; had a Palestinian State that included a sizable piece of Jerusalem been created; had the construction of Jewish settlements on the West Bank and elsewhere been rolled back; had Hamas and other Palestinian groups stopped killing Israeli civilians—then it might be time to begin talking about political forgiveness between Palestinians and Israelis. These did not happen, of course, and the recent warfare has pushed the horizon for discussion of forgiveness back by years if not decades. It does not make sense to pursue political forgiveness when Palestinians are subject to political and economic containment, not to mention military attacks on civilians, and Israelis daily fear for their lives.

Therefore, the application of a model like mine—one of deep reconciliation—to this context will have to be limited. The situation in Palestine is not transitional in the sense that I have been using this word. That said, I would affirm that elements of the model are quite relevant to the work of peacemaking while a nation is still undergoing extreme conflict. To illustrate the point, let us reflect on acts one and three of my drama of forgiveness.

First, act one. We can say that there has been a very large amount of truth-telling regarding the Palestinian-Israeli conflict. The nature and origins of the hostilities have been analyzed and debated incessantly in the Middle East and elsewhere. All this has not produced a durable peace, let alone the beginning of reconciliation. Does this mean that the work of truth-telling should be abandoned for the time being, perhaps until a working peace is achieved? There is some merit to this idea. The kind of truth-telling taking place at this point largely consists of Palestinians (and their sympathizers) crying out against Israeli oppression, and Israelis (and their supporters) protesting the terrorism to which they are subjected and pointing out how the Palestinian leadership is complicit. While there is much truth to what both camps are saying, neither is gaining much of an audience on the other side. Instead the two programs of complaint, and the violent actions they spawn, are sustaining mutually reinforcing fundamentalisms that preclude peace. Reeling in the fervent rhetoric would be a step in the right direction.

But I am still not prepared to surrender the view that appropriate forms of truth-telling are needed—indeed crucial—at this time. One thing required now is truth-telling by Israelis that is empathetic to the plight of Palestinians and truth-telling by Palestinians that is empathetic to the situation of Israelis, especially the former. While this is certainly not the time for a truth commission or similarly grand exercise, the creation of "islands of truth" by courageous members of each nation would be invaluable. Of course, small numbers of individuals have been trying to do just that on both sides of the disputed borders. The growing ranks of "refuseniks" serves as a prominent example, as do the efforts of Rabbis for Human Rights and other groups to publicize and eliminate human rights abuses by the Israeli army on the West Bank.[14] Such truth-telling will take courage, especially on the part of Palestinians. Those who publicly sympathize with the suffering of Jews or who call for their own country to turn away from terrorism are placing themselves in physical jeopardy. But physical bravery is not the only kind of valor needed; it takes unusual intellectual clarity and courage to be capable of empathy for one's "enemies" in a context like the Middle East, where citizens cannot avoid being immersed in fervent nationalist polemic.

Truth-telling by international observers is also crucial. One very important form is the documenting of human rights abuses and war crimes by international NGOs. It is essential, for example, that incursions by Israeli military forces into Palestinian territories be revealed for what they are: extremely high-impact interventions that annihilate physical infrastructure and countenance great numbers of civilian casualties. This too is terrorism. Attempts to pass off these incursions as surgical strikes against terrorist targets must be challenged, especially in the US media. The Middle East policy of the United States government is extremely important to the conflict. Therefore, so is American public opinion. Equally important is opinion in other Arab and Islamic countries. The growing lionization of suicide bombers in the Islamic world is truly disturbing and dangerous, and reinforces the urge to extreme vengefulness by Palestinians. Muslim clerics and other leaders who portray these measures as mad and "anti-Islamic" need to be celebrated for their form of truth-telling.

Equally relevant to the Israeli-Palestinian context is the task of justice-building. Perhaps what is needed most at this time is some retributive justice measures that will curb the increasingly ruinous cycle of vengeance. During much of 2002 we have watched it happen: A suicide bomber kills Israeli civilians; a few hours or days later the Israeli military strikes a target in the West Bank or Gaza, and a number of civilians die from "collateral damage"; then another young Palestinian willing to make the ultimate sacrifice is dispatched. By now it has become clear that the trainers and dispatchers of suicide bombers will not be prosecuted by the Palestinian Authority unless it is forced to do so. The Israeli officers who plan strikes against civilian targets will enjoy equal impunity, as will Israeli soldiers who beat or torture Palestinians and Mosad agents who carry out assassinations.

From where, then, will retributive justice come? It appears it will have to come from outside, if at all. Will the new International Criminal Court have the power and the will to try Israeli and Palestinian war criminals? Will action be launched in the courts of another nation—as was the case when General Pinochet of Chile was charged in Spain? A failed attempt has already been made to bring Ariel Sharon to justice in Belgium for his role in the Sabra and Shatila refugee camp massacres twenty years ago in Lebanon. As with the Pinochet case, the outcome of this legal action may have been disappointing, but the effort itself combines with momentum from the War Crimes Tribunal in The Hague and the creation of the International Criminal

Court. We can hope that there is a real historical drift toward the prosecution of crimes against humanity by legitimate international tribunals. Again, US policy is of central importance here. At present, it serves as the most significant barrier to such a drift.

What about restorative justice? Generally, restorative measures are taken after the commission of crimes has ended and they have been acknowledged. At present, the historical crime against the Palestinians is ongoing and "crimes against humanity" are being perpetrated by both sides. If a lasting peace is ever reached, that will be the time to discuss sweeping restorative measures like the return of land to Palestinians and compensation for social, infrastructural, and economic devastation. Despite this, I would argue that some restorative measures are appropriate today, especially those that carry powerful symbolic value. One such initiative is being undertaken by the Israeli Coalition for the Prevention of Home Demolitions, which is seeking to find "adopting families" for the thousands of Palestinians who currently have demolition orders on their homes. Jews and Palestinians in other parts of the world could also take measures. A joint effort to memorialize children and other innocent civilians lost in both nations would be a powerful sign.

To some extent the heuristic value of my model for contexts like Israel arises from the hope that they will someday be transitional. It can inform current decisions about truth-telling, justice-building, and so on with a view to a better time. Even for societies like Palestine, where peaceful and democratic coexistence would be a very great improvement over the current state of affairs—and should be the immediate goal that informs peace-building—political forgiveness still hovers on a far horizon. It may be many generations away, but peacemakers should not totally ignore that horizon. It can serve to orient closer horizons and therefore current efforts.

APPLYING THE MODEL TO NORTHERN IRELAND

Let us shift our attention to a context where that horizon is somewhat closer. It is difficult to know if we can rest assured that Northern Ireland is a transitional society. It has some good signs: a great reduction in the level of violence; the renewal of institutions of governance; the growth of "democratic reciprocity" and forums for "deliberative democracy";[15] the launching of reparations programs; reform of policing agencies; and so on. But there is a pervasive feeling that the achievements to date are very fragile and that there could be a descent back into "the troubles." As I write, Northern Ireland's Assembly is still suspended. There have been some recent acts of violence, including killings. The Irish government has indicated that it believes the IRA is still active, causing David Trimble and other leaders of Protestant unionist parties to walk out of talks designed to renew the peace process and reopen the Assembly. Also disturbing is the endurance of the marching culture. The large number of unemployed youths who are attracted to sectarian gangs and communal violence is an ongoing problem. The recent eruption of violence in Derry after a soccer match was a clear sign of lingering volatility.

Although the Good Friday Agreement—the historic agreement of 1998 that advanced the peace process and led to the establishment of the Northern Ireland Assembly—was a watershed event, it did not mark the movement from one era to another as clearly as the 1994 election in South Africa, for example. If an irreversible turn toward peace does take place, the importance of that development will likely become clear only through hindsight decades later. So it is only with a certain timidity that we can apply a model like mine to Northern Ireland. With that qualification, let us see how it relates.

Concerning act one, truth-telling, we can say that Northern Ireland does not have to overcome the same kind of systematic state disinformation and propaganda program that operated in South Africa. Also, since "the troubles" began in 1969, there has been a sizable amount of investigation into the nature and causes of the conflict by media organizations, international agencies, and even commissions of inquiry. This does not mean, however, that there is no need for an extensive process of truth-telling. Many things are still not known. With regard to the British government and its military forces, there needs to be revelation concerning the role of intelligence operatives, collusion with loyalist paramilitaries, mistreatment of IRA prisoners, and the culpability of soldiers and senior officers in incidents like Bloody Sunday. Clarification of similar questions concerning Ulster police forces is also needed. The participation of off-duty police officers in sectarian violence is an important issue. With regard to Catholic and Protestant paramilitaries, there are the issues of sources of funding, details about the planning and carrying out of bombings and assassinations, and connections to international terrorist organizations and spy networks.

Let us move to act two. The July 2002 statement in which the IRA made a sharp about-face, apologized for violence against "noncombatants," and offered condolences to the families of its civilian victims was met by some with scorn, but it was also heralded by commentators and politicians as "astonishing" and as an important building block. I am not really aware of how much apologizing has gone on in Northern Ireland, but it seems clear that more gestures like the one by the IRA could help. Given the sectarian nature of the conflict, the hard-line stance of clergymen like Ian Paisley, even the implication of some clerics in violent attacks, a joint or mutual apology from Roman Catholic and Protestant leaders would be a powerful act. At least equally significant would be an apology from British Prime Minister Tony Blair for his country's historical treatment of Ireland and abuses by British soldiers in Ulster.

The great value of acts like the IRA apology, besides their potential for inspiring the surrender of resentment and other retributive emotions, is that they display a willingness to claim responsibility. This inspires confidence that more responsible behavior is to follow and therefore hope of progress. In the late nineties Irish Prime Minister Bertie Ahern was calling for Tony Blair to apologize for the actions of British soldiers at the Bloody Sunday massacre in 1972. As far as I know, no apology was ever issued, but the Blair government launched an inquiry into the incident. The judicial inquiry has been extremely thorough and will still be hearing testimony in 2003. Even this measure, which shows a willingness to be proven guilty of a past transgression, is a significant step. It not only implies a disposition to accept responsibility, but it also opens the door to justice-building, our third act.

Since the violence began three and one-half decades ago, Northern Ireland has not gone without retributive justice. Hundreds of IRA and loyalist paramilitary operatives have been convicted of their violent crimes and sent to jail. These punishments seemed to do little to curb vengeance, however. This may be attributable in part to nationalist perceptions that the Ulster police and the British government did not have legitimate authority. Protestant loyalists may have felt the need to act violently because the jailing of IRA agents was having little deterrent effect. In the nineties it was not the expansion of punitive measures but rather the success of peace negotiations that seemed to curb the cycles of vengeance.

This does not mean that the expansion of retributive justice would have no value today. In fact, if a government and a police force broadly seen as legitimate by both Protestants and Catholics can be established, and if it can inspire confidence in its ability to bring to justice those who continue to commit sectarian violence, this should not only deter revenge-taking but should also advance the kind of stability required for socioeconomic recovery. On the other hand, a case can be made for a certain suspension of punitive justice. The willingness of the British government to lessen the sentences of IRA prisoners and to provide amnesty for "on-the-runs" seems to have boosted the peace process and softened the IRA position. Would a turn away from punishment for those who committed crimes before the 1998 accord and a vigorous pursuit of those committing human rights violations since then meet the antithetical needs? Would some kind of creative compromise like the amnesty provisions in South Africa fit the bill?

Perhaps *restorative* justice could be advanced if those who admit to human rights violations or other offenses can be engaged in restitutive measures. This is tricky business, and trite forms of community service for offenders would only inspire contempt, but imagine the symbolic and integrative value of having former enemy combatants work side by side in service to the larger community. Protestants and Catholics are already working together on a number of initiatives, like the Mediation Network for Northern Ireland, and the joint educational programs of the Irish Council of Churches (Protestant) and the Irish Commission for Justice and Peace (Roman Catholic). Former militants could perchance be drawn into these ventures.

Ambitious reconstruction programs have been launched. In 1995, in cooperation with the relevant member states, the European Union began its Special Support Programme for Peace and Reconciliation. It had two strategic objectives: "(i) promote the social inclusion of those who are at the margins of social and economic life; (ii) exploit the opportunities and address the needs arising from the peace process in order to boost economic growth and advance social and economic regeneration."[16] This program ran until 1999 and focused on the following areas: employment, urban and rural regeneration, cross border development, social inclusion, and productive investment/industrial development. When its time-line ended, this program was replaced with a similar one called the EU Programme for Peace and Reconciliation in Northern Ireland and the Border Counties of Ireland 2000-2004 (Peace II). The budget for this initiative is 531 million euros, which amounts to more than the three billion Rand needed for the TRC reparations program.[17]

While this is not a reparations program for individuals and families, like the TRC plan, it can certainly be seen as a venture in restorative justice. It can also be seen as an attempt at national healing. It serves as a bridge from act three to act four of my model.

Besides dealing with reparations, the discussion of national mending (act four) in Chapter 8 focused on the healing of the trauma suffered by individuals, communities, and society as a whole. These two things go together; ideally, they should be intimately linked. For individuals and communities to move beyond trauma, they need to feel safe and to have solid relationships. Without economic improvement that reduces underemployment and poverty, a community will suffer from too many social ills and will be too prone to violence for a sense of safety to become pervasive. On the other side of the coin, the lingering effects of trauma, which in families and communities can be multi-generational, generate too much dysfunction and instability for real socioeconomic recovery to take hold.

I do not have nearly enough "on the ground" knowledge of Northern Ireland to know if the integration of therapeutic measures with economic reconstruction efforts is taking place, but my experience in other contexts makes me think it is unlikely. The EU programs mentioned above have a "life skills" component, but this does not appear to be therapeutic. It seems that the dominant paradigm for reconstruction programs around the world today is overly focused on economic development. The greatest priorities are to generate investment and integration into the world economy and to give the citizenry the necessary skills to make the country "competitive." This is all well and good; economic improvement will moderate noxious social ills (unless it generates more inequality), but economics are only one dimension of life. Despite the promises inherent in the mythology that is spreading with global capitalism, marketplace success cannot heal all our wounds.

There is one aspect to the dominant reconstruction paradigm that is quite helpful, however, and it can serve as a corrective for my model. Governments and international agencies like the World Bank and the International Monetary Fund (IMF) are coming to recognize the value of civic capacity and social capital. While these terms can be troublesome (*social capital,* for example, implies the reduction of broad human talents and capacities to something that can be managed and exchanged like money), the growing currency of these notions indicates a recognition of the need to strengthen and integrate community and a wide range of social institutions. In contexts like Northern Ireland the goal is the generation of civic capacity and social capital that crosses sectarian boundaries and binds formerly alienated parties together in mutual appreciation and hearty cooperation.

Although it uses a different vocabulary to name it, the Northern Ireland peace movement has been aware of this goal for a long time. For thirty years groups involved in this movement have worked in schools and elsewhere to bring Catholic and Protestant children together and have sponsored inter-neighborhood and interdenominational projects. The Mediation Network, for example, seeks to build peace "from the bottom up," slowly, over time. It is critical of "event driven" initiatives launched from "above" by politicians, seeking rather to methodically form strategic relationships that cross the borders of conflict.[18]

The formation of such relationships is something that has not received enough attention in my model. It is implied in Chapter 8 during discussions of community healing and reparations, but its value could be stated more thoroughly; it could be a more integral part of act four. In Northern Ireland both the stability of peaceful coexistence and the potential for political forgiveness will depend upon a mending of the fabric of society that does not simply reweave old patterns. Only the emergence of a new design that brings Protestants and Catholics together in affinity and collaboration, into a certain level of communion, can make the cloth more durable and less prone to further tearing. Such a cloth will be both stronger and more beautiful.

Every time I turn my mind to a new context of rending, and I see the depth of hurt and the breadth of harm, I despair of the notion of political forgiveness. I wonder if I should settle for a four-act drama. This happened again when I began to look at Northern Ireland. I think, Perhaps those who say forgiveness talk is folly are right. How can deep reconciliation ever come to a place like this? I wonder again if peaceful coexistence is not the most that can be aspired to. But something in me rises and protests that this is not enough. It is not enough as the ultimate hope for a society. It is not enough as a vision to inspire new generations. It is not enough to orient the courageous work of peacemakers. This is easy for me to say, sitting at a long and safe distance from that troubled society, but a quick survey of Irish peace-making initiatives has reinforced my view. Perhaps for peace-building "from above"—for the work of politicians, jurists, and EU bureaucrats—it is enough. Perhaps they should limit their focus to economic reconstruction, civic capacity, and deliberative democracy. But for those who have been working at the grassroots, those like the Corrymeela Community—an intentional community of Protestants and Catholics that worships together and engages in a very impressive range of peacemaking activities—it is not enough. Work that requires that level of passion, commitment, and sacrifice needs a more profound vision.

This is a vision of a deep rapprochement that frees a people for a new journey. Now we are talking about political forgiveness. Only those deeply enmeshed in Northern Irish society can know the sources of inspiration for such a vision. It will take Irish equivalents of Desmond Tutu, Nelson Mandela, and Antjie Krog to rework narratives of identity, symbol systems, and theologies such that a new understanding of nationhood emerges and new visions plant seeds of forgiveness. (I have no doubt that they are there.) As in my discussion of South Africa, I balk at becoming prescriptive when I arrive at act five. The movement into the final act of the drama is a move onto more sacred ground.

What can be reflected upon is the arrangement of truth-telling, responsibility-claiming, justice-building, and healing initiatives such that the possibility of political forgiveness is strengthened. As outlined above, all of these kinds of initiatives are being carried out, but it seems to me that there is a certain danger in allowing each to follow its own historical path without some attempt at alignment. I am not arguing for a grand and coordinated venture like the TRC, but, given that such imperatives as truth-telling and justice-seeking can work in concert with each other or in opposition to each other, there is a strong argument for intervening with a view to concord.

For political forgiveness to be possible, large numbers of people will need to surrender both fear and resentment. This will require the broadening of truth-telling. As long as citizens feel that there are hidden paramilitary networks with weapons caches, they will continue to be afraid. The exposition of the membership of such networks and the revealing of who did or who planned what will go a long way to assuage fears. This was certainly the case in South Africa. Even better would be an owning up to covert activity or human rights violations by the members of these networks. Similar revelations about the role of Ulster police forces and the British army are also needed. At the same time, citizens need to see that new acts of violence will be punished and that the administration of justice will be evenhanded. Is punishment for past acts the necessary deterrent? As mentioned in Chapter 7, some commentators would say yes to this. They believe that criminal trials for past transgressions are the best way to combine the goals of truth-telling and retributive justice. My view is different. It seems to me that, as with South Africa, the trial option would lead to less rather than more revelation. It would also have the potential to derail the peace process. The former combatants also want to feel safe.

Blanket amnesty does not seem to be a very good option either. In March 2002 Tony Blair was floating an amnesty plan for IRA "on-the-runs." It met with strong opposition from Protestant politicians, including David Trimble. Others had pointed out that this was more of a travesty of justice than early release for IRA prisoners, because the prisoners had at least been convicted of crimes. The spending of even one night in jail is a "no" from society to what they did. Trimble was willing to compromise, however; he could accept the return of up to forty "on-the-runs," and their evasion of jail, as long as they were required to face some kind of judicial process.[19]

What kind of process would this be? If the returnees were to avoid jail, what would they face? The genius of the TRC process was that it turned an imposed amnesty into an opportunity to extend truth-telling and the imposition of accountability—even if in a soft form. Is there a similarly ingenious arrangement for the Irish situation? Could it be even better? Is there a way to trade the avoidance of jail for both truth-telling and a stronger form of accountability? Some kind of restitution perhaps?

Another real strength of the TRC process was that it did not rest with forensic truth-telling. It also gave both perpetrators and victims opportunities to share their stories and perspectives. It opened the door to empathy. It seems to me that a series of formal inquiries like the Bloody Sunday Inquiry and the Patten Commission on Policing, both of which seem to have performed their assigned tasks well, would not give sufficient opportunity for such sharing. For surrender of fear and resentment to happen, truth-telling forums that inspire empathy will be required. It will be necessary for Catholics to come to know the pain of Protestants and vice versa. Opportunities for soldiers, militia members, sectarian gang members, clergy, teachers, community leaders, and others to come together and accept responsibility for spreading rancor or for simply not doing enough to stop the hate would also be very valuable. In all likelihood these things are already happening at low-visibility, community-level forums. These kinds of encounters can be just as valuable as TRC-style hearings given great national visibility—if there are enough of them.

Besides opening participants to transformation and empathy, such encounters can also open them to deep wells of pain or rage. One of the shortcomings of the TRC process was that sufficient provisions for therapy were not put into place. If Northern Ireland does engage in deep and broad truth-telling, it is to be hoped that it will be more prepared. Even though it has not enjoyed the same economic boom as the Republic of Ireland, the resources available to it far outstrip those in South Africa.

Finally, I will repeat the points about the value of reparations programs that integrate the work of healing with the work of socioeconomic reconstruction and about the belief that such programs are of greatest value when they build civic capacity and social capital across the frontiers of conflict. These kinds of programs seem to hold the greatest potential for bringing people from alienated communities toward an understanding and appreciation of one another. Such knowledge is invaluable for the surrender of fear and resentment.

It remains to be seen if Northern Ireland will truly become a transitional society. We can hope that decommissioning will be extended, that the Assembly will reopen and firm up its ability to govern, and that the peace process will be replaced by reconstruction and reconciliation processes. If this happens, it would be wonderful to see Catholic and Protestant leaders coming together to integrate restorative and reconciliatory initiatives into a more cohesive framework. It would be even more wonderful if such cooperation freed people on both sides to turn toward forgiveness. In the meantime, I hope that this tentative interface between my model and my inexpert knowledge of Northern Ireland has had some heuristic value, both for understanding the challenges that confront that nation and for flushing out the contours of the model.

Afterword

In the fall of 2001, as I was finishing the doctoral dissertation that has been developed into the core of this book, I turned on the television and discovered that four airplanes had been hijacked in the United States and that two of them had crashed into the World Trade Center, one into the Pentagon, and one into the countryside of Pennsylvania, causing thousands of horrible, senseless deaths. In the months since those attacks international attention has shifted away from peacemaking and reconciliation toward "the war against terrorism." First there was the war in Afghanistan. Then there was the Iraq war, which bypassed the United Nations and was launched from very questionable grounds in terms of international law. And the war is being fought on many other fronts. Missiles are lobbed into Yemen—an execution without judicial process. Moneys are poured into Colombia, making its people fear the biggest bloodletting yet. The prime minister of Australia considers preemptive strikes in other countries. Officials from the American Department of Defense and State Department turn up the rhetorical heat on Syria. New terrorist attacks have occurred in Saudi Arabia and Morocco.

It seems that the West and the Islamic world are being dragged into a conflict of great historical proportions, even though most citizens on both sides do not want this. The potential rending of such a conflict is so great that the repair required afterward would make the reconciliation process in South Africa seem small and simple. But rapprochement will have to come, someday, between those who hold to the "American dream" and those who are willing to kill and to die to stay its advance. Or at least between their descendants.

Forgiveness will have to become a greater part of human reality if we are to be spared endless cycles of violence. More and more people are coming to hold this view. My model of political forgiveness is intended to be a contribution to the discourse being opened by these people. It is influenced, of course, by my own predilections and formation, but I would like to think that it is shaped even more by the lessons being taught to the world by South Africans. My hope is that it will be compared with models, theories, and ideas developed in other parts of the world, and that this exercise will clarify the challenges faced wherever people are trying to countermand the violence of history.

Because of recent events, I am afraid that the promise of reconciliation, only now capturing the world's attention, will be pushed from view as a taste

183

for war spreads. The history of South Africa teaches us that such setbacks are an all-too-real possibility. But it also teaches us that enemies tire of the fight and prophets of peace find their following. When they do, the imperative to forgive rises to consciousness.

Notes

I   INTRODUCTION

1. The terms used to designated racial groups in South Africa are somewhat ambiguous and in a state of evolution. I use the term *African* to refer to the majority population of South Africa whose ancestry belongs to the African continent. *Coloured* is a term commonly used in South Africa to designate people of mixed race. Like a growing number of South Africans, I prefer to say simply *mixed race*. *Indian* refers to people of East Indian descent. I use the term *black* to include members of all three of these groups.

2. The "people's courts" were established in black communities, often with leadership from members of the ANC or other anti-apartheid organizations, as an alternative to the "justice" meted out by the apartheid regime. Those who were believed to have cooperated with the security police were often brought before these tribunals. People accused of other offenses—rape, for example—were tried there as well.

3. Throughout the book I relate the experiences and opinions of a number of private individuals in South Africa. I interviewed almost all these people personally between January and May of 2000. Some of their names and biographical details have been changed to ensure confidentiality; one or two of the life stories presented are amalgams.

4. Donald W. Shriver Jr., *An Ethic for Enemies: Forgiveness in Politics* (New York: Oxford University Press, 1995), 3.

5. Hannah Arendt, *The Human Condition*, 2d ed., intro. Margaret Canovan (Chicago: The University of Chicago Press, 1958), 236-43.

6. Desmond Tutu, "Address to the First Gathering of the Truth and Reconciliation Commission," TRC website (December 16, 1995) <www.truth.org.za>.

7. Ibid.

8. "Transcript of Heidelberg Tavern Massacre Amnesty Hearing," TRC website (October 27-31, 1997) <www.truth.org.za>.

9. Most of the field research took place in South Africa between January and May of 2000. During that time more than fifty formal, taped (or recorded through note-taking) interviews took place with a sample of South Africans. Care was taken to make this sample representative in terms of sex, race, age, religion, political affiliation, and economic circumstance, but perfect representation was not achieved. Muslim women and practitioners of traditional African religion are under-represented, for example. Most of the interviews were in the Western Cape. Beside these extensive interviews, many shorter or less formal queries took place during breaks at TRC hearings, at NGO meetings, at the breakup of religious services, with university researchers, and so on. Observation of the hearings, meetings, and services themselves was also invaluable. This less formal process of data gathering took place in 1997

185

as well. All of the data gathering was determined by methods of qualitative research. The interviews themselves were "semi-structured" and designed to encourage the interviewees to generate as much narrative as possible.

10. Here my thinking has been strongly influenced by Nicholas Tavuchis's description of the process of apology and forgiveness (see Nicholas Tavuchis, *Mea Culpa: A Sociology of Apology and Reconciliation* [Stanford, Calif.: Stanford University Press, 1991]).

11. I will not explain here why I chose these two additions. The relevant chapters, as well as the theoretical discussion in the next chapter, should make those reasons clear.

2   THEORETICAL ISSUES

1. Jeffrie G. Murphy and Jean Hampton, *Forgiveness and Mercy* (Cambridge: Cambridge University Press, 1988).

2. Jeffrie G. Murphy, "Forgiveness and Resentment," in Murphy and Hampton, *Forgiveness and Mercy*.

3. See Joseph Butler, *Fifteen Sermons* (London, 1726), especially Sermon VIII, "Upon Resentment," and Sermon IX, "Upon Forgiveness of Injuries."

4. Murphy, "Forgiveness and Resentment," 24.

5. Jean Hampton, "Forgiveness, Resentment, and Hatred," in Murphy and Hampton, *Forgiveness and Mercy*, 36-37 (emphasis added).

6. Hampton, "Forgiveness, Resentment and Hatred," 42.

7. Evert L. Worthington Jr., "The Pyramid Model of Forgiveness: Some Interdisciplinary Speculations about Unforgiveness and the Promotion of Forgiveness," in *Dimensions of Forgiveness: Psychological Research and Theological Perspectives*, ed. Evert L. Worthington Jr. (Philadelphia: Templeton Foundation Press, 1998).

8. Another caution that needs to be made relates to survivors of mistreatment who suffer from traumatic stress disorders. Such victims often repress their strong feelings and dissociate emotional life and all its connections. For them a reconnection to strong emotion is a central challenge. Worthington's intervention would not only bypass this essential treatment step, but it might well reinforce or entrench dissociation in novel forms. Also, trauma therapists in South Africa warn that the healing process of trauma survivors is sometimes truncated by recourse to fantasies of forgiveness that do not constitute a real surrender of anger and grief but rather serve as a technique for avoiding them. See Chapter 8 for further discussion of these issues.

9. The model outlined by Worthington is not the only forgiveness intervention being tested and refined. Robert Enright and his colleagues are working on the "Process Model of Forgiveness." While this model resembles Worthington's in many ways, it appears to give more attention to moral and ethical dilemmas along the way and to offer more opportunities for the client to pause and evaluate whether or not further journeying toward the end goal of forgiveness is the most appropriate action (see Robert D. Enright and Catherine T. Coyle, "Researching the Process Model of Forgiveness within Psychological Interventions," in Worthington, *Dimensions of Forgiveness*).

10. Molly Andrews, "Forgiveness in Context," *Journal of Moral Education* 29 (2000): 75-86.

11. Hannah Arendt, *The Human Condition*, 2d ed., intro. Margaret Canovan (Chicago: The University of Chicago Press, 1958).

12. Miroslav Volf, *Exclusion and Embrace: A Theological Exploration of Identity, Otherness, and Reconciliation* (Nashville, Tenn.: Abingdon Press, 1996); Robert J. Schreiter, *Reconciliation: Mission and Ministry in a Changing Social Order* (Maryknoll, N.Y.: Orbis Books, 1992); L. Gregory Jones, *Embodying Forgiveness: A Theological Analysis* (Grand Rapids, Mich.: Eerdmans, 1995); Donald W. Shriver Jr., *An Ethic for Enemies: Forgiveness in Politics* (New York: Oxford University Press, 1995).

13. Martha Minow, *Between Vengeance and Forgiveness: Facing History after Genocide and Mass Violence* (Boston: Beacon Press, 1998).

14. Shriver, *An Ethic for Enemies*, 4.

15. Here Shriver and I do not agree. In my treatment forgiveness involves reconciliation, indeed "thick" reconciliation.

16. For a thorough discussion of this shift, see Nicholas Tavuchis, *Mea Culpa: A Sociology of Apology and Reconciliation* (Stanford, Calif.: Stanford University Press, 1991).

17. Shriver, *An Ethic for Enemies*, 91.

3   HISTORICAL OVERVIEW

1. For a very thorough academic history, see T. R. H. Davenport, *South Africa: A Modern History*, 4th ed. (Toronto and Buffalo: University of Toronto Press, 1991). Another fine work is Allister Sparks's *The Mind of South Africa: The Story of the Rise and Fall of Apartheid* (London: Arrow Books, 1997).

2. Davenport, *South Africa*, 3-7.

3. Ibid., 6-8.

4. Ibid., 8-9.

5. Trekboers were the first people of Dutch descent who broke away from the Cape Colony to explore and settle lands to the north. They play a prominent role in Afrikaner mythology.

6. Davenport, *South Africa*, 12-18.

7. Thomas Pakenham, *The Boer War* (New York: Avon Books, 1979), xix.

8. African Independent Churches combine elements of Christian belief and worship with elements of traditional African belief and practice (see Hennie Pretorius and Lizo Jafta, "'A Branch Springs Out': African Initiated Churches," in *Christianity in South Africa: A Political, Social, and Cultural History*, ed. Richard Elphick and Rodney Davenport (Berkeley and Los Angeles: University of California Press, 1997); see also Jim Kiernan, "The African Independent Churches," in *Living Faiths in South Africa*, ed. Martin Prozesky and John de Gruchy (Cape Town and Johannesburg: David Philip, 1995).

9. Davenport, *South Africa*, 335.

10. Ibid., 332-36.

11. Allister Sparks, *Tomorrow Is Another Country* (Sandton: Struik Book Distributors, 1994), 23-26.

12. South Africa had by the mid-1980s moved to a presidential form of governance. The UDF was an umbrella organization of anti-apartheid groups with close ties to the ANC.

13. The IFP is an organization made up almost entirely of Zulus. Before the 1994 election (as today) its constituency was located in Natal and the Zulu homelands (now KwaZulu-Natal). Its organization extended to other areas where Zulu workers had migrated, especially the mines near Johannesburg.

14. Davenport, *South Africa*, 356-60, 364-65.

15. The actions of some ANC/MK operatives or cells clearly contradicted this philosophy. According to Davenport, ANC violence passed through three phases between the late 1970s and the end of the 1980s. In the late 1970s it went through a period of establishing cells and setting up arms caches. This was followed by a period of attacks on infrastructural targets like oil refineries and power stations and on security-force targets. As this phase of operations progressed, the ANC became less careful to avoid civilian casualties. A car bomb outside Air Force Headquarters in Pretoria killed nineteen people and injured two hundred. By 1989 the ANC had reduced its sabotage operations and was focusing on mass action organized by movements like the UDF (ibid., 427-28). The ANC has also been criticized for its creation of paramilitary bands, called Self-Defence Units, in response to the ANC-IFP violence. The TRC has accused these units of contributing to the spiral of violence that engulfed South Africa during the early 1990s (see Anthony Sampson, *Mandela: The Authorised Biography* [London: HarperCollinsPublishers, 1999], 436-39).

16. Davenport, *South Africa*, 378.

17. Sparks, *Tomorrow Is Another Country*, 25; Davenport, *South Africa*, 376-77.

18. Davenport, *South Africa*, 418-21.

19. Sparks, *Tomorrow Is Another Country*, 7.

20. Ibid., 12-14.

21. Venda is one of the former homelands in South Africa's north near the border with Zimbabwe.

22. Kader Asmal, Louise Asmal, and Ronald Suresh Roberts, *Reconciliation through Truth: A Reckoning of Apartheid's Criminal Governance* (Cape Town and Johannesburg: David Philip Publishers, 1996), 2.

23. Danish Ministry of Foreign Affairs, "Strategy for Danish-South African Development Cooperation," 1995.

24. Julian May, ed., *Poverty and Inequality in South Africa: Meeting the Challenge* (Cape Town: David Philip Publishers, 2000), 133-39.

25. Jeremy Baskin and Vishwas Satgar, "South Africa's New LRA: A Critical Assessment and Challenges for Labour," *South African Labour Bulletin*, 19/5 (1995), 51.

26. "The Employment Equity Act" (1998), no. 55.

4   ACT ONE: TRUTH-TELLING

1. Kader Asmal, quoting Nobel laureate Derek Walcott.

2. Kader Asmal, Louise Asmal, and Ronald Suresh Roberts, *Reconciliation through Truth: A Reckoning of Apartheid's Criminal Governance* (Cape Town and Johannesburg: David Philip Publishers, 1996), 10.

3. Alex Boraine, *A Country Unmasked: Inside South Africa's Truth and Reconciliation Commission* (Oxford: Oxford University Press, 2000), 289-91.

4. Asmal, Asmal, and Roberts, *Reconciliation through Truth*, 9.

5. Ibid., 10.
6. Walter Wink, *When the Powers Fall: Reconciliation in the Healing of Nations* (Minneapolis, Minn.: Fortress Press, 1997), 53-54.
7. Priscilla B. Hayner, *Unspeakable Truths: Confronting State Terror and Atrocity* (New York and London: Routledge, 2001), 6.
8. Ibid., 185-95.
9. Ibid., 24-25.
10. Ibid., 61-62.
11. Ibid., 64-66.
12. Ibid., 38-40.
13. "Constitution of the Republic of South Africa" (1993), Act 200.
14. See Hayner, *Unspeakable Truths*, 60-64.
15. Johnny de Lange, "The Historical Context, Legal Origins, and Philosophical Foundation of the South African Truth and Reconciliation Commission" in *Looking Back, Reaching Forward: Reflections on the Truth and Reconciliation Commission of South Africa*, ed. Charles Villa-Vicencio and Wilhelm Verwoerd (Cape Town: University of Cape Town Press, 2000), 20.
16. For a thorough description and discussion of the consultation process, see Boraine, *A Country Unmasked*.
17. Dumisa Ntsebeza, "The Struggle for Human Rights: From the UN Declaration of Human Rights to the Present," in Villa-Vicencio and Verwoerd, *Looking Back, Reaching Forward*, 6.
18. Truth and Reconciliation Commission, *Final Report*, vol. 4, chap. 3.
19. Tutu's willingness to push for forgiveness may have been problematic. This issue will be discussed in Chapter 8.

5   ACT TWO: APOLOGY AND THE CLAIMING OF RESPONSIBILITY

1. "Transcript of National Party Recall, Political Party Hearings," TRC website (May 14 1997).
2. Russell Daye, "Forgiveness as a Political Process: Rending and Reconciliation in South Africa," *Journal of Religion and Culture* 12 (1998): 61-91.
3. Nicholas Tavuchis, *Mea Culpa: A Sociology of Apology and Reconciliation* (Stanford, Calif.: Stanford University Press, 1991).
4. Ibid., 7.
5. Ibid., 8, 12-14.
6. Some of the material in this section has been adapted from an earlier publication (see Russell Daye, "An Unresolved Drama: Canada's United Church Seeks Reconciliation with Native Peoples," *The Ecumenist* 36/2 [April-May 1999]).
7. UCC, "Brief to the Royal Commission on Aboriginal Peoples" (October 27, 1993), 4-5.
8. Stanley McKay and Janet Silman, "A First Nations Movement in a Canadian Church," in *The Reconciliation of Peoples: Challenge to the Churches*, ed. Gregory Baum and Harold Wells (Maryknoll, N.Y.: Orbis Books, 1997), 174.
9. Ibid., 175.
10. The national Native consultations identified a need for (and a dream of) Native self-government within the church. The organizational structure of the UCC moves from pastoral charge (parish), to presbytery, to conference (twelve conferences cover

the geography of Canada), to General Council. The move to self-government began with the formation of Keewatin Presbytery, an all-aboriginal presbytery in the Manitoba and Northwestern Ontario Conference. More presbyteries of this kind were formed in other areas, and in 1988 the ANCC became the UCC's thirteenth conference. Unlike the other twelve, its boundaries are not defined by geography. It has approximately thirty-five congregations from Quebec to Alberta. They come together annually at what is called the Grand Council. The Native congregations in the British Columbia Conference did not join the ANCC, but most of them come together as part of Prince Rupert Presbytery. While the ANCC is considered a conference within the national structure of the UCC, its functioning has many unique aspects. The ANCC operates through a consensus model of decision-making and honors both Christian and aboriginal spiritual traditions.

11. Ibid.; see also UCC, "Brief to the Royal Commission on Aboriginal Peoples."

12. The line of thought in this paragraph is mine, not that of Tavuchis.

13. Tavuchis, *Mea Culpa*, 19-23.

14. Ibid., 46, 71, 99-109.

15. Ibid., 109-15.

16. UCC, "Brief to the Royal Commission on Aboriginal Peoples," 7.

17. "A Question of Repentance," *United Church Observer* (October 1997).

18. UCC press release, October 27, 1998.

19. This encounter was televised by the South African Broadcasting Company during its nationally viewed evening news journal. It was shown in South Africa in the autumn of 2000. My account is based on my memory of the broadcast. Some of the details may be inaccurate, but the general contours of the encounter remain painfully clear.

20. "Transcript of Business Sector Hearing Transcripts," TRC website (November 13, 1997).

21. Ibid.

22. Ibid.

23. For more on the employment of violence by the ANC, see Chapter 3.

24. Kader Asmal, Louise Asmal, and Ronald Suresh Roberts, *Reconciliation through Truth: A Reckoning of Apartheid's Criminal Governance* (Cape Town and Johannesburg: David Philip Publishers, 1996), 28.

25. It is difficult to know just how high this proportion is. My impressions are based on my interviews and conversations during my visit, the voting patterns of white South Africans, and the vocal opposition from privileged citizens to affirmative action programs.

26. Register of Reconciliation, TRC website (December 11, 1997).

6   ACT THREE: BUILDING A TRANSITIONAL-JUSTICE FRAMEWORK

1. This episode was recounted to me by Mr. Bizos during an interview in Johannesburg in April 2000. He tells the same story in the epilogue to his book *No One to Blame? In Pursuit of Justice in South Africa* (Cape Town: David Philip Publishers, 1998).

2. It is easy to forget this restraint and concern for reconciliation in light of more recent developments. It must also be noted that Mugabe's forces were much more severe in their treatment of members of certain other black liberation movements.

One also wonders whether the current turmoil and oppression in Zimbabwe would be so bad if the country had undertaken strong truth-telling and transitional justice measures (like legitimate land reform) at the time of liberation.

3. Donald W. Shriver Jr., *An Ethic for Enemies: Forgiveness in Politics* (New York: Oxford University Press, 1995), 30-31.

4. Ibid., 31.

5. Ibid.

6. TRC, *Final Report*, vol. 1, chap. 1, paras. 21-23.

7. Elizabeth Kiss, "Moral Ambition within and beyond Political Constraints," in *Truth v. Justice: The Morality of Truth Commissions*, ed. Robert I. Rotberg and Dennis Thompson (Princeton, N.J.: Princeton University Press, 2000), 77.

8. See "Transcript of Political Party Hearings," TRC website (May 6, 1998).

9. TRC, *Final Report*, vol. 1, chap. 1, paras. 26-30.

10. Ibid., para. 29.

11. Kiss, "Moral Ambition within and beyond Political Constraints," 77.

12. TRC, *Final Report*, vol. 1, chap. 4, para. 23.

13. "National Promotion of Unity and Reconciliation Act of 1995," Section 1(1)(x), quoted in Charles Villa-Vicencio and Wilhelm Verwoerd, "Constructing a Report: Writing up the 'Truth,'" in Rotberg and Thompson, *Truth v. Justice*, 292 n. 7.

14. Ibid.

15. Ibid., emphasis added.

16. These principles come from Carl Norgaard, a president of the European Human Rights Commission.

17. Richard Lyster, "Amnesty: The Burden of Victims," in *Looking Back, Reaching Forward: Reflections on the Truth and Reconciliation Commission of South Africa*, ed. Charles Villa-Vicencio and Wilhelm Verwoerd (Cape Town: University of Cape Town Press, 2000), 186-87.

18. Antjie Krog, *Country of My Skull: Guilt, Sorrow, and the Limits of Forgiveness in the New South Africa* (Toronto: Random House, 1998), 154.

19. Ibid., 159.

20. Hugh Corder, "The Law and Struggle: The Same But Different," in Villa-Vicencio and Verwoerd, *Looking Back, Reaching Forward*, 101-2.

21. Mary Burton, "Making Moral Judgements," in Villa-Vicencio and Verwoerd, *Looking Back, Reaching Forward*, 77-78.

22. "Amnesty Plan for SADF Generals," News 24 website (June 10, 2001).

23. "Pardoned Prisoners' Names Released," South African Broadcasting Company website (May 19, 2002).

24. See "Transcript of Amnesty Hearing for Brian Mitchell," TRC website; see also "Mitchell's Application for Amnesty Accepted," *South African Press Association* (October 16, 1996); "PAC Condemns Mitchell's Release," *South African Press Association* (December 11, 1996); "SAPOHR Welcomes Mitchell's Release, Victims' Families Bitter," *South African Press Association* (December 11, 1996); and "Brian Mitchell to Meet Trust Feed Community," *South African Press Association* (April 23, 1997).

25. In this vignette I follow the account of Krog, *Country of My Skull*, 92-97. All quotes come from these pages.

26. I am aware of no statistics that indicate the percentage of successful and unsuccessful applications among those that were given a public hearing. From perusing the decisions of the Committee on Amnesty, my impression is that a higher

percentage of them were successful than applications that were not given a hearing.

27. Ronald C. Slye, "Amnesty, Truth, and Reconciliation: Reflections on the South African Amnesty Process," in Rotberg and Thompson, *Truth v. Justice*, 172-73.

28. Ibid., 173.

29. Ibid., 174-75.

30. Ibid., 177-78.

31. The CCB was one of the front agencies for the South African security forces that were designed to combat anti-apartheid groups. It purported to be a liaison group between government and business but actually employed former policemen and other agents. In their service to the CCB, these agents plotted and carried out assassinations of anti-apartheid activists and other human rights violations, including bombing a day-care center.

32. "Where Have All the Bastards Gone?" *Weekly Mail and Guardian* (June 15, 2000).

33. There were, of course, amnesty hearings in which the perpetrators were black and the victims white. While there certainly were expressions of sympathy for victims, I would argue that the perpetrators did not lose face in the same way as white offenders because their actions, albeit sometimes extreme or unwarranted, were carried out in service to a just cause: the end of apartheid.

34. Yazir Henry's story and perspective on the reconciliation process are recounted in Chapter 4. At nineteen years of age, when he was an ANC operative, he was captured and tortured and threatened until he revealed the location of another operative. He was then forced to witness his comrade's murder.

35. Yazir Henry, "Where Healing Begins," in Villa-Vicencio and Verwoerd, *Looking Back, Reaching Forward*, 170.

36. Ibid., 171.

37. Ibid.

7   ACT THREE: BUILDING A TRANSITIONAL-JUSTICE FRAMEWORK

1. By the term *transitional justice,* I mean a form of justice particular to contexts that are moving from civil war or large-scale oppression to stability and a more democratic form of governance. It is an inclusive term, which incorporates imperatives normally associated with retributive, restorative, distributive, and other forms of justice. By *transitional democracy* I mean new and democratic arrangements of governance that have been established in the wake of war or large-scale oppression.

2. Jeffrie G. Murphy (among others) asserts that resentment is a response to injuries that carry a message from an offender that he or she is more important than the victim. The resentment, then, is an internal counter-claim, an assertion of one's self-respect (see Jeffrie G. Murphy, "Forgiveness and Resentment," in Jeffrie G. Murphy and Jean Hampton, *Forgiveness and Mercy* [Cambridge: Cambridge University Press, 1988], 14-34).

3. For a fascinating and evocative discussion of vengeance, including a thorough survey of its literary treatment, see Susan Jacoby, *Wild Justice: The Evolution of Revenge* (New York: Harper & Row, 1983).

4. Ibid., 5.

5. I agree with Jacoby's assertions that retributive desires should be seen as legitimate, and that it is the rightful role of the state (in a just configuration) to satisfy these

desires. I also agree that there is an association between the acceptance of retributive motivations and the ability to harness them in a legitimate judicial system. I would add, however, that both private vengeance *and* state legal systems are sometimes employed to protect a social disequilibrium or, to phrase it differently, an immoral equilibrium. Apartheid South Africa provides a clear example of this. When blacks, through either individual action or organized political resistance, asserted rights that were illegitimately denied them, they were regularly retaliated against through private revenge-taking and/or state-administered punishment. In both cases the supporters of apartheid who "punished" them were acting to protect or to reestablish a social equilibrium that provided great privileges to the few at an enormous cost to the many.

6. Ibid., 12-13.

7. Background information on the CCB for this vignette was gleaned from Jacques Pauw, *Into the Heart of Darkness: Confessions of Apartheid's Assassins* (Johannesburg: Jonathan Ball Publishers, 1997).

8. See the beginning of Chapter 6 for a description of Bizos.

9. Jean Hampton, "The Retributive Idea," in Murphy and Hampton, *Forgiveness and Mercy,* 117; see also J. L. Mackie, "Morality and the Retributive Emotions," *Criminal Justice Ethics* (1982), 3-9.

10. Hampton, and her partner in dialogue, Jeffrie G. Murphy, were contributors to our theoretical discussion on forgiveness in Chapter 2 (see the section "Interpersonal Forgiveness").

11. Hampton, "The Retributive Idea," 117-18.

12. Ibid., 123.

13. Murphy, "Forgiveness and Resentment."

14. Hampton does not fully accept Murphy's theory of resentment, but she accepts the parts I describe in this paragraph.

15. Hampton, "The Retributive Idea," 122-25.

16. Ironically, these are often the very same ends championed by supporters of retributive justice. This shows that the restoration *vs.* retaliation debate is partially a false one.

17. Alex Boraine, cited in Dumisa B. Ntsebeza, "The Uses of Truth Commissions: Lessons for the World," in *Truth v. Justice: The Morality of Truth Commissions,* ed. Robert I. Rotberg and Dennis Thompson (Princeton, N.J.: Princeton University Press, 2000), 164-65.

18. Amnesty International, "Policy Statement on Impunity," in *Transitional Justice: How Emerging Democracies Reckon with Former Regimes,* 3 vols., ed. Neil J. Kritz (Washington, D.C.: United States Institute of Peace Press, 1995), 1:290-91.

19. Elizabeth Kiss, "Moral Ambition Within and Beyond Political Constraints: Reflections on Restorative Justice," in Rotberg and Thompson, *Truth v. Justice,* 79.

20. Jennifer J. Llewellyn and Robert Howse, "Institutions for Restorative Justice: The South African Truth and Reconciliation Commission," *University of Toronto Law Journal* 49/3 (1999). Available online at the University of Toronto Press Journals Division website.

21. Ibid.

22. I interviewed Rashied Omar in early 2000 in Claremont, Cape Town. Quotes come from this interview.

23. José Zalaquett, "Confronting Human Rights Violations Committed by Former Governments: Principles Applicable and Political Constraints," in Kritz, *Transitional Justice,* 1:3-31.

24. Ibid., 1:10-11.

25. Paul van Zyl, "Justice without Punishment: Guaranteeing Human Rights in Transitional Societies," in *Looking Back, Reaching Forward: Reflections on the Truth and Reconciliation Commission of South Africa*, ed. Charles Villa-Vicencio and Wilhelm Verwoerd (Cape Town: University of Cape Town Press, 2000).

26. Ibid., 49.

27. Eric Harper, a therapist at The Trauma Centre for Survivors of Violence and Torture in Cape Town, whom I interviewed in early 2000, believes that a significant proportion of family and community violence in black communities arises from rage that has political violence and oppression as its source. He is not unique in this belief. A number of other interviewees made similar assertions (see Chapter 8).

28. Kiss, "Moral Ambition within and beyond Political Constraints," 71.

29. Amy Gutmann and Dennis Thompson, "The Moral Foundations of Truth Commissions," in Rotberg and Thompson, *Truth v. Justice*, 35-36.

30. See Chapter 8 for a discussion of inequality, the need for socioeconomic reconstruction, and the work of the TRC's Committee on Reparations and Rehabilitation.

31. Ibid., 36.

32. An Amnesty International document entitled "Preserving the Gains for Human Rights in the 'War Against Crime': Memorandum to the South African Government and South African Law Commission on the Draft Anti-Terrorism Bill, 2000" provides an interesting discussion of this situation and the government response (Amnesty International website [December 6, 2000]).

33. See Chapter 8 for a discussion of this link.

34. Juan J. Linz, "The Breakdown of Democratic Regimes: Crisis, Breakdown, and Reequilibration," in Kritz, *Transitional Justice*, 1:125.

35. See Desmond Tutu, *No Future without Forgiveness* (London: Rider, 1999), 55-57, especially the quote from Judge Mahomed.

36. This spectrum is outlined and discussed in the opening section of Chapter 6; see also Donald W. Shriver Jr., *An Ethic for Enemies: Forgiveness in Politics* (New York: Oxford University Press, 1995), 30-31.

8   ACT FOUR: FINDING WAYS TO HEAL

1. "HRV Transcript, Hiedeveld," TRC website (April 22-25, 1996), This last statement by Baba Sikwepere may be the most repeated piece of testimony from all of the TRC hearings. It has become a part of public memory and has been reproduced in a number of articles and books, including Antjie Krog, *Country of My Skull: Guilt, Sorrow, and the Limits of Forgiveness in the New South Africa* (Toronto: Random House, 1998) and Desmond Tutu, *No Future without Forgiveness* (London: Rider, 1999).

2. Judith Herman, *Trauma and Recovery* (New York: Basic Books, 1992).

3. Ibid., 33.

4. Ibid., 34.

5. Ibid., 3-4.

6. Ibid., 37-50.

7. Ibid., 37-38.

8. Ibid., 1.

9. Ibid., 75-76.

10. Herman, *Trauma and Recovery*, 77.

11. American soldiers in Vietnam who committed or witnessed atrocities were much more likely than other soldiers to suffer post-traumatic stress disorder (see Herman, *Trauma and Recovery*, 54).

12. For a discussion of national trauma, individual trauma caused by political events and circumstances, and the interconnectedness of the two, see David Becker et al., "Therapy with Victims of Political Repression in Chile: The Challenge of Social Reparation," in *Transitional Justice: How Emerging Democracies Reckon with Former Regimes*, 3 vols., ed. Neil J. Kritz (Washington, D.C.: United States Institute of Peace Press, 1995), 1:583-91.

13. Harper was interviewed at the Trauma Centre in early 2000.

14. Herman, *Trauma and Recovery*, 133.

15. Ibid.

16. Ibid., 134.

17. Ibid., 135. Becker et al. also make this point strongly (see "Therapy with Victims of Political Repression in Chile," 587).

18. Herman reports that some survivors of traumatic injuries undertake a mission to aid sufferers of similar injuries or to transform the social conditions that produce or permit those violations. Often for these survivors, the mission becomes an integral part of the healing process. It is her observation that these survivors are often among those who have the most successful recoveries (Herman, *Trauma and Recovery*, 73).

19. Not everyone agrees with this perspective. For an interesting exchange on this topic, see the comments of Tina Rosenberg, Lawrence Weschler, and Brinton Lykes in *Truth Commissions: A Comparative Assessment—An Interdisciplinary Discussion Held at Harvard Law School in May 1996* (Harvard Law School Human Rights Program, 1997), 26-27.

20. "Like any abstract concept, these stages of recovery are a convenient fiction, not to be taken too literally. They are an attempt to impose simplicity and order upon a process that is inherently turbulent and complex" (Herman, *Trauma and Recovery*, 155).

21. Ibid., 155-74.

22. Ibid., 175-95.

23. Ibid., 155.

24. This can be said with confidence about the survivors who testified at hearings. The majority of survivors who made victim statements, however, made them in a one-on-one interview with a TRC staff person. It is more difficult to know what happened during these sessions, but, based on limited anecdotal evidence, my impression is that TRC interviewers were, with exceptions, generally sympathetic and supportive.

25. Rosenberg et al., *Truth Commissions*, 26.

26. Ibid.

27. Herman, *Trauma and Recovery*, 181-83.

28. The APLA, an armed organization affiliated with the PAC, appeared to use violence against whites to strengthen its tenuous position in negotiations between the government and the liberation organizations.

29. Priscilla B. Hayner, *Unspeakable Truths: Confronting State Terror and Atrocity* (New York and London: Routledge, 2001), 170-71; see also the TRC *Final Report*, vol. 5, chap. 5, para. 11-18.

30. Hayner, *Unspeakable Truths*, 170-71.

31. Martha Minow, *Between Vengeance and Forgiveness: Facing History after Genocide and Mass Violence* (Boston: Beacon Press, 1998), 93.

32. TRC, *Final Report*, vol. 5, chap. 5, para. 3.

33. TRC press statement, "Policy Framework for Urgent Interim Reparation Measures," TRC website (November 11, 1996).

34. TRC press statement, "Introductory Notes to the Presentation of the Truth and Reconciliation Commission's Proposed Reparation and Rehabilitation Policies," TRC website (October 23, 1997).

35. Ibid.; see also TRC, *Final Report*, vol. 5, chap. 5.

36. "Apartheid Victims 'Not Happy' with TRC," *The Cape Times* (April 16, 2003).

37. TRC press statement, "TRC Statement on Justice Budget Vote Yesterday," TRC website (June 7, 2000); "TRC Needs R3bn For Reparations," *Mail and Guardian* (March 16, 2001); "TRC Closure Ends Saga of Atrocity," *The Star* (May 30, 2001); "TRC Reparations Report Due Soon," *South African Press Association* (June 6, 2001); "Apartheid Victims' Group Files Suit Against Tutu," South African Broadcasting Company website (June 27, 2002); "Mbeki to Approve Apartheid Reparations," South African Broadcasting Company website (August 16, 2002).

38. "TRC Needs R3bn," *Mail and Guardian* (March 16, 2001).

39. For a discussion of this dispute, see Chapter 7, the section entitled "The Implementation of Measures to Ensure Accountability."

40. Wendy Orr, "Reparation Delayed Is Healing Retarded," in *Looking Back, Reaching Forward: Reflections on the Truth and Reconciliation Commission of South Africa*, ed. Charles Villa-Vicencio and Wilhelm Verwoerd (Cape Town: University of Cape Town Press, 2000), 244. Orr was a TRC commissioner assigned to the Committee on Reparations and Rehabilitation.

9   ACT FIVE: EMBRACING FORGIVENESS

1. See Wilhelm Verwoerd, *My Winds of Change* (Randburg: Ravan Press, 1997). I interviewed Dr. Verwoerd in February 2000.

2. Rajeev Bhargava, "Restoring Decency to Barbaric Societies," in *Truth v. Justice: The Morality of Truth Commissions*, ed. Robert I. Rotberg and Dennis Thompson (Princeton, N.J.: Princeton University Press, 2000), 61.

3. Miroslav Volf, *Exclusion and Embrace: A Theological Exploration of Identity, Otherness, and Reconciliation* (Nashville, Tenn.: Abingdon Press, 1996).

4. African Initiated Churches combine elements of Christian belief and worship with elements of traditional African belief and practice (see Hennie Pretorius and Lizo Jafta, "'A Branch Springs Out': African Initiated Churches," in *Christianity in South Africa: A Political, Social, and Cultural History*, ed. Richard Elphick and Rodney Davenport [Berkeley and Los Angeles: University of California Press, 1997]; see also Jim Kiernan, "The African Independent Churches," in *Living Faiths in South Africa*, ed. Martin Prozesky and John de Gruchy [Cape Town and Johannesburg: David Philip, 1995]).

5. There are some powerful counter-examples to this refusal. I met a number of whites who were involved in deep soul searching and were calling on their fellows to do so collectively. Antjie Krog's *Country of My Skull: Guilt, Sorrow, and the Limits of Forgiveness in the New South Africa* (Toronto: Random House, 1998)

and Rian Malan's *My Traitor's Heart: A South African Exile Returns to Face His Country, His Tribe, and His Conscience* (New York: Vintage International, 1990) are prominent literary examples of such soul searching, both by Afrikaners. Wilhelm Verwoerd's journey, which I portrayed at the beginning of this chapter, is another prominent example.

6. Volf, *Exclusion and Embrace*, 17.

7. Ibid., 58-64.

8. Ibid., 64-68.

9. Ibid., 72-78, 35-37.

10. Ibid., 113-19.

11. Volf's portrayal of forgiveness is somewhat different from mine. For him, forgiveness heals the wounds that acts of exclusion have inflicted, but it leaves a space of neutrality between people. It leaves the choice of going separate ways or falling into embrace. In my treatment, forgiveness goes further; it includes the level of reconciliation that Volf describes as "embrace."

12. Volf, *Exclusion and Embrace*, 119-25.

13. Ibid., 125-31.

14. Ibid., 131-40.

15. Ibid., 140-44.

16. There were some prominent counter-examples, the writing and political activity of Alan Paton, author of *Cry, the Beloved Country*, being one.

17. Michael Battle, "A Theology of Community: The Ubuntu Theology of Desmond Tutu," *Interpretation* 54/2 (2000), 177.

18. Included within this group are the Zulu-Xhosa-Swazi, the Sotho-Tswana, the Venda, the Shona, and others (Jim Kiernan, "African Traditional Religions in South Africa," in Prozesky and de Gruchy, *Living Faiths in South Africa*, 19).

19. Michael Battle, *Reconciliation: The Ubuntu Theology of Desmond Tutu* (Cleveland, Ohio: Pilgrim Press, 1997), 39.

20. Ibid.

21. Desmond Tutu, *No Future without Forgiveness* (London: Rider, 1999), 34-35.

22. Battle, *Reconciliation*, 40.

23. Ibid.

24. Ibid., 40-42.

25. Desmond Tutu, "Response at Graduation of Columbia University's Honorary Doctorate," address (August 2, 1982). Quoted in Battle, *Reconciliation*, 43-44.

26. Ibid., 43-45.

27. Ibid., 45-47.

28. Desmond Tutu, "Where Is Now Thy God?," address at Trinity Institute, New York (1989). Quoted in Battle, *Reconciliation*, 47.

29. Tutu, *No Future without Forgiveness*, 213.

10   CONCLUSION

1. James L. Gibson and Helen Macdonald, "Truth—Yes, Reconciliation—Maybe: South Africans Judge the Truth and Reconciliation Process," research report, Institute for Justice and Reconciliation (Rondebosch: IJR, 2001). Available online at the IJR website.

2. Ibid., 7.

3. An A. C. Nielsen-Market Research Africa survey garnered much attention (see Robert I. Rotberg, "Truth Commissions and the Provision of Truth, Justice, and Reconciliation," in *Truth v. Justice: The Morality of Truth Commissions*, ed. Robert I. Rotberg and Dennis Thompson [Princeton, N.J.: Princeton University Press, 2000], 19).

4. Gibson and Macdonald, "Truth—Yes, Reconciliation—Maybe," 7-9.

5. Ibid., 6.

6. It is ironic that joint amnesty is being contemplated considering the consternation on the part of ANC leaders over the fact that the TRC did not more clearly distinguish between violence committed in defense of apartheid and violence committed in an attempt to end it.

7. Gibson and Macdonald, "Truth—Yes, Reconciliation—Maybe," 10.

8. See my discussion of the work of Gutmann and Thompson in Chapter 7.

9. I do not want to give the impression that international commentary regarding the TRC is unanimous in its praise. It also has its critics.

10. Gibson and Macdonald, "Truth—Yes, Reconciliation—Maybe," 15.

11. Ibid., 18. Note that the authors of the study do not use the same terms as I do to denote race. Their use of "black" equates with my use of "African," and their use of "Coloured" equates with my use of "mixed race."

12. Ibid., 18-19.

13. Walter Wink, *When the Powers Fall: Reconciliation in the Healing of Nations* (Minneapolis, Minn.: Fortress Press, 1997), 18.

14. Rabbis for Human Rights is only one of a number of Israeli groups engaged in this kind of activity. For more information see its website and the websites of the following groups: The Israel Coalition to End House Demolitions, Oz VeShalom, Bat Shalom, Gush Shalom, Coalition of Women for a Just Peace, and Peace Now (Shalom Achshav),

15. These terms are taken from Amy Gutmann and Dennis Thompson, "The Moral Foundations of Truth Commissions," in Rotberg and Thompson, *Truth v. Justice*. See Chapter 7 herein for a discussion of their work.

16. "The Special Support Programme for Peace and Reconciliation" (July 1998); program summary is available online.

17. "EU Programme for Peace and Reconciliation in Northern Ireland and the Border Counties of Ireland 2000-2004 (Peace II)," Department of Finance and Personnel European Division website.

18. Brendan McAllister, "Encountering the Strange: Mediation and Reconciliation in Northern Ireland's Parades Conflict," paper presented at the Promoting Justice and Peace through Reconciliation and Co-existence Alternatives Conference at The American University, Washington, D.C., February 20, 1999. Available on the Mediation Network for Northern Ireland website.

19. "Deal over Amnesty for IRA Fugitives Now Near," *The Guardian* (March 29, 2002).

Bibliography

Amnesty International. "Policy Statement on Impunity." In *Transitional Justice*, 290-91. *See* Kritz.

Andrews, Molly. "Forgiveness in Context." *Journal of Moral Education* 29 (2000): 75-86.

Arendt, Hannah. *The Human Condition*. 2d ed. Chicago: The University of Chicago Press, 1958.

Asmal, Kader, Louise Asmal, and Ronald Suresh Roberts. *Reconciliation through Truth: A Reckoning of Apartheid's Criminal Governance*. Cape Town and Johannesburg: David Philip Publishers, 1996.

———. "When the Assassin Cries Foul: The Modern Just War Doctrine." In *Looking Back, Reaching Forward*, 86-98. *See* Villa-Vicencio and Verwoerd.

Baskin, Jeremy, and Vishwas Satgar. "South Africa's New LRA: A Critical Assessment and Challenges for Labour." *South African Labour Bulletin* 19/5 (1995): 50-56.

Battle, Michael. *Reconciliation: The Ubuntu Theology of Desmond Tutu*. Cleveland, Ohio: The Pilgrim Press, 1997.

———. "A Theology of Community: The Ubuntu Theology of Desmond Tutu." *Interpretation* 54 (2000): 172-82.

Baum, Gregory, and Harold Wells, eds. *The Reconciliation of Peoples: Challenge to the Churches*. Maryknoll, N.Y.: Orbis Books, 1997.

Becker, David, Elizabeth Lira, Maria Isabel Castillo, Elena Gomez, and Juana Kovalskys. "Therapy with Victims of Political Repression in Chile: The Challenge of Social Reparation." In *Transitional Justice*, 583-91. *See* Kritz.

Bhargava, Rajeev. "Restoring Decency to Barbaric Societies." In *Truth v. Justice*, 45-67. *See* Rotberg and Thompson.

Bizos, George. *No One to Blame? In Pursuit of Justice in South Africa*. Cape Town: David Philip Publishers, 1998.

Boraine, Alex. *A Country Unmasked: Inside South Africa's Truth and Reconciliation Commission*. Oxford: Oxford University Press, 2000.

Burton, Mary. "Making Moral Judgements." In *Looking Back, Reaching Forward*, 77-85. *See* Villa-Vicencio and Verwoerd.

Corder, Hugh. "The Law and Struggle: The Same But Different." In *Looking Back, Reaching Forward*, 99-106. *See* Villa-Vicencio and Verwoerd.

Danish Ministry of Foreign Affairs. "Strategy for Danish-South African Development Cooperation." 1995.

Davenport, T. R. H. *South Africa: A Modern History*. 4th ed. Toronto and Buffalo, N.Y.: University of Toronto Press, 1991.

Daye, Russell. "Cracking Open Identity, Truth, and God: Reflections on South Africa's Reconciliation Commission." *ARC: The Journal of the Faculty of Religious Studies, McGill University* 28 (2000): 67-89.

――――. "Forgiveness as a Political Process: Rending and Reconciliation in South Africa." *Journal of Religion and Culture* 12 (1998): 61-91.

De Lange, Johnny. "The Historical Context, Legal Origins, and Philosophical Foundation of the South African Truth and Reconciliation Commission." In *Looking Back, Reaching Forward*, 14-31. See Villa-Vicencio and Verwoerd.

Enright, Robert D., and Catherine T. Coyle. "Researching the Process Model of Forgiveness within Psychological Interventions." In *Dimensions of Forgiveness*, 139-61. See Worthington.

Gibson, James L., and Helen Macdonald. "Truth—Yes, Reconciliation—Maybe: South Africans Judge the Truth and Reconciliation Process." Research report, Institute for Justice and Reconciliation. June 11, 2001. Available on IJR website.

Gutmann, Amy, and Dennis Thompson. "The Moral Foundations of Truth Commissions." In *Truth v. Justice*, 22-44. See Rotberg and Thompson.

Hayner, Priscilla B. "Same Species, Different Animal: How South Africa Compares to Truth Commissions Worldwide." In *Looking Back, Reaching Forward*, 32-41. See Villa-Vicencio and Verwoerd.

――――. *Unspeakable Truths: Confronting State Terror and Atrocity.* New York and London: Routledge, 2001.

Henry, Yazir. "Where Healing Begins." In *Looking Back, Reaching Forward*, 166-73. See Villa-Vicencio and Verwoerd.

Herman, Judith. *Trauma and Recovery.* New York: Basic Books, 1992.

Human Rights Program Harvard Law School, and World Peace Foundation. *Truth Commissions: A Comparative Assessment—An Interdisciplinary Discussion Held at Harvard Law School in May 1996.* Cambridge: Harvard Law School Human Rights Program, 1997.

Jacoby, Susan. *Wild Justice: The Evolution of Revenge.* New York: Harper & Row, 1983.

Kiernan, Jim. "The African Independent Churches." In *Living Faiths in South Africa*, 116-28. See Prozescky and de Gruchy.

――――. "African Traditional Religions in South Africa." In *Living Faiths in South Africa*, 15-27. See Prozesky and de Gruchy.

Kiss, Elizabeth. "Moral Ambition within and beyond Political Constraints." In *Truth v. Justice*, 68-98. See Rotberg and Thompson.

Kritz, Neil J., ed. *Transitional Justice: How Emerging Democracies Reckon with Former Regimes.* Vol. 1. Washington, D.C.: United States Institute of Peace Press, 1995.

Krog, Antjie. *Country of My Skull: Guilt, Sorrow, and the Limits of Forgiveness in the New South Africa.* Toronto: Random House, 1998.

Linz, Juan J. "The Breakdown of Democratic Regimes: Crisis, Breakdown, and Reequilibration." In *Transitional Justice*, 123-31. See Kritz.

Llewellyn, Jennifer J., and Robert Howse. "Institutions for Restorative Justice: The South African Truth and Reconciliation Commission." *University of Toronto Law Journal* 49/3. 1999. Available online.

Lyster, Richard. "Amnesty: The Burden of Victims." In *Looking Back, Reaching Forward*, 184-92. *See* Villa-Vicencio and Verwoerd.

Malan, Rian. *My Traitor's Heart: A South African Exile Returns to Face His Country, His Tribe, and His Conscience.* New York: Vintage International, 1990.

Martin, Stephen W. "The TRC and Its Legacy: Report on the Debate at the Goedgedacht Forum, 21 August 1999." *Journal of Theology for Southern Africa* 105 (1999): 57-63.

May, Julian, ed. *Poverty and Inequality in South Africa: Meeting the Challenge.* Cape Town: David Philip Publishers, 2000.

McKay, Stanley, and Janet Silman. "A First Nations Movement in a Canadian Church." In *The Reconciliation of Peoples: Challenge to the Churches*, edited by Gregory Baum and Harold Wells, 172-83. Maryknoll, N.Y.: Orbis Books, 1997.

Minow, Martha. *Between Vengeance and Forgiveness: Facing History after Genocide and Mass Violence.* Boston: Beacon Press, 1998.

————. "The Hope for Healing: What Can Truth Commissions Do?" In *Truth v. Justice*, 235-60. *See* Rotberg and Thompson.

Murphy, Jeffrie G., and Jean Hampton. *Forgiveness and Mercy.* Cambridge: Cambridge University Press, 1988.

Ntsebeza, Dumisa. "The Struggle for Human Rights: From the UN Declaration of Human Rights to the Present." In *Looking Back, Reaching Forward*, 2-13. *See* Villa-Vicencio and Verwoerd.

Orr, Wendy. "Reparation Delayed Is Healing Retarded." In *Looking Back, Reaching Forward*, 239-49. *See* Villa-Vicencio and Verwoerd.

Pakenham, Thomas. *The Boer War.* New York: Avon Books, 1979.

Pauw, Jacques. *Into the Heart of Darkness: Confessions of Apartheid's Assassins.* Johannesburg: Jonathan Ball Publishers, 1997.

Pretorius, Hennie, and Lizo Jafta. "'A Branch Springs Out': African Initiated Churches." In *Christianity in South Africa: A Political, Social, and Cultural History*, edited by Richard Elphick and Rodney Davenport, 211-26. Berkeley and Los Angeles: University of California Press, 1997.

Prozesky, Martin, and John de Gruchy, eds. *Living Faiths in South Africa.* Cape Town and Johannesburg: David Philip Publishers, 1995.

Research Institute on Christianity in South Africa. "Faith Communities and Apartheid." In *Facing the Truth*, 15-77. *See* Cochrane, de Gruchy, and Martin.

Robertson, Mary. "An Overview of Rape in South Africa." Centre for the Study of Violence and Reconciliation. Available online.

Rotberg, Robert I. "Truth Commissions and the Provision of Truth, Justice, and Reconciliation." In *Truth v. Justice*, 3-21. *See* Rotberg and Thompson.

Rotberg, Robert I., and Dennis Thompson, eds. *Truth v. Justice: The Morality of Truth Commissions.* Princeton, N.J.: Princeton University Press, 2000.

Sampson, Anthony. *Mandela: The Authorised Biography.* London: HarperCollins, 1999.

Shriver, Donald W., Jr. *An Ethic for Enemies: Forgiveness in Politics.* New York: Oxford University Press, 1995.

Slye, Ronald C. "Amnesty, Truth, and Reconciliation: Reflections on the South African Amnesty Process." In *Truth v. Justice*, 170-88. *See* Rotberg and Thompson.

South African Defence Force Contact Bureau. *Analysis of the TRC Report by the SADF Contact Bureau*. May 28, 1999.

Sparks, Allister. *The Mind of South Africa: The Story of the Rise and Fall of Apartheid*. London: The New Hotfire Trust, 1990; reprint, Arrow Books, 1997.

——. *Tomorrow Is Another Country*. Sandton: Struik Book Distributors, 1994.

Tavuchis, Nicholas. *Mea Culpa: A Sociology of Apology and Reconciliation*. Stanford, Calif.: Stanford University Press, 1991.

Truth and Reconciliation Commission. *Final Report*. Cape Town, 1998.

——. *Heidelberg Tavern Massacre Amnesty Hearing Transcript*. Available on the TRC website.

Tutu, Desmond. Address to the First Gathering of the Truth and Reconciliation Commission. December 16, 1995. Truth and Reconciliation Commission website.

——. *No Future without Forgiveness*. London: Rider, 1999.

United Church of Canada. "Brief to the Royal Commission on Aboriginal Peoples." October 27, 1993.

Van Zyl, Paul. "Justice without Punishment: Guaranteeing Human Rights in Transitional Societies." In *Looking Back, Reaching Forward*, 42-57. *See* Villa-Vicencio and Verwoerd.

Verwoerd, Wilhelm. "Individual and/or Social Justice after Apartheid? The South African Truth and Reconciliation Commission." *The European Journal of Development Research*. 11 (1999): 115-40.

Villa-Vicencio, Charles, and John W. de Gruchy, eds. *Resistance and Hope: South African Essays in Honour of Beyers Naude*. Cape Town and Johannesburg: David Philip Publishers, 1985.

Villa-Vicencio, Charles, and Wilhelm Verwoerd. "Constructing a Report: Writing up the 'Truth.'" In *Truth v. Justice*, 279-94. *See* Rotberg and Thompson.

Villa-Vicencio, Charles, and Wilhelm Verwoerd, eds. *Looking Back, Reaching Forward: Reflections on the Truth and Reconciliation Commission of South Africa*. Cape Town: University of Cape Town Press, 2000.

Volf, Miroslav. *Exclusion and Embrace: A Theological Exploration of Identity, Otherness, and Reconciliation*. Nashville, Tenn.: Abingdon Press, 1996.

Wink, Walter. *When the Powers Fall: Reconciliation in the Healing of Nations*. Minneapolis, Minn.: Fortress Press, 1997.

Worthington, Evert L., Jr., ed. *Dimensions of Forgiveness: Psychological Research and Theological Perspectives*. Philadelphia: Templeton Foundation Press, 1998.

——. "The Pyramid Model of Forgiveness: Some Interdisciplinary Speculations about Unforgiveness and the Promotion of Forgiveness." In *Dimensions of Forgiveness*, 107-37. *See* Worthington.

Zalaquett, Jose. "Confronting Human Rights Violations Committed by Former Governments: Principles Applicable and Political Constraints." In *Transitional Justice*, 3-31. *See* Kritz.

Index